# His Brother's Keeper

# His Brother's Keeper

Israel and Diaspora Jewry
in the Twenty-first Century

YOSSI BEILIN

SCHOCKEN BOOKS  NEW YORK

All rights reserved under International and Pan-American Copyright
Conventions. Published in the United States by Schocken Books,
a division of Random House, Inc., New York, and simultaneously in
Canada by Random House of Canada Limited, Toronto. Distributed by
Pantheon Books, a division of Random House, Inc., New York. Originally
published in Israel as *Moto Shel Hadod Me'america* by Yediot Achronot,
Tel Aviv, in 1999. Copyright © 1999 by Yossi Beilin.

Schocken and colophon are registered trademarks of
Random House, Inc.

Library of Congress Cataloging-in-Publication Data

Beilin, Yossi.
[Moto shel ha-dod me-Amerikah. English]
His brother's keeper: Israel and Diaspora Jewry in the
twenty-first century/Yossi Beilin
p.     cm.
Includes bibliographical references and index.
ISBN 0-8052-4175-2
1. Israel and the diaspora. 2. Jewish diaspora. 3. Jews—Attitudes toward
Israel. 4. Jews—Identity.    I. Title.
DS132.B3413   2000
305.892'4—dc21
99-089429

www.schocken.com

*Book design by Cassandra J. Pappas*

Printed in the United States of America
First American Edition
2   4   6   8   9   7   5   3   1

*For Yinon*

# Contents

# Foreword

ON ISRAEL'S FIFTIETH BIRTHDAY, I found myself at a country club in Omaha, Nebraska. I was meeting with members of the local Jewish community at this club—now a "mixed" club, though originally all Jewish—to discuss the future of relations between Israel and the Jews of America. The moderator began by thanking me for making the effort to come to Omaha, where only about 6,000 Jews live, on such a festive day for Israel. Then he interrupted his introductory remarks and turned to me to ask, half in jest, half in earnest, "Why did you come to *us* on Israel's Independence Day?"

I responded to this question in an equally jocular manner, refraining from providing the deeper answer. Essentially, there were two factors that explained my presence in Omaha on Israel's jubilee birthday. On the one hand, it was very difficult for me to rejoice at home when the prime minister was Benjamin Netanyahu, a native Israeli of my own generation who was leading my country backwards in the peace process, damaging Israel's international standing, and undermining the rule of law. And on the other hand, I felt it was important for me to be with a small community, especially on such an occasion, rather than at the resplendent receptions sponsored by larger Jewish communities. Meeting with the small Jewish community in Omaha provided an opportunity for me to express my ideas on Jewish issues, and to hear and discuss their views. I saw this as a modest contribution toward bridging the wide gap between Israel and American Jewry, the two largest Jewish communities in the world, which have been separated—consciously—by their leaders. Establishing a real connection between these two communities in the twenty-first century could have a dramatic impact on the future of both.

We are tourists in each other's countries. Israelis tour New York, reach the West Coast, and sometimes stay in the United States for several years to study. They return home with a greater mastery of the English language and know more about American sports, but they do not necessarily return home with a better understanding of American Jewry. American Jews tour Israel as individuals or in groups, learn how to say a few phrases in Hebrew, and go home, still strangers to Israelis.

We are very careful not to interfere in each other's affairs. Even if it is clear to us as Israelis that a significant number of the groups in the Conference of Presidents of Major Jewish Organizations comprise little more than post-office boxes, we treat this framework as if it really represented the Jews of America. Even when American Jews are convinced that the policies of the government of Israel are misguided—that Israel is naïvely pursuing peace or unnecessarily provoking its Arab neighbors—they stick essentially to the principle that whatever government is in power in Israel deserves their unequivocal support. They save their criticism for the pages of their memoirs.

The sort of dialogue established in the 1950s and sixties by the leaders of the two large Jewish communities—Israeli and American Jewry—is inappropriate today and needs to undergo a major overhaul. Continuing to follow a policy of nonintervention in each other's affairs, and continuing to remain content with sponsoring the same sort of UJA missions and black-tie Israel Bonds dinners, could have a tragic impact on the future of the Jewish world—a world largely dependent on its two greatest communities.

Just thirty or forty years ago the situation was different. The United States was then home to the largest Jewish community in the world, more than three times the size of the community in Israel. The institutions of American Jewry were still relevant for the most part, and the rate of assimilation in America was low. There were still close family ties between many of the Jews living in Israel and the United States. Telephone conversations, visits, and letters helped to maintain a real connection between the two communities.

Today the two communities are about the same size. The American Jewish community is assimilating, many of its institutions are no longer relevant, and the number of nonaffiliated American Jews exceeds the number of affiliated ones. Family ties with Israelis are often distant, separated by three or four generations. If we do not meet in Omaha on Israel's Independence Day, if we do not find ways to establish new connections, if we do not build a bridge over the Atlantic Ocean, if we do not abandon the foolish pledge to avoid involvement in each other's affairs, we will soon be forced to accept a Jewish world confined to the borders of our own countries.

Only a serious, institutionalized, and frank dialogue between the two communities can create a new situation and enable the continued existence of a Jewish world. This type of dialogue requires some acute introspection on the part of each community, with an honest recognition of each community's strengths and weaknesses. This dialogue must be conducted in a new forum, one that encourages informal contacts, supports joint projects, and examines new ideas.

The obsolescence of many Jewish institutions not only makes them less and less relevant, it also distances the individual Jew from the community. These institutions were formed to deal with specific problems but have remained in their original configuration even while seeking new challenges to justify their existence. Some have found new challenges and some are still searching; few have disbanded or merged. The leaders of many organizations continue to give exaggerated reports on the size of their membership, while the true picture is one of widespread attrition.

The aging leadership has not changed. There are no internal democratic mechanisms, and it is nearly impossible for young Jews to reach leadership positions. Young Jews in America view these organizations as old-age homes and keep their distance from them. Jewish professionals, usually in their fifties, earn substantial salaries for managing these organizations and amuse themselves by rotating the presidents of their organizations every two years in order to give their large donors the feeling that they are not only affluent but also "leaders."

The recent merger between the Jewish federations and the United Jewish Appeal is an expression of fresh thinking. On the other hand, discussions on combining the American Jewish Congress and American Jewish Committee have led nowhere. Neither the Committee (established to assist in the absorption of Jews from Germany), nor the Congress (convened to arrange democratic elections among American Jewry), nor the much older B'nai B'rith organization (formed in response to the exclusion of Jews from other clubs) would be created today if they did not already exist. By focusing their energies in other directions—aid for Jews in distress throughout the world, international relations, human rights issues, connections with Israel, and so on—these old organizations have extended their existence long after their original goals were realized. But in light of their dwindling and aging membership, inertia has become the main reason for the continued existence of these organizations.

The Zionist movement in America is another example of a weak and problematic framework whose elderly membership is steadily declining in numbers. For a century, this movement has taught that there is no necessary connection between Zionism and immigration to Israel. It is hard to imagine that the Zionist movement in the United States has ever actually helped any American Jew to decide in favor of making *aliyah*. It has always been much more helpful for American Jews considering *aliyah* to be in direct contact with Israel, since the American Zionist movement is still debating the anachronistic party politics of the previous generation.

This irrelevant existence of institutions dealing with the link between the Jews of America and Israel is a luxury we cannot afford. The organizations mentioned above, along with others, are responsible for the illusion that there is, ostensibly, an extensive network of connections spanning the vast geographic divide. Only when these institutions are dismantled will it become clear that although there are many trees, there is no forest. A new framework must be created if ever a forest of connections is to exist. This new framework—or frameworks—can serve as a bridge for two-way traffic and provide the unifying vitality that is missing today.

We know each other, but not really. It is not surprising that our acquaintance is superficial, with the exception of those few among us who have spent some years in both communities. The truth is, we do not even know how to persuade one another, much less to win favor.

The day after my stop in Omaha, I visited Atlanta to meet with the leaders of the local Jewish federation. We met in the office of Steve Selig, the president of the federation. A copy of the city's major newspaper, the *Atlanta Constitution,* was on his desk; it featured a picture of Selig riding a camel down Atlanta's main street during Israel's Independence Day celebrations. Selig was very proud of the picture, and his colleagues shared this excitement.

I was furious. My high-tech Israel, the world's number-three producer of start-ups (after California and Massachusetts), whose standard of living is comparable to that of Great Britain, is epitomized on its Independence Day by a camel ride! Selig and his federation colleagues could not comprehend my anger. They were sure that once I saw the camel, I would be reminded of Israel and feel flattered . . .

If we abide such camel rides for another generation, while doing nothing to revamp our shrinking and aging institutions, we may miss the precious opportunity to build a bridge. The camel ride must end now. We must replace this theater of the absurd that characterizes the relations between Israel and American Jewry, with its faded set and dreadful conservatism, and do so quickly.

We would be making a mistake to take an arrogant approach with one another, thinking that either of us has all of the solutions for the other side. Both communities have the right to be proud of their great achievements, but they must also recognize their major failures. Neither community—even if it tried—could succeed in refashioning the other in its own image. Yet if we tried to exploit the advantages of cooperation, we could derive great benefits merely from the fact that we are not giving up on each other. The book before you seeks to contribute to the creation of such cooperation.

This book is written with great love for the tormented people into which I happened to be born. It is intended to describe the current situation of Jewry at the dawn of the twenty-first century, to take a peek into the third millennium and to anticipate events likely to occur at its outset. It offers several proposals aimed at changing the frameworks for dealing with the "Jewish problem" in its new form.

The positions I have held during the past two decades have afforded me the opportunity to visit dozens of Jewish communities. I have discovered a wonderful and fascinating world that is carrying forward an ethos that is one of the most beautiful in human history. At the end of the first half of the twentieth century, it underwent an unprecedented trauma. At the beginning of the twenty-first century, it seems to be simply disappearing of its own accord.

There are those who are not concerned with this and explain that the Jewish contribution to the world does not necessarily require Jews. The contribution of ancient Greek culture is not carried forth by the Greeks, yet its influence on the world is enormous. The same is true of the cultures of Egypt, Babylon, and Rome.

There are those who are worried by the diminishing numbers but are convinced that this is an inevitable phenomenon about which nothing can be done. From the moment that the world began accepting the Jews and moving away from anti-Semitism, the wide gate of assimilation was open. Nevertheless, despite great efforts, no one has succeeded in finding a secular substitute for religion, while the definition of the Jew in the secular world remains largely one of negation. Anti-Semitism, as Herzl believed, preserves the Jews, and its disappearance could bring about the disappearance of Jews who do not live in a sovereign Jewish community.

Others, like myself, are concerned yet believe that we should not resign ourselves to this eventuality. I understand that we are dealing with a trend, and that this trend will continue, but I believe we can mount a serious effort to minimize its dimensions and perhaps even change its direction.

I OWE a great debt of gratitude to the late Isaiah Berlin, Arthur Hertzberg, Shimon Peres, Theo Klein, George Weidenfeld, and others with whom I held long discussions in recent years on the future of the Jewish people. I am also grateful to many others— community leaders and rabbis from the various religious streams, and Jewish student representatives—who shared with me the dilemmas they are facing as Jews living outside of Israel.

In the process of writing this book and bringing it to publication, I was assisted by Ruti Zussman, Ira Moskowitz, and Seymour Rossel and I would like to thank them for their part in it.

# Personal Introduction:
# 24 Kalischer Street

ON MAY 14, 1946, a short, stocky, bald man with a large head, holding a cane, exited the taxi that brought him from the Savings and Loan Bank at the corner of Herzl and Lilienblum in Tel Aviv to his home on Kalischer Street. He returned home, as usual, at three in the afternoon, had a light meal, and took a short nap. When he got up, he felt chest pains. He died at eight o'clock that evening. Two years later—to the day—his life dream was realized as the State of Israel was established.

My grandfather, Avraham Yosef Bregman, was a familiar figure in the community. He managed the Savings and Loan Bank for eighteen years in a commanding fashion and was a great expert in banking cooperatives. A determined man, he was easy to anger and easy to please. The front pages of the daily newspapers reported his death in large headlines. *Davar* referred to him as "one of the endearing figures from the early period of Russian Zionism. . . . A tireless preacher of Zionism, he was continually traveling to cities and towns, explaining, arguing, and organizing." The *HaTzofeh* daily knew to report that he was the grandson of two rabbinical sages—the rabbi of Chernobyl on his father's side and the rabbi of Stolin on his mother's.

The *Forward* in New York also announced the death of Yosef Bregman, the well-known Zionist in Tel Aviv, and noted his closeness to Chaim Weizmann (1874–1952) and his resolute opposition to Theodor Herzl's Uganda plan. *Yedioth Ahronoth* described Bregman as "stormy and explosive as lava . . . When encountering hesitation, he would arise full of excitement and fury to bring the matter to a decision."

His fame did not last. He had written books about cooperative credit unions that were forgotten as these cooperatives disappeared. His contemporaries took their memories of him to their graves and he himself wrote no memoirs. If he had, they undoubtedly would have been like those of his contemporaries for whom Zionism became a religion.

This grandchild of two rabbinic sages was born in 1880 in Pinsk, White Russia. His lifelong nickname, "Yossel Hosid," contained a reference to his ancestry, as well as his status as a *hasid* (fervent follower) of Zionism. After learning in a *cheyder* (elementary religious school), he taught himself by reading books and became fluent in Russian and German with the help of private tutors. He read history voraciously and became attracted to the principles of cooperatives. From an early age, he began to work in a bank and, prior to World War I, he became a director of the savings and loan bank in Pinsk.

Following the publication of Herzl's *The Jewish State*, he helped to found a Bnei Zion organization in Pinsk. He also began to travel from town to town, preaching Zionism to the Jewish residents.

In 1901, he was elected to the Fifth Zionist Congress as a representative of the town of Shklov in the Mogilev region and traveled to Basel for the first time. He joined the "Democratic Faction" led by Leo Motzkin (1867–1933), Martin Buber (1878–1965), and

Chaim Weizmann, organized at that time to counter the one-man rule of Theodor Herzl in the Zionist movement, and was an enthusiastic supporter of the Jewish National Fund, established during this congress. He listened with great emotion as Max Nordau (1849–1923) spoke about the physical and spiritual deterioration of the Jews. Nordau explained that this spiritual and physical condition would not improve until a national normalization transpired.

In August 1902, he participated in the Minsk conference, the first and last conference of Russian Zionists that was legally approved by the government of Russia. Bregman, then twenty-two years old, argued against the cultural Zionist approach popularized by Ahad Ha'am (pseudonym of Asher Ginzburg, 1856–1927) and found himself a part of the political approach represented by Chaim Weizmann. He remained close and loyal to Weizmann for the rest of his life.

Contrary to his parents' desires, he held Zionist meetings in his spacious home and assisted Hebrew teachers in Pinsk who founded the "improved *cheyder*" in the face of stubborn opposition by the *haredim* (ultra-orthodox). He was no longer religious, but still continued to visit and preach Zionism in synagogues. Bregman established the *Poalei Zion Yemin,* the "Right-wing" of the Workers of Zion, with some friends, though he never considered himself particularly political.

Two issues filled his life: Zionism and banking. In both, he was zealous, impatient, and uncompromising.

Bregman traveled to Basel with other Russian representatives in August 1903 to attend the Sixth Zionist Congress after being elected again in Shklov. Herzl arrived in Basel after concluding a long tour of Russia, where he was treated as a king by the Jewish masses. Indeed, Herzl had no way of anticipating the battle waiting to erupt at the congress.

On the eve of the congress, the British Colonial Office issued the famous announcement about the possibility of establishing a Jewish settlement in Africa. The British government would allow a Jewish delegation to visit Africa in order to look for an available tract of land under British control. If land were found, and if approved by the British government, a Jewish settlement could be established where Jewish national traditions could be maintained and local affairs managed by a Jewish official.

The proposal, called the "Uganda Plan," looked toward the land between Nairobi and the slopes of Dunn. Herzl asked the congress only to accept the proposal to send a delegation. Not all of the Russian delegates rejected the idea. Yehiel Tschlenow (1863–1918), for example, was excited that a powerful country was finally ready to recognize the Jewish people. At the beginning of the congress, the proposal was received in a positive way. Herzl explained that Uganda was not a substitute for the Land of Israel but that a place must be found for those who had an immediate need to emigrate. He tried to make it clear that what was under consideration was only the decision to send a delegation, not a preference for East Africa over Palestine.

Max Nordau spoke, as usual, more effectively than Herzl. He noted that it was not only a question of responding politely to the British government's gesture, but a practical, if temporary, solution in face of the gathering storm. Nordau referred to the Uganda Plan as *"Nachtasyl,"* and Bregman, already fluent in German, understood that the Zionists were being offered a "place of nighttime refuge" in Africa.

Nordau attempted to dispel concerns and promised that Zion would always be the goal. However, he warned that soon the gates of the West would close—in England, in America—and the situation of the Jews in Eastern Europe would worsen without any solution in sight. Here, perhaps, was an opportunity to establish temporary Jewish sovereignty and provide a place of refuge for any Jewish immigrant.

Bregman was among those who worried about the "Rabbi Amnon syndrome." According to legend, Amnon, a tenth-century rabbi, brought martyrdom on himself. The bishop of Mainz was so persistent in asking Amnon to accept Christianity that the rabbi finally requested three days to consider the matter. But his conscience was so troubled that he failed to appear on the third day and had to be brought before the bishop by force. Amnon begged, "Cut out my tongue, since I did not refuse you at once." The bishop replied, "It was your legs which did not bring you to me," whereupon Amnon's legs and arms were amputated and he subsequently died a martyr. Bregman feared that an agreement to consider the Uganda Plan would be a betrayal of the Zionist idea and believed that even if it were feasible to establish a Jewish state in Africa, the Zionists must not agree to this. He joined a group of Russian delegates led by Weizmann against the attempt by Herzl and Nordau to solve the plight of the Jews now. Weizmann argued that it would be better to wait for the British to approve the transfer of Jews to the Land of Israel. If the Jews had waited this long for their state, they could wait a bit longer and see their state established in the Land of Israel.

It was a revolt of the young Zionists. Weizmann, twenty-nine, along with other young delegates like Bregman, twenty-three, confronted Nordau, fifty-four, and a weak and sickly Herzl, forty-three. The young Zionists were in no hurry, preferring to wait for Zion later rather than opt for a partial, imperfect solution now. The Russian delegates met in heated debate, and when the plenary session of the congress reconvened, it appeared that they were intent on breaking up the assembly since Herzl enjoyed majority support. They almost succeeded, entering the famous casino hall with loud shouts and then singing Russian songs. Some of them stood on chairs, singing and hollering, while others threw pamphlets from the balconies. From a side entrance, dozens of young Russian girls appeared and began shouting as well. When the chairman of the session came down to the floor in an attempt to quiet the disruption, he was simply carried off on their shoulders and not allowed to return to the podium. In order to calm things down, someone turned off the lights. In the early hours of the morning, the voting was concluded: 295 delegates supported Herzl's recommendation to send a delegation to East Africa, while 178 voted against and 130 abstained.

Bregman did not stay to hear Herzl speak after the vote. The Russian delegates regarded the leader of the Zionist movement as a traitor. As Herzl stood on the podium quoting Psalm 137, "If I forget thee, Jerusalem, let my right hand forget its cunning . . ." they were already planning their next steps in one of the side rooms.

However, they could not take their next step without their leader—and Bregman's patron—Menahem Ussishkin (1863–1941). When the congress was being held, Ussishkin was in Palestine working—unsuccessfully—to establish the first prestate political institutions. Upon his return, he championed the rebellion. In a letter to Herzl, Ussishkin wrote that although he was still prepared to serve on the executive committee of the Zionist movement, he did not accept the Uganda decision. This was not a simple matter: one of the leaders of this six-year-old voluntary organization, whose representatives were elected by hundreds of thousands of members, was rejecting the right of the majority to decide!

Herzl was quick to reply, with a letter in which he contended that the acquisition of land in Palestine was not essentially different from the purchase of land by Jews in Russia. It would not make Palestine Jewish so long as there was not Jewish sovereignty in Palestine. Ussishkin and his colleagues were far from persuaded, and their position became more extreme. In opposition to Zionists who turned their backs on Zion, the Zionei Zion, Zionists for Zion, movement was founded. Bregman was one of its leaders—in open opposition to Herzl. Ussishkin admired Bregman's passion.

In October 1903, at the Kharkov conference in Ukraine, Ussishkin led the fight. The Russian delegates decided to form an alternative Zionist movement if Herzl did not abandon the Uganda Plan. On December 31, Ussishkin sent a message to Herzl calling for him to meet with three Russian delegates in order to hear their demands. The three were known as "Ussishkin's Cossacks." Bregman was one of them. Herzl refused to meet with them and viewed the formation of this delegation as a personal insult. He would agree only to meet with each of the three Zionists individually.

Bregman presented the demands in a private meeting with Herzl. He, of course, had no idea that this would be the last time that he would see Herzl, who would die within several months at age forty-four. Bregman was very angry with Herzl and did not feel nervous about the meeting. He presented unequivocal demands: the leader of the Zionist movement should consult the Executive Committee on his decisions and not act alone, and should commit in writing that the Zionist Congress would not be asked in the future to adopt any plans for Jewish sovereignty outside of Palestine and Syria.

Bregman and Herzl discussed the differences between Zionism and Hovevei Zion—which in Hebrew means "Lovers of Zion." (Bregman was one of the leaders of Hovevei Zion in Pinsk.) Herzl spoke of the struggle to gain approval for establishing a Jewish state that could absorb the Jewish masses, and contrasted this ambitious plan with the activities of Hovevei Zion, which had been holding meetings for more than twenty years and had raised some money for settlements in Palestine but had not offered a real solution to the plight of the Jews. He sought a solution for a real problem and was not interested in a partial and protracted process. Herzl said that he was not enthusiastic about Uganda and would not press the next congress to approve the plan and transfer Jews there. He remained committed to the original "Basel Plan" and the establishment of a Jewish state in Palestine.

Bregman and the other two members of the delegation felt reassured. At the meeting of the Zionist Executive Committee in

April, Herzl reiterated his commitment to returning to Zion and it was decided to defer the Uganda issue to the Seventh Zionist Congress.

On July 3, 1904, Herzl died and the Seventh Zionist Congress was convened without him in Basel at the end of July. Bregman was part of a large majority that defined the "Basel Plan" as the congress's singular goal and maintained that no alternative plan of settlement outside of Palestine would be considered. This time it was the "territorialists" (who backed the Uganda Plan) who threatened to leave the Zionist movement and establish a separate movement of their own.

In 1905, following pogroms in the Ukraine, Yosef Bregman was sent to several Ukrainian cities to report on the condition of the Jews there. The full report of his trip appears in the two-volume *Book of Russian Pogroms* edited (and mainly written) by Leo Motzkin in 1909–10. In December 1906, Bregman was a delegate to the annual assembly of Russian and Polish Zionists in Helsinki. Here he again found himself in the minority when it was decided that Zionists should support and participate in the liberation movements of Russian nationalities, following the revolution of 1905, in order to ensure national rights and cultural autonomy for the Jews of Russia. Bregman viewed all of this as a deviation from the main goal. He was not interested in the affairs of other peoples and viewed Jewish autonomy in Russia as an undesirable alternative to the Zionist cause.

During all of these years, he was still an active member of Hovevei Zion in Pinsk, and a member of the Association of Enlightenment Disseminators and emigration board of the Jewish Colonization Association. Bregman founded vocational schools in his city and waged battles against the anti-Zionist Bund socialists for the support of the youth. He was a leader of Zeirei Zion since its inception in 1903, rented a space for this youth movement to meet in, and gave Jewish history lessons on Saturdays.

In August 1907, he was again a delegate to the Eighth Zionist

Congress, which met this time at The Hague, home of the new president of the movement, David Wolffsohn (1865–1914). Bregman supported the proposal to establish a Palestine Office of the Zionist movement, to be headed by Dr. Arthur Ruppin (1876–1943). During this time, Zionist activities in Russia had become impossible. The authorities prohibited Zionist conferences and allowed only local meetings of Hovevei Zion. In 1908, Bregman took the bold step of convening an illegal national meeting of Russian Hovevei Zion in one of the luxury hotels in Odessa. It was, in fact, an illegal, nationwide assembly of Russian Zionists. Subsequent meetings took place in Vilna.

The Ninth Zionist Congress took place in December 1909, in Hamburg, Germany. It was convened in the shadow of failed talks with the Turkish authorities and increasingly severe European restrictions on emigration to Palestine. The Russian delegates, including Bregman, constituted an opposition to Wolffsohn. They advocated focusing on settling Palestine and practical Zionism, instead of courting the Turks in hope of receiving a concession for Jewish immigration to Palestine. The Russian delegates regarded Wolffsohn, who was the banker to the Dutch royal family, as a tyrant, and as lacking Herzl's vision. Wolffsohn complained that the Russian opposition hurt him, as it had Herzl; he accused them also of failing to raise money for financing the Zionist movement.

During the tenth congress, held in Basel in August 1911, Wolffsohn, suffering from heart disease and exhaustion, resigned. He was replaced by Professor Otto Warburg (1859–1938), who, since he favored practical Zionism and settlement in Palestine, was supported by the Russian delegates. This represented a victory for "synthetic" Zionism—a fusion of practical and diplomatic goals—as espoused by Chaim Weizmann. Bregman was pleased by this change. (Returning home utterly dispirited, Wolffsohn died two years later.)

Max Nordau also retreated to the sidelines. Although he continued to appear at Zionist forums, he no longer played a central role in the debates and decision-making. He witnessed the collapse of the vision he had shared with Herzl, of attaining a temporary place of refuge for the Jews even while the young Russians enthusiastically encouraged the gradual settlement—legal or otherwise—of Palestine. At the tenth congress, Hovevei Zion defeated the political Zionists.

The tide had shifted. The eleventh congress, held in Vienna in September 1913, now dealt with issues of concern to the working settlements in Palestine. Weizmann and Ussishkin, the dominant figures at this congress, proposed the idea of establishing the Hebrew University of Jerusalem.

This was the last Zionist congress that Bregman attended. He had a long talk with Ussishkin and informed him that he intended to emigrate to Palestine. Ussishkin, however, said that first he had an important task for Bregman to fulfill—the management of a savings and loan bank in his home city of Yekaterinoslav. Bregman, already thirty-three years old, was faced with the choice of following his heart to Palestine or carrying out his mentor's instructions and postponing his emigration for several years. He chose to follow Ussishkin's directive.

During these years, Bregman had made his home in Pinsk, where he married Rivka in 1906. His son Baruch Lev was born in 1907, followed three years later by a daughter, Zehava Golda—my mother. From 1907, he managed the savings and loan bank in Pinsk. In 1914, while he was preparing to move to Yekaterinoslav, World War I erupted.

The young Bregman family had to relocate several times during the war, finally arriving in Yekaterinoslav after the 1917 revolution. (The new Bolshevik regime had already renamed the city Dnepropetrovsk in its campaign to wipe out vestiges of the czarist regime.) The new government did not look kindly upon either banks or Zionism. Bregman managed the bank in Ussishkin's city for only a short period of time before he was forced to relocate to Moscow. He was able to return to Pinsk only after the war.

It was in 1923 that Bregman and his family finally emigrated to Palestine, only to face initial hardships. They rented an apartment in Tel Aviv and Bregman found employment in a bakery. At this stage in his life, he found himself working nights beside sweltering ovens. But this difficult period was not destined to last long.

Their fluency in the Hebrew language helped the Bregmans to adjust. No other language was permitted in the home—not in Pinsk, Yekaterinoslav, Moscow, or Tel Aviv. Everyone in the family spoke and wrote Hebrew. After several months in the bakery, Bregman found a job as a clerk in the Mashbir, the important retail organization of the cooperative movement. He returned to his vocation in 1928, when he began managing a savings and loan bank in Tel Aviv. Bregman purchased a home next to the bank. His son, Baruch, became a fierce champion of the "brigade for defending the [Hebrew] language" and also began to work in banking. Bregman's daughter, Zehava, attended the Girls' School and continued her studies at the Herzliya High School.

The family's travels had disrupted Zehava's studies and she only completed her matriculation examination in 1930, at age twenty. When she received her matriculation certificate, her father was on business in Jerusalem and she mailed him a letter about her future plans. From the language of the letter, it appears that Zehava found it easier to put these words in writing than to confront her father in person:

Dear father!

Yesterday I completed my course of studies. After returning from the celebrations, and while straightening up the house, I began to ponder various thoughts that came to mind. I thought back to the first day we came to this land, how we rode in a carriage from the port, how we first arrived at Herzl Street and I had my first glimpse of the high school. Mother looked admiringly at the school and said that she hoped that Baruch and I would be able to study there. This was mother's ambition and maybe yours as well. In the early days, when you visited the Girls' School, you would often ask me—what do you plan to do, my daughter?

I would respond by saying that when I finish the Girls' School, I would like to study at the high school and then at the university, which I was sure would eventually open.

My dear father! Perhaps you hoped to hear something different from me. You would have liked to hear that I wish to study agriculture, join a *kvutzah,* a *moshav,* and work the land. I realize that our young people must return to work the soil, to be agriculturists. This is a holy duty that we owe to the homeland, and to the Jews of the Diaspora, who are counting on the young people in Palestine. However, each person has his or her own special inclinations. I have no penchant for agriculture. I am prepared to work for the homeland, for the benefit of my people and land, but in a different path.

I have different plans and dreams . . . and in order to achieve all of these things, I'll need to learn the languages of the East.

My father! At the bottom of my matriculation certificate it says that this document entitles its holder to gain entrance to the Hebrew University without requiring an examination. These words constitute an obligation of sorts. Would you really not allow me to study at the Hebrew University on Mount Scopus?

Your daughter,
Zehava

Yosef Bregman wrote back to his daughter on "the third day of Av, 5690" (according to the Jewish calendar), on stationery from the Tel Aviv Hotel in Jerusalem:

My daughter Zehava!
I received your letter today—it made me cry and made me

happy. What can I tell you? Your request is certainly, certainly justified, but have you forgotten or don't you realize that I have always sacrificed my own personal interests and those of my wife, son, and daughter when the interest of building up the land—or more precisely, Zionism—demanded this of me?

As of now, I have yet to form an opinion on this question, and it seems that the two of us will need to find an opportunity as soon as possible to have a long conversation about this.

Your father,<br>
Yosef

Accept my congratulations on graduating from the Herzliya school in the first Hebrew city.

Father and daughter did indeed have a subsequent conversation on this matter and a decision was made. Zehava moved to Jerusalem and studied the history and languages of the Middle East at Hebrew University on Mount Scopus. She later left the field of Middle East studies to become a Bible scholar.

Yosef Bregman was the ultimate Zionist activist. He was a board member of the Geula High School and other educational institutions, the Zerubavel Bank, the port warehouses, and the Joint Council of Cooperatives in Palestine. He was among the founders and a board member of the HaMifade HaEzrahi (a fund established in 1938 to help small businesses) and was on the Endowment Committee of the Jewish National Fund. No one knew which political party he supported. He viewed party activism as detrimental to the overriding goals of Zionism.

My grandfather was very sure of his chosen path: promoting cooperative credit as the way toward progress, and championing practical Zionism. He was nostalgic about Pinsk and proud that many Zionists originated there. Despite his being completely secular, he was close to the Karlin Hasidim. His obituary in *HaBoker* read, in part:

He loved the Karlin Hasidim and looked after them wherever they were. I was walking in the alleys of Tiberias one time this year and came across the Karlin synagogue. There I learned of Bregman's devotion to this Hasidic sect. He took care of their external affairs, as well as their ritual needs. He made regular "pilgrimages" to the Karliners in Tiberias, distributing contributions and gifts to the needy, sometimes anonymously. In this way, he always lived within his own personal past—in the spirit of his father's home.

Bregman suffered from heart disease for ten years until he succumbed, at the end of a work day, in his home in Tel Aviv.

Two years later, I came into this world and was immediately assigned the task of carrying on the name of my grandfather, Yosef. Upon my arrival at the family's home on 24 Kalischer Street, I met his widow, Rivka, who was now my grandmother, and found his daughter, Zehava, my mother. His son-in-law, Zvi, was my father, and his grandson, Ynon, my brother. It seemed, however, as if they were waiting not for me but for him.

When you are born into a particular home, it seems natural to you that this is the way it is supposed to be. Years pass before you are able to make comparisons and understand that your home is well-educated or ignorant, rich or poor, crowded or spacious. Only from a distance did I begin to understand how much the house was a shrine to Yossel Hosid, Yosef Bregman. Nothing was changed since his death: in his study, or "the cabinet," were his massive, glass-topped desk, bookcases, leather chair, pictures from all of the Zionist congresses he attended, pictures of Weizmann at various stages of his life, pictures of Herzl, of Ahad Ha'am, and a giant picture of the historian Ze'ev Ya'vetz. His walking stick was leaning against the wall as if he would soon take it into his hands and again head off to the bank.

When they explained to me that all of these things belong to

"Grandfather Yosef," I asked when he would finally arrive. A story was then invented for me so that I would not be sad—this before I understood the concept of death. According to the story, grandfather was on a trip to America. I waited for him until age four or five. I dreamed about the moment when this man from the pictures would meet me for the first time. So familiar to me was he from the many photographs, I could see myself run to his open arms and tell him that I am his grandson.

I wanted to be worthy of this important man who had to leave us for such a long time. For hours, I would look at the pictures that covered the walls of the five rooms of our home. They were not pictures spontaneously taken during the course of a meeting, but studio photos in which Herzl is sitting with members of the "Democratic Faction," or posing with congressional delegates. The pictures of those who attended the meeting but missed the photo session were later pasted in by the photographer so that no one would be left out.

I was particularly enchanted by one of the rooms in the house—the library. I would run my fingers across the covers of the Russian encyclopedia and browse through its volumes, especially where there were color plates of animals and plants protected by rustling transparent paper. I wanted to impress him with all the things I knew about him. I was really stunned when finally informed of his death, years after he had actually died.

I read all of the books he had written on credit cooperatives. They were thin, black books, with many pictures, and written in simple language so that the general public could understand them. I read everything written about him in all of the "who's who" books of the *yishuv,* all of the eulogies devoted to him, and all of the hundreds of condolence telegrams that my brother pasted in a black album, on thick black pages.

My mother continued to revere my grandfather Yosef all of her life. She felt such immediate excitement over everything happening in the country that she could easily have appeared in any Jewish Agency movie about the wonders of the country. My father, a loyal Haganah veteran and member of the Watchmen, was a loyal advocate of assertive nationalism. On every birthday, Zehava and Zvi gave each other books, in which they noted—instead of the date—the number of years since Israel's independence. When I came home on my first vacation leave from the army after the Six-Day War, I received *The Knesset: Israel's Parliament* by Asher Zidon as a present from my parents. The dedication they wrote in it includes: "For your first vacation leave after the Six-Day War and redemption of the Land. Love, Mother and Father."

It was impossible to be more nationalist, more Zionist, or more convinced that our path was just. Ussishkin was the height of infallibility, along with David Ben-Gurion (1886–1973). Weizmann was a positive figure, while Herzl always remained tainted by the Uganda incident, though his untimely and sudden death earned him a reprieve of sorts. Wolffsohn and Nordau represented the assimilated intelligentsia who did not understand the essence of Zionism. Ze'ev Jabotinsky (1880–1940) was a dreamer. Ahad Ha'am was smart, though mistaken in emphasizing Israel as a spiritual center for the Jewry of the Diaspora. Dr. Moshe Sneh (1909–1972) was intelligent and charismatic, but outside the camp. Menachem Begin (1913–1992) was a dangerous schemer.

Quite a few years passed before I was able to see things in a different perspective from the one that prevailed so convincingly at 24 Kalischer Street. I now believe Zionism was the right course and that Hovevei Zion was mistaken. The difference between these two approaches was enormous a hundred years ago: Hovevei Zion wanted, first of all, to possess the Land of Israel, while the highest priority for the Zionists was to save the Jews of Europe. Hovevei Zion was, to a large extent, a national liberation movement. Herzl's Zionism was a Jewish rescue movement. Hovevei Zion was not in a hurry. Zionism had no time to spare.

When Herzl wrote in his diary that the Jewish state would be established within five years—and if not, it would take another fifty years—he did not really expect that his dream would only be realized decades after his death. He really meant five years. The last thing he could have suspected was that he would be the visionary of a Jewish state founded fifty years later and three years after most of European Jewry was annihilated.

There could be no greater failure for the Zionist movement than the Holocaust. Like a person who dreams about a nice pair of new shoes but receives them after his legs are amputated, so was the Jewish state founded after the Holocaust. Instead of a natural and orderly flow of Jewish immigrants, the new state had to search for Jews in the world and persuade them to come.

It is no coincidence that discussion of the Holocaust was largely suppressed in Israel (including during the prestate period) until it appeared center stage in the Eichmann trial. It was impossible to completely portray Israel as a success story against the backdrop of the destruction of European Jewry. To dispel the notion that the state of Israel was a direct result of the Holocaust, Israelis made two new assertions: first, the Holocaust would not have occurred if the State of Israel had been in existence; and, second, that the victims of the Holocaust went to their deaths passively, as sheep to the slaughter, and thus were partly to blame for their helplessness and victimization.

In fact, it is hard to believe that Israel would have been established had it not been for the Holocaust. The British government's White Paper of 1939 was unprecedented in its severe restrictions on Jewish immigration and settlement, and, if implemented, the idea of a Jewish state in Palestine would likely have petered out. And, of course, the Jews of Europe had no real alternative other than to march to their deaths; even Jewish heroism in the ghettos of Warsaw and Bialystok ended in the death of most of these heroes. The closing of the world's gates before the Jews—in the

United States, Canada, and most of the other immigrant nations, including Palestine—constituted the real death knell for the Jews of Europe.

Herzl, the assimilating journalist shocked by the hatred of Jews expressed at the Dreyfus trial during a period of secularization; David Wolffsohn, the Dutch banker who joined Herzl in the effort to persuade world leaders to grant a place of refuge for the Jews; and Max Nordau (born Simcha Zeidfeld), a Hungarian doctor who became a writer in Paris, and who died in solitude in 1923 after trying unsuccessfully to convince his friends of the urgent need for emigration—all were correct in foreseeing the coming tragedy. The Russian Zionists, including my grandfather, were the ones who erred.

This was a mistake committed by a wonderful group of people. They were enthusiastic believers who lived modestly and put aside many personal goals for the sake of the community. None of them would have supported the long process of practical Zionism if they could have foreseen the approaching Holocaust. The determination of these good people to oppose any "night refuge" outside of Palestine places them in an uncomfortable position vis-à-vis the judgment of history, even though the Uganda Plan was probably impractical in any case.

Israel is a fantastic success story of generations of Hovevei Zion. The significance of Herzl's failure, however, is that six million Jews perished. Perhaps if Herzl and his colleagues had received more serious consideration, more than just a technical majority, it might have been possible to find a "night refuge" to save most of the European Jews while also building a Jewish state. We'll never know.

This mistake by the Russian Zionists was kept secret from us. Of course there was no conspiracy to do this, but most of Israel's leaders were people like my grandfather, and believed as he did, though perhaps with an added dose of socialism. For them, the

Uganda Plan was treason, and the intellectual and assimilated leadership of the Zionist movement was bourgeois and alienated. The policy of "acre by acre, goat by goat" remained the correct path in their view, even in the wake of the Holocaust. Their Zionist outlook focused on immigration to Israel. Investment in the Diaspora, in Jewish education, and in organizing Jewish institutions was viewed as unnecessary and even counterproductive, as it only helped to perpetuate the Diaspora.

These Zionist "Mensheviks," opposed to Uganda, who constituted a minority in the historic vote at the Sixth Zionist Congress, were the ones who survived and wrote the history, teaching us to believe that they were right and that their actions saved the Jewish people. Those who voted with the majority eventually surrendered to the enthusiasm of the Russian delegates or else became "territorialists" (for whom the task of finding a haven for Europe's threatened Jews was the top priority) and left the Zionist camp.

This mistake, this stubborn determination to refuse to even consider the "night refuge" option, should teach us to be more modest in our approach to the problems of today. When Herzl spoke of the need to save the Jews and find a "night refuge," the Russian Zionists responded by arguing that, after waiting so many years in the Diaspora, it would be better to build the Zionist entity in the Land of Israel in stages rather than hurrying to adopt a different option. Today, when the rate of assimilation in the Jewish world is reaching distressing proportions, some of our leaders respond with a similar solution for the well-established Jews of the West: immigrate to Israel!

This solution is too glib and impractical. It is similar to the previous error. If the existence of the Jewish people is still important to us in the twenty-first century, we must think of additional answers. This book seeks to examine the development of the Jewish people over the past generation, to assess the direction in which it is heading, and to propose ways of changing this direction. It

is dedicated to the man whose name I carry but never met—
an irascible and poetic man, domineering and wise, daring
and miscalculating. It is thanks to Yosef Bregman that I was
born in one of the most wonderful and fascinating places in the
world.

# His Brother's Keeper

# CHAPTER 1

# Basic Assumptions on Jewish Identity and Continuity

The importance of the Jewish people's existence is a basic premise underlying the writing of this book. I do not ask here "Why be a Jew?" or "Why is it important to preserve Judaism?" For me, it is a foregone conclusion. I do not wish to burden the reader with explanations regarding the necessity of the Jewish people's continued existence. Like almost all other Jews, I did not become Jewish by choice, and it is quite reasonable to suppose that I would be busy promoting a different heritage had I been born in a different place, into a different family.

There is no rational analysis that could convince someone that the Jewish people should take precedence over any other people. It is not a case of capitalism versus social democracy, or one political party versus another. My one and only answer to the question "Why be Jewish?" is: "Because I was born that way." Jews who do not regard their Jewishness with more importance than, for example, their high school graduating class, will probably choose to ignore this book. I cannot find fault with them.

A person born into this world needs anchors. These anchors are family and extended family. Extended family includes tribe, people, and state. A person's identity is derived from his or her surroundings. Naturally, one looks with pride on one's identity and "roots." Indeed, people often find themselves exaggeratedly glorifying their background in order to enhance their self-confidence and their connection with the world. Even though it may seem largely irrelevant, individuals like it to be known that they are the descendants of someone important. They identify with their people's victory in important battles that occurred hundreds of years ago, and want to believe that the culture they began learning as children is superior to other cultures.

Meanwhile, it is very difficult, perhaps impossible, to be a citizen of the world in a general sense and to live as a citizen of the world in a general sense, especially as everyone else has his or her own anchors. When a Christian brings home a Christmas tree, a Jew feels compelled to light the Hanukkah menorah. When Arabs in a neighboring country raise their flag, Israelis feel the need to raise their own. To a large extent, therefore, self-definition is negatively motivated: since Arabs or Christians live around me, I feel the need to strengthen my Jewish identity. It is easy to suppose that we would not be developing our own culture so aggressively if the people surrounding us had no significant national or religious consciousness.

Since our self-identity is important to us, and since the fact that we are Jews and our national pride are both part of this identity, it is important for us that Jews continue to exist in the world. It is important to us that there will be people able to discuss the Jewish future and continue to contribute to the world as Jews. The continued existence of a sizable enough Jewish people and the preservation of its culture is in our interest as people who were born Jews and as people who need anchors. We feel an instinctive need to impart our feelings about being Jewish to our children and hope that our grandchildren continue in this path and thus prove that we were not mistaken.

There is much that is beautiful in the Jewish heritage. Each of us can find in this heritage various aspects and values that appeal to us. Some of these are also to be found in other cultures, and a smaller number are indeed unique. One such unique Jewish cultural aspect is a legal ruling that requires that a defendant be set free if the Great Sanhedrin unanimously sentences him to death! This ruling has fascinated me for years, and I have found no parallel ruling in any other culture, as much as I continue to investigate. On the contrary, in societies with jury systems, efforts are made to attain full agreement among jury members, and such a consensus is required for carrying out the death penalty. The earlier Jewish idea, that unanimity may suggest that something has run afoul, speaks much more to me than the idea that consensus assures a correct verdict.

Can it be said that this is the reason that I am a Jew, or remain a Jew? Certainly not—I am a Jew because I was born one. And I have not stopped being a Jew, because I feel that this would profoundly damage my identity. In addition, no one in my surroundings would receive me more favorably if I changed my identity. Such is my understanding. I realize, of course, that this is not exactly the case for all Jews in today's world.

There is, it may be said, a Jewish "club" with its own interests: it seeks prestige and tries to impart a feeling of pride in membership so that its members will want to remain part of the club. It seeks to ensure its exclusivity; it includes only those who wish to join— these are generally the sons and daughters of club members. The club seeks to be attractive enough so that the next generation will indeed be interested in joining.

For this reason, we glorify the past, focusing on the highlights of our history, referring to ourselves as the "chosen people" and taking pride in the "Jewish genius." We also emphasize our common historic suffering (the exile, the Inquisition, the persecution, the pogroms, and, of course, the Holocaust). This is mainly due to the fact that persecution by others is greatly effective in securing a sense of unity and identity.

It is not surprising that the Six-Day War in June 1967 marked the high point of identification with Israel for world Jewry. For many Jews, it was the first time that they publicly identified with the Jewish people. The convincing victory over the neighboring Arab states enabled the Jews of the world to view themselves as participants in victory. No longer was the popular image of the Jews as chronic losers, forced to pay a heavy price for their mere survival, being reinforced. The generation of the 1960s in the Jewish world was much more comfortable identifying with amazing strength than with devastating loss. Thus, the Six-Day War changed the way many Jews related to themselves, the Jewish people, and Israel. If we overlook its troubling political implications, there is no doubt that the war helped significantly to delay the shrinking of world Jewry.

The future is no less important to us. If our children will not be part of the Jewish people, despite the values and knowledge we invest in them, we will feel disconnected from them, that we have failed and erred. We see our perpetuation in the future of the Jewish people, which is the future of our children. As Jews, both religious and secular, we would feel awful if we were to learn that the Jewish people would soon cease to exist as a result of assimilation. Even though the comparison would not be appropriate, many of us would then say that the embrace of liberal, Western society completed the work of Hitler.

Not only does our "club" have a great interest in the continuation of the Jewish people, but during the last decade we have been urgently searching for ways to preserve this people. After all, there would be no reason to maintain the "club" today if it had no future.

Leaving aside philosophical questions about whether religions are necessary, about the nature of relations between state and religion, and so on, I believe that we can think of ourselves as a sort of "parents' committee," seeking to promote the welfare of our children's schooling for their benefit. This is the situation in which many of the Jews of the Diaspora find themselves, along with those Israeli Jews who are concerned about the problems of world Jewry. Clearly, Israel is itself becoming more and more important as the common denominator in the Jewish world, so one hope for ensuring the future of the Jewish people lies in institutionalizing the connection between Israel and the Diaspora.

For a very long time, the work of the "parents' committee" was quite simple. All of the Jews belonged to the same "club" or "school," lived similar lifestyles, and were congregated in Jewish communities. All that was necessary was to pass the torch from one generation to the next, teaching the stories of the past, to ensure continuity. The task of the "parents' committee" is much more difficult in a world where most Jews are not traditionally observant and thus do not need to live in close proximity with each other, and in a world in which we are exposed to a proliferation of intermarriage. In the twenty-first century, these challenges will demand a great deal of creativity.

There are those who say that the continuation of the Jewish world is essential in order to preserve the rich Jewish heritage. There are several problems with this contention. First, no one can approach an individual Jew and demand that he or she continue to be a Jew in order to preserve cultural treasures. No one has been assigned this task or should feel obligated to do this only because he or she happened to be born Jewish. In addition, it is quite possible that Jewish cultural treasures can be maintained without the need for Jews. After all, there are departments of Jewish studies in universities in the world that have neither Jewish faculty nor Jewish students.

To religious Jews it is easier to say that a divine mandate requires them to preserve their Judaism. Yet such talk of divine sanctions cannot be expected to influence secular Jews. When a secular Jew falls in love with a non-Jew, the "parents' committee of the Jewish people" has no argument to present that would stop the couple from marrying. As liberal people who believe in the inherent equality of humankind, we even react against the pretension of those who would separate lovers only on account of their divergent religious backgrounds.

Nor can the Holocaust be invoked perpetually as an excuse for Jewish survival. The sort of secular contention that maintains that "We need to prove that Hitler failed" is also not persuasive. We cannot require generation after generation to continue to live in a certain way because the Jewish people suffered such a terrific tragedy in the 1940s. The future cannot live for the sake of the past. In the end, the "parents' committee" must be able to persuade Jews, as individuals, that it offers ways to live a better and fuller life. It is impossible to come to these individual Jews with historical or collectivist arguments.

We know that the growing scope of intermarriage is liable to bring an end to the Jewish people, at least in the Diaspora. But our efforts must focus on connecting the next generation with their roots, with presenting opportunities for young Jews to meet one another and establish family units. We should not be attempting to separate people who have already fallen in love.

There is no longer any doubt as to the importance of the State of Israel for the future of the Jewish people. There are at least two aspects to this. First, during the twenty-first century, Israel will become the largest Jewish community in the world. This assertion is based on Israel's high rate of natural growth, continued immigration by Jews in distress, and the continuing tendency toward assimilation of the Jewish community in America. It is natural that the largest community also assumes the greatest importance.

Everything that happens in Israel will in the future reflect upon the entire Jewish world, even more so than it does today.

The second aspect derives from Israel's success. This special, unprecedented experiment was destined to fail, but it has turned into a success thanks to determination, vision, courage, historical circumstance, and luck. The arguments concerning practical Zionism versus political Zionism or synthetic Zionism ended long ago. Israel's existence as a spiritual center, as Ahad Ha'am (Asher Ginzburg) advocated, is also no longer an issue. Israel is, first and foremost, a center of life for millions of Jews. Only peripherally does Israel seek a special spiritual role.

The argument between Zionists and anti-Zionists in the Diaspora is also a thing of the past. Most Jews in the world look upon Israel favorably, though they do not prefer it as a place to live. Israel is not a burden on the Jewish world as perhaps it was perceived to be during the early years of its existence. The financial contributions of world Jewry to Israel today amount to only 0.5 percent of the state's annual budget. On the other hand, Israel participates in educational and other programs in Jewish communities throughout the world.

Israel is also proof that secular Jews can survive as Jews. It is one of the only places in the world—if not the only one—where a secular Jew is not worried about whether his or her grandchildren will remain Jewish. The Jews of the world live with Israel. Since most of them do not make regular use of Jewish community services or strictly adhere to Jewish tradition, their principal Jewish identification is with the Jewish state. They are proud of Israel's achievements and, in difficult times, make apologies on its behalf. They are anxious about its future when Israel is attacked and see it as their home in time of distress. Many of them admit today that they need Israel more than Israel needs them.

Nonetheless, they are not prepared to invoke concepts that hint at the primacy of Israel, or at the need for them to immigrate to the Jewish state. The word *exile* is no longer used to define the Jews living outside of Israel and "Diaspora" is no longer a comfortable designation for many. They wish to see a Jewish world dealing with the challenges of the day, while part of this world lives in Israel and part of it lives in other places. This is especially true of the Jewish community in North America, which regards the United States as the fulfillment of the original Zionist dream to win equality while preserving Jewish identity.

Of course, there are Jews in important positions throughout the world in government, science, communications, and culture, but there is no Jewish spiritual authority—religious or secular—outside of Israel who has influence over the entire Jewish world. Israel has become the decision-maker in world Jewish affairs, and its influence is even greater than in the past, especially as many Jewish leaders in the Diaspora feel less self-assured in the face of an assimilation they are unable to prevent. This demonstrated weakness gives a natural priority to Israel, where such processes of assimilation do not exist.

The fact is that Conservative and Reform Jews raise a cry each time the "Who is a Jew?" issue appears again on the agenda in Israel, although decisions taken in Israel would seem to have no impact on their daily lives. Complaints like "My grandchild would not be considered a Jew in Israel" are very often expressed, even if it is clear to the speaker that his or her grandchildren would never live in Israel and perhaps not even visit. The conflict with the Israeli leadership that resurfaces periodically, and the threat of a rift with Israel if it decides to recognize only Orthodox conversions, only serve to highlight the Diaspora's dependence on Israel.

Israel has grown accustomed to, and comfortable with, the fact that Jews occupy positions of influence and power in other countries at a time when a fairly large Jewish state exists. There are those who even say that this is the ideal situation—that a strong American Jewish community is more important to Israel than immigration from America. This contention is voiced mainly by Diaspora

Jews who feel the need to justify why, as Zionists, they do not fulfill their Zionism by immigrating to Israel.

The Israeli leadership has always preferred that Jews immigrate to Israel rather than remain in the Diaspora to provide assistance to Israel. If world Jewry, with its enormous human and economic capacities, immigrated to Israel, Israel would become a country of some thirteen million Jews, with a standard of living ranked among the highest ten states in the world. However, it is clear that this is not about to happen, and thus Israel looks to exploit the strength of the Diaspora in other ways.

The economic assistance Israel has received from world Jewry since its early days—including the United Jewish Appeal in the U.S.A., the Foundation Fund (Keren HaYesod) in Europe, and the Jewish National Fund (Keren HaKayemet)—has helped it to absorb masses of new immigrants, purchase land, and build its economic strength and security. In the 1950s, the Israel Bonds organization began making loans available on comfortable terms.

As the years passed, this economic aid became a less significant percentage of Israel's gross national product and government budget. Today, most of the money collected in the Diaspora is allocated not for projects promoting immigration, but for the internal needs of the local community, including social welfare programs and education. In addition, some contributions from the Diaspora to Israel are earmarked for universities, hospitals, museums, and so on, and are not channeled to the state through national organizations.

Political support for the State of Israel has been no less essential, nor has its importance decreased over the years. During the fifty years prior to the establishment of the state, British Jews served an important role in the effort to persuade the Mandatory government to act favorably toward the leadership of the *yishuv*, though they met with little success. On the eve of Israel's establishment, and during the years since 1948, the Jews of the United States have played a central—and far more successful—role in the effort to lobby their home government for the benefit of Israel. This effort has been conducted primarily via the American Israel Public Affairs Committee (AIPAC), an American Jewish organization aimed at promoting good relations between the United States and Israel.

The influence of American Jews in their country is much greater than their proportion in the population (only about 2 percent). This is not the case in other Jewish centers in the world. Jews do hold important government positions in other countries, but the fact that they are Jews has only marginal significance, and there are no Jewish or pro-Israel pressure groups in these countries. European Jews are trying to exert influence through the framework of the European Community, but their attempts to form an effective Europe-wide lobby have not fared well.

Jews of the former Soviet Union had no opportunities to influence the old regime, and they have still not found their voice in the new political system. It is not clear how many of these Jews will emigrate and how many will remain and try to build influential community organizations like the American Jewish federations. In most communities in the world, organized Jewish political activity takes on the character of an appeal for assistance, while in the United States this activity is effective enough to imply a threat.

The existence of Jews throughout the world enables Israel to be not only a Jewish state but also the state of the Jews, providing world Jewry with the feeling that they have a second home. The dialogue with the Jewish world can contribute to the Jewish nature of the state. Anti-Semitic activities in the world strengthen Zionist feelings. Identification with Jewish distress in the world raises the level of internal Jewish solidarity in Israel.

Israel is involved in the security problems of the Jewish communities in the world, as well as in their educational issues, and sends emissaries worldwide for all types of purposes—*aliyah* emissaries, educators, and others. Still, the connection between Israel and the Diaspora is not a topic on the national agenda in Israel. It surfaces from time to time around the recurrent issue of

"Who is a Jew?" or following acts of violence against Jews in the world, and then quickly disappears. Most Israelis are not concerned about assimilation statistics in the Diaspora, are not familiar with Jewish communal life outside of Israel, and follow a narrow "Canaanite" outlook without ever having consciously adopted this ideology.

# CHAPTER 2

# One Hundred Years of Zionism: A Critical Assessment

A century has passed since the First Zionist Congress, and Israel's fifty-year jubilee is already behind us. This is an appropriate time for Israel to do some national soul-searching and assessment, to take pride in the success of our special mission, and to admit our failures.

It is possible that Zionism would have developed without Theodor Herzl. (We Israelis are very fond of calling him by his Hebrew name, Benjamin Ze'ev, but if someone had called him this in the street during his lifetime, it is unlikely that he would have even turned his head in response.) After all, Hibbat Zion and Leo Pinsker (1821–1891) preceded him, as did the First Aliyah. The Second Aliyah occurred despite Herzl and not because of him. Indeed, if the gates of America had remained open to Jewish immigration after the 1920s, the Zionist movement might have been little more than an episode in Jewish history. If it were not for the Holocaust, the State of Israel might not have been established in 1948 and no one would recall Herzl's prediction that a Jewish state would come to be in fifty years, or his famous motto "If you will it, it is no dream."

Even in retrospect, it is difficult to fully understand this enigmatic man who died at age forty-four, brokenhearted and betrayed. The more one studies his life, the more complicated it seems. A visit to his study, relocated on Mount Herzl in Jerusalem, does little to shed light on the man. Nor does a look around his small room in the Three Kings Hotel in Basel, left intact to memorialize his stay there during the First Zionist Congress—complete with the hotel bill written in German, beer glasses he used, the single bed, the famous balcony, the river.

Herzl, the first Zionist, was more, much more, cut out to become the last Jew. The diligent Paris correspondent for the *Neue Freie Presse* was born in 1860 to assimilating parents. As a child, he hated his Jewish studies so much that his parents were forced to transfer him to a regular school at age ten. At thirteen, Herzl had a "confirmation" ceremony in his home, and there is no evidence that he visited a synagogue on this occasion. He himself volunteered that if it were up to him, he would have been born a Prussian aristocrat, and indeed, he behaved as such throughout his entire life. He internalized anti-Semitic attitudes, admired the music of Wagner, regarded Bismarck as a model leader, and identified with the rising German nationalism. When his son was born, he did not bother with a ritual circumcision (*brit milah*) of the child in accordance with Jewish tradition.

In his personal life, Herzl was somewhat repulsive. He was terribly childish, living with his parents and in their shadow. Herzl consorted with prostitutes and contracted gonorrhea. Worst of all, he fell in love with eight- and nine-year-old girls and was unable to maintain real relationships with adult women. His married life was marked by unsuccessful attempts to reach a divorce agreement with his wife, Julie, and his children witnessed the fierce arguments between their parents. He would disappear from home for months at a time, under all sorts of pretenses, simply to distance himself from his wife.

After his death at age forty-four from heart failure, the family disappeared from the scene of world history without a trace. His wife, suffering from mental illness, died in 1907, at the age of thirty-seven. Herzl's son, Hans, converted to Christianity and committed suicide in 1930. His sister, Paulina, was addicted to drugs and also took her own life that same year. Trude, his third daughter, spent many years in mental hospitals and was killed in a Nazi concentration camp in 1943. Her only child, Peter Theodor, committed suicide three years later.

Herzl was a cynical dandy, dependent on his parents. He was a mediocre playwright who fled from his wife and children. He distanced himself from his Jewishness, and at one point even proposed leading an operation to convert European Jewry to Christianity. Such was the man who became the first Zionist. A coincidence of circumstances, combined with Herzl's genius and extraordinary organizational talents, left an amazing impact after a very brief period of time. Herzl's nine Zionist years, 1895 to 1904, changed his short life, and the life of the Jewish people.

Herzl had been born in the midst of a new phenomenon, unprecedented in the life of the Jewish people: only a few years before, Jews were permitted to leave the ghetto, to study and to teach without formal restrictions. He did not suffer from harsh anti-Semitism in his youth, and so he thought it would be possible to live in the modern world alongside Christians as an assimilated Jew. Later, he became convinced that assimilation would not mean a normal life and that the Christian world was not ready to open its arms to people like him. From this moment, he devoted the rest of his life to finding a solution for his Jewish brethren, so that they could live normal lives.

Herzl was not seeking a way to preserve the enormous spiritual treasures of the Jewish people. He did not dream of a spiritual center or of a chosen people. He was not at all concerned with the question of Jewish continuity or Judaism. He was only interested in Jews as people. If the world had welcomed Jews as people, and the Jews then gave up their Jewishness, no one would have been happier than Herzl.

Herzl is an extreme example of a man who appeared on the stage of history only due to the circumstances of his time. He was disappointed by the results of Jewish emancipation and encountered personal difficulty in becoming part of non-Jewish society, even under a legal system that officially permitted this. Today, Herzl would not have acted as he did in his own time. In a world in which Jews can assimilate into non-Jewish society in most nations, Herzl would not have dreamt of proposing that they congregate in their own state, nor would he have written *The Jewish State.*

Herzl would not have denied this—his entire foundation was negative. Everything began and ended with anti-Semitism. On the one hand, he felt superior to other Jews and internalized some aspects of anti-Semitism. On the other hand, anti-Semitism horrified him. Whoever reads *The Jewish State,* first published in 1896, soon realizes that there is only one motive driving the Zionist idea of the movement's leader: the threat of anti-Semitism. He was pragmatic and cynical. He did not marvel at Jewish history, and it is unclear whether he ever fully exchanged the German nationalism he met at the university for Jewish nationalism. He encountered anti-Semitism and decided that he was capable not only of describing the problem as a journalist, not only of bemoaning it as a Jew, but capable also of solving it as a leader who, meanwhile, had yet to enlist a single follower. In the end, he became the prophet of the Jewish state, the new Moses, a leader of the Jewish people, yet he was very close to becoming just another dreamer like Pinsker.

It is customary to attribute Herzl's personal conversion, culminating in Zionism, to his experience as a journalist covering the

Dreyfus trial in France. According to this view, Herzl came to understand during the course of the trial that even an assimilated Jew like Dreyfus was unable to escape his Jewishness—and the anti-Semitism directed against him as a Jew—and therefore Herzl decided that the only way left for the Jews was to establish a state of their own.

Shlomo Avineri argues that Herzl was predominantly influenced by events that occurred in the Austro-Hungarian Empire in the closing decades of the 1800s, such as the election of Dr. Karl Lueger, an outspoken anti-Semite, to the important position of mayor of Vienna, the repeated calls for anti-Jewish legislation in Hungary, and anti-Semitic occurrences in Czechoslovakia.

In any case, Herzl adopted a deterministic view of anti-Semitism as a permanent phenomenon:

> Perhaps we could completely assimilate into the peoples surrounding us if they left us alone for at least two generations. But they won't leave us alone. . . . Only the pressure makes us emotionally cling to our origins, only the hatred of those around us makes us alien again. Whether we like it or not, we have always been and still remain an historic community sharing a clear affiliation. We are a people—the enemy forges us as a people against our own will—and thus it has always been in history. In times of distress, we band together and suddenly display our strength. And yes, we have the strength to build a state, even an exemplary state. We have all of the means—human and material—necessary to achieve this.

The Jewish state, in the eyes of its prophet, was a fallback that could have been established in Uganda, Argentina, the Sinai, or even the Land of Israel. It is the result of the Jewish failure to integrate in the world, not the two-thousand-year-old dream of returning home in song and joy. Anti-Semitism is the sole and sufficient motive for the Zionist movement: "Therefore there will be no need for a special effort to ignite the movement," he writes.

> Anti-Semitism will take care of this for us. All they need to do is to continue to behave as they have and the desire of the masses to emigrate will awaken in those places where it has not yet done so and will strengthen where it already exists.

Herzl had no illusions. If he had fully appreciated the potential for immigration to the United States, he would simply have encouraged this immigration and would not have spent the rest of his life trying to gain permission from the world powers to transfer Jews to a state of their own. But he was not familiar with the United States or the emerging immigration trends at the time he outlined his program.

Herzl's real dream was for something like the American dream—to enable Jews to live like human beings and to assimilate since everything is so good! In many ways, he envisioned Jewish life in America much more than he envisioned a real Jewish state:

> For those who wish to see the Jews disappear through intermarriage, there is only one way. The Jews must first reach a great level of economic strength that will help overcome the prejudice of the old society.

Herzl's vision of his Jewish state is derived, of course, from his worldview as a liberal European, a son of late-nineteenth-century German culture. His main idea was to form a "Jewish Company" sponsored by the government of England, which would handle the disposition of Jewish real estate in Europe while the Jews were moving to their new state. The Jewish Company would ensure that the properties were sold at the best price possible. In exchange, the Jewish immigrants would be able to purchase land and build homes in the new state. A real population transfer—scientific and orderly—was envisioned. Each community, led by its own rabbi, would move to the state in turn. The Jewish Company would build homes for the middle class. Unskilled workers would build wooden homes for themselves and would become owners of these homes if "they behave properly for three years."

The workday would be seven hours. In order to prevent unemployment and crime, those in need of work would be provided unskilled labor jobs. The system of government Herzl favored was a monarchy. Since this was not practical, he advocated an aristocratic republic similar to medieval Venice, where the Doge ruled for life, in consultation with a council of aristocrats. Each person would speak his own language, as was customary in Switzerland. Herzl considered Hebrew impossible to speak and thought that Yiddish should be abolished. In the end, the language that proved most useful would gain predominance.

Rabbis would be forbidden from interfering in the affairs of state. The Jewish state would be politically neutral, with only a professional standing army. The state would have a constitution, and its flag would be white with seven gold stars to represent the seven hours of the workday.

Herzl's vision was not realized. No Jewish Company ever sold the property of Jews in the Diaspora and thus there were no earnings to transfer to new immigrants. Immigration to Palestine was not orderly and entire communities did not immigrate together. No great power awarded the Jews a concession enabling unlimited immigration to Palestine. In fact, except for a few years, immigration during the prestate period was severely restricted.

The story of Israel is ultimately one of national and military struggle. This aspect was scarcely acknowledged in Herzl's vision. Israel has not turned out to be the safest place for Jews. In fact, it is the only state in the world today where Jews are attacked simply for being Jews. There is no constitution, rabbis are actively involved in the political system, compulsory military service is the longest of any democratic country, and the state flag is not even white with seven gold stars.

If Herzl's vision had been fulfilled, the Jews would have abandoned Europe prior to World War II. For this reason, the failure to realize his vision constitutes a lost opportunity of enormous consequences, as the most horrible of all scenarios was not prevented. The culture that Herzl venerated, in the city that he so loved, produced the Nazi beast that herded six million Jews to their death, accompanied by the music so dear to Herzl. Immigration to pre-state Israel occurred without the consent of the world powers and was in large part illegal. It was also opposed, to a large extent, by the veteran Zionist leadership, which remained in Europe and viewed practical Zionism as a mistake, clearly preferring political Zionism. In the end, practical Zionism prevailed.

The British Mandate, which the Zionist movement saw as a savior, moved further and further away from any readiness to establish a Jewish state. It placed hurdles before immigration and prevented Jews from purchasing land. Were it not for the Holocaust, it is hard to imagine that the world would have acquiesced in the establishment of a Jewish state in Palestine. But even the world's consent was not enough, and the state was only founded after a bloody war in which an entire generation of young Israelis—six thousand—lost their lives, a full 1 percent of the Jewish population in 1948.

Would all this have occurred without Herzl? We'll never know. He contributed the dream, the feeling that change was possible, the organization, and the effort to raise international awareness for the issue. The World Zionist Organization, the Jewish National Fund, the various economic instruments and the Zionist leadership played an important role in establishing the Jewish state, but not a central one. Relatively few Zionists immigrated to Israel before the state was founded, mainly young people looking for a challenge and a new life, along with immigrants rejected by other countries.

In 1917, the atmosphere in Britain was favorable enough to allow for the issuance of the Balfour Declaration, which expressed support for the establishment of a national home for the Jews in Palestine. In time, the British cooled to this idea as they became entangled in the contradictory promises they gave to the Arabs, the French, and the Jews during World War I. They withdrew their support for the Peel Report, which proposed establishing both a small Jewish state and an Arab state in the area west of the Jordan River, later issuing the White Papers that would have brought an end to the Zionist dream.

The first White Paper was published in 1922 and awarded the eastern part of Palestine to the emir Abdallah (1882–1951). It also stipulated that Jewish immigration to Palestine would be restricted to the country's ability to absorb the immigrants within its own economy, adding that there was no intention of making Palestine as Jewish as "England is English." The second White Paper, issued in 1930, sought to prevent any additional Jewish settlement resulting from the conflict of interests between the Jews and Arabs, and advocated the formation of a legislative council comprised of a majority of Arab representatives. Protests from the Jewish Agency and Zionist leadership led to the cancellation of this White Paper.

In 1939, a White Paper was published that limited land sales to Jews in Palestine; and in February 1940, Jewish land acquisition was completely prohibited in certain areas of Palestine. The British plan permitted the immigration of 75,000 Jews to Palestine during the next five years, with any subsequent immigration to be conditional upon Arab approval.

Could a small community of 500,000 Jews have established a Jewish state if not for World War II and the Holocaust of European Jews? It appears doubtful. Zionists and the children of Zionists met their death in the concentration camps in Europe. Whoever waited in Europe for a "red carpet" to be spread out before the Jews paid the ultimate price. It was, then, the Holocaust that kept most of the nations of the world from opposing the establishment of a Jewish state.

If not for the Holocaust, the Jews of Palestine would likely have remained a permanent minority, without rights to purchase land. Upon conclusion of the British Mandate, an Arab state would have been established. At that juncture, the Jews, or a large number of them, would have left Palestine for Europe or America, if immigration were allowed.

A mistake on a different scale pertained to the Arab issue. The early Zionists did not completely ignore this problem, but neither did they foresee its severity, preferring to portray it in a more positive light than was warranted by reality. In *The Jewish State,* Herzl wrote:

> Palestine is our unforgettable historic homeland. This itself would constitute a strong rallying cry for our people. If His Majesty the Sultan were to grant us Palestine, we could promise in return to completely organize the financial situation of Turkey. For Europe, our presence there would be part of a wall of defense against Asia. We would be a bulwark of civilization against barbarism.

In his fictional work about Palestine, *Altneuland* (The Old-New Land), written in 1902, Herzl presents an idyllic picture of relations between Jews and Arabs. Thus, he reveals that he was aware of the problem but believed that it would be possible to negotiate a solution. Rashid, a handsome Arab, thirty-five years old, who recently completed his studies in Berlin, represents the Arabs in the novel. When one of Herzl's characters asks, "Don't you view the Jews as foreign intruders?" Rashid offers this amazing response:

> "Is this the way you would view a person who takes nothing away from you and brings you something? The Jews have enriched us, so why should we even be angry with them? They live with us as

brothers, why should we not even love them? . . . Our houses of prayer stand one beside another, and I have always believed that, when our prayers start to rise to heaven, they join somewhere up above and continue together until they reach our Father in heaven."

Ahad Ha'am responded to this in a sarcastic critique of *Altneuland*:

> How nice is this ideology! How clever was the new society to find enough land for the millions of Jews returning from the Diaspora, while all of the lands the Arabs were previously cultivating—that is, most of the good land in Palestine—still remains in their hands, and nothing was taken from them. . . .

Herzl does not stop at this. Rashid is tested with another question, more difficult than the first: "All this is very well and good, and appropriately said. But you are an educated man. You studied in Europe. Yet, I assume that your views are not the same as those of the simple urban and village dwellers?" Rashid is not confused and answers:

> "These views apply even more to them than to myself. . . . Tolerance I did not learn in the West. We, the Muslims, have always lived in peace with the Jews. . . . From the time the first Jewish settlers appeared here, at the end of the previous century, Arab rivals would sometimes choose a Jew as an arbitrator or would appeal directly to the council of the Jewish community in order to seek advice, aid or a ruling."

The novel *Altneuland*—named for the famous synagogue in Prague, the *Altneushul*—describes Palestine in utopian terms and, as a work of literature, should not be subjected to a political analysis. It is not a political essay like *The Jewish State*. Still, two points become clear here: first, Herzl was aware of the problem of Palestine's Arabs and devoted some thought to how the Arabs would relate to the Jewish immigrants. He did not imagine that Palestine was an uninhabited land. Second, Herzl hoped that by bringing their assets and achieving modernization, the Jews would create such prosperity for the Arabs that they would feel grateful to the new immigrants and want to live with them in peace.

This was also the view of Max Nordau, who saw Zionism as an extension of European culture into Asia. His assessment—like that of Dov Ber Borochov (1881–1917), on the opposite end of the political spectrum—was that the power of the culture the Jews brought with them would assimilate the Arabs living in Palestine. In his view, the Arabs would be absorbed into the Jewish society since "the means of production" (in his Marxist terminology) are stronger among the Jews. There would be those, of course, who would not assimilate, and they would be treated fairly and even enjoy autonomy. Nordau did not foresee a national awakening among the Arabs of Palestine.

Ahad Ha'am thought differently. In his 1891 article "The Truth from Palestine," he presents a complex picture of Arab-Jewish relations in Palestine. The Arabs are, for the moment, willing to accept the Jewish immigration since it improves their economic situation and is small in scope. But if the number of immigrants increases, the tension is liable to explode. There is potential for this in the harsh attitude of the Jewish farmers toward their Arab workers.

As Ahad Ha'am explained it,

> The Arab, like all Semites, is smart and cunning. . . . The peasants
> are happy with the formation of a Hebrew colony in their midst
> since they receive good wages for their work, and are prospering
> from year to year . . . and the landowners are also happy with us

since we pay them a high price for their land of rock and sand, a price beyond anything they had ever dreamed. However, if the time comes when the life of our people in Palestine develops so much that it displaces—to a small or great extent—the [Arab] inhabitants, then they will not give up their place easily.

In this important article, he showed more long-range vision than the founders of the Zionist movement did. He warned against provoking the anger of the Arabs through the "disgraceful acts" of Jewish farmers, who were exploited in the Diaspora and now seek to exploit the Arabs of Palestine. These farmers "act towards the Arabs with animosity and cruelty, trespass without justification, shamefully beat them without any sufficient cause, and even brag about doing so."

Yitzhak Epstein (1862–1943), a teacher and agriculturist, was one of the first to identify the Arab question as the central problem facing Zionism and advocated an alliance with the Arabs. At the time of the Seventh Zionist Congress in 1905, he declared that Palestine belongs to "those two old Semitic peoples," Jews and Arabs, and called for an end to land acquisition where it entails the dispossession of Arab peasants. Instead, he advocated only purchasing uninhabited land that was not already under cultivation by Arab fellahin.

According to Epstein, the Jewish people could assist the Arabs, liberate them from illiteracy, and bring them progress under the condition that Jews would not act like colonialists. The Jews could establish educational, health, and cultural institutions and help the Arabs integrate into these. They could help make peace between the various Arab sects, and even promote their national consciousness and recognize their right to self-determination. In Epstein's dream, the Arab nationalist movement would not be anti-Jewish if the Jews helped in its development.

Thirty years passed before the Zionist movement understood

that the Arab nationalist movement in Palestine posed a real threat. Not only was it impossible to establish a Jewish state as long as there was a massive Arab majority in western Palestine, real hatred for the Jews developed among the Arabs of Palestine. Fearful about the large waves of immigrants, they became ready to fight to prevent continued immigration and land purchase.

After the Balfour Declaration, in 1917, by which Britain appeared to give its approval for a Jewish state, the main question, it seemed, was how to develop an economic base in Palestine for mass immigration from Europe. By 1936, however, it was clear that the central problem was the struggle between the Arabs and Jews in the face of the British fear of Arab demands. In 1947, two years after the Holocaust of European Jews ended, the Zionist movement wanted to believe that the world would grant the Jews their coveted state. But it soon became apparent that a war with the Arab countries would be necessary in order to attain statehood, and it was hard to predict whether the Jews would emerge victorious from this war.

It was wrong, or naïve, to think that the Jews were coming to an uninhabited land, or that the small Arab population, anxious to improve their economic conditions, would welcome the Jewish immigrants. The case of the untrained and ill-equipped Holocaust survivors who, soon after arriving in Palestine, died in attempts to capture the Kastel police fortress on the road to Jerusalem is only one of many examples of how the "Altneuland" was mistaken in its portrait of an idyllic haven for Jews. These examples also include: the War of Independence in 1948, the Sinai Campaign in 1956, the Six-Day War in 1967, the War of Attrition until 1970, the Yom Kippur War in 1973, the Lebanon War in 1982, and the Gulf War in 1991 (in which Israel participated only as a victim).

The immediate price was paid in human life. In total some 20,000 Jewish soldiers were killed in Israel's wars. Thirty percent of these fell in the War of Independence, which was the most difficult war of all. The loss of this large part of the 1948 generation had a significant impact on the state's early days. My childhood in Israel in the 1950s was shadowed by the loss of the six million killed in the Holocaust and the six thousand killed in the War of Independence. The new memorial days—Holocaust Day and the Memorial Day for IDF Soldiers—became, in time, the defining characteristics of being Israeli.

If we add the thousands of people permanently injured as a result of wars and hostilities, it becomes clear that practically every home in Israel has directly experienced bereavement or disabling injuries. This is the most horrible aspect of the Israeli experience. It was not part of the plan. It never appeared in the darkest nightmares of the Zionist leaders. No one can say whether they would have persisted in their Zionist vision had they known that Israel would become the only place in the world where Jews are endangered simply because they are Jews, where dozens of missiles would crash into Tel Aviv, destroying the homes of innocent residents, and where citizens would stand in line waiting to receive gas masks fifty years after the previous generation was destroyed in gas chambers.

On the one hand, it is true that the Holocaust of European Jews would not have occurred if the Zionist vision had been realized before World War II. On the other hand, the Holocaust might also have been prevented if the gates to the United States had remained open to European Jews. In any case, we cannot deny that it is more dangerous to be a Jew in Israel than in any other place in the world. As long as this situation does not change, it is Zionism's paradox and its most painful failure.

Israel's defense budget (relative to its gross national product) is the highest of any democratic country. It was quite low during the 1950s, rose during the late 1960s, and peaked after the Yom Kippur War, which cost the Israeli economy the equivalent of one year of GNP! Current defense expenditures, together with defense-related loan payments, make the Israeli budget to a large extent inflexible.

As a result, heavy taxation is necessary, making it difficult to enact sweeping economic reforms. Much of the large investment in defense does not contribute to economic growth and constitutes a very heavy burden on the Israeli economy.

The economy suffers in productivity due to the requirements of military service. Israel has the longest compulsory military service of any Western nation (three years), plus thirty years of reserve duty (one month per year). Young people at the height of their intellectual ability are required to interrupt their education for military service, returning to their studies in their early twenties, when young people their age in other countries have already graduated.

Reserve military service burdens the economy since people in senior as well as less senior positions are required to stop their work and return to uniform for a period of several weeks. This sometimes causes considerable damage to important economic systems. Nevertheless, the prevailing attitude is that there is no alternative, since security is indeed more important than the economy.

The security threat has produced an economy with autocratic characteristics and a siege mentality. There is a huge price to be paid for a society that needs to produce its weapons itself, that needs to develop agricultural and other products that would be cheaper to import, and that needs to stockpile oil and other essential resources.

Part of the problem of Israel's economy stems from a feeling that by focusing on those areas in which we have a competitive advantage, Israel would become too dependent on the outside world. In the event of a blockade, Israel would be unable to hold out against its enemies.

Israel has failed, so far, to win recognition from parts of the Muslim world for the legitimacy of its right to exist. It is therefore the only country in the world that official political leaders—like those in Iran—openly speak of annihilating. In an age when nuclear, chemical, and biological weapons of mass destruction come into play in regional conflicts, Israel's survival is even more endangered. Israel's tremendous military accomplishments and conquests, and the development of the most effective army in the Middle East, become shadows against this array of destructive threats.

The collapse of the Soviet Union and the transition of Eastern Europe to a democratic region under NATO influence has not made the world any easier for Israel. In a world that is no longer bipolar, Israel's unique role as the trusted ally of the United States in the Middle East has eroded. Control over weapons of mass destruction is almost impossible in this new world. The only long-term solution, without a doubt, is to complete the circle of peace with our immediate neighbors and, later, with our more distant ones.

Countries like Iran and Iraq are likely to seek the support of fellow Muslims in future conflicts by claiming that their fight is against the "Zionist enemy." Iraq did just that in 1991, when it fired thirty-nine SCUD missiles into the heart of Israel. The assumption is that if their battle is perceived as anti-Zionist, the Muslim world—especially the Arab states—will not be able to stand on the side-lines. But Arab countries that have concluded peace agreements with Israel would be much less likely to answer this call, and this, in turn, would lower the likelihood of an attack initiated by the radical states on Israel's periphery. All of this underlines, once again, the importance of completing the initial circle of peace with Israel's neighbors, including Syria and Lebanon.

Israel has sent its soldiers to battle every ten years, and is still suffering casualties in Lebanon. Israeli citizens are still forced to cope with Palestinian terror and threats of destruction. It is no wonder, therefore, that Israelis put a high value on "security." Like a healthy person who learns to value his health only after a severe illness, Israelis appreciate security after experiencing so much insecurity.

The energies of Israel's best intellects are directed toward solving security problems—how to deal with Palestinian demonstrators, or roadside bombs in Lebanon; the production of sophisticated and impenetrable fences, night-vision equipment, antimissile technology; and so on. Security concerns reduce the scope of tourism to Israel and deter families with children approaching enlistment age from considering immigration. If a parent faces the choice between a country that allows an eighteen-year-old to attend university and one that requires the same young person to enlist for three years of army service, the parent must be an ardent Zionist to choose the second option.

Security has also become an excuse. When in Israel it is said that something is impossible, canceled, or prevented due to security considerations, this is taken as a sufficient answer. Security was used to justify the travel restrictions imposed on the Arab citizens of Israel during the "Military Government" of 1948–66. It is still used today to justify norms that are difficult to accept in a democratic state, such as administrative detention (until the high court of justice banned it in 1999) and the use of force by the General Security Service (GSS) in interrogating suspects.

The distinction between security rationale and security pretense is sometimes blurred. This was the case, for example, in the 1986 episode of the Route-300 bus, when GSS agents killed several terrorists after they were captured alive. When this serious case was exposed, the agents did not stand trial but were instead released from the security service under a presidential pardon.

Israel, which was to be a bulwark of democracy, human rights, and minority rights, receives critical reports each year by organizations like Amnesty International and the local B'Tzelem group for its harsh treatment of Palestinians. Due to its siege mentality and the feeling that "all the world is against us," Israel decided to ally itself with "pariah" states and was subsequently defiled by their depravity.

Israel's relations with apartheid-era South Africa, Pinochet's

Chile, the Shah's Iran, and Somoza's Nicaragua all resulted from a feeling that only these states were sincerely interested in us, while the rest of the world was cynical and hypocritical. Yet these relations made it very difficult for the only democracy in the Middle East to speak about justice and human rights. The United Nations became our greatest enemy, and important international organizations like UNESCO turned us away. The combination of a difficult struggle for survival and wars that involved the conquest of territories, turned Israel into a virtual pariah state for many years.

The cynical attitude we Israelis have developed toward the world—the jaundiced view we take of international organizations and their double standards, the reports of various human rights groups, and the real meaning of so-called "freedom fighters" in different parts of the world—has made us into a state that is quite apart from the "spiritual center" envisioned by Ahad Ha'am, for example. The originators of the Zionist idea never anticipated the security problem or the constant fight for survival. Moreover, a reading of Herzl suggests that he would not have proposed a "Jewish state" if he had thought that this dream could only be realized by means of an ongoing struggle for the state's existence. His remarks on the military (in *The Jewish State*) were quite succinct: "The Jewish state should be a neutral state. It only requires a permanent army, which would indeed be equipped with all of the modern weaponry to maintain order, on both the foreign and domestic fronts." This is all that Herzl has to say on the security issue! In another place, where he talked about the future bureaucracy in the Jewish state, he noted in parentheses:

> (By bureaucrats, I also include officers of the army of defense, whose numbers should always be equal to about ten percent of the male immigrants. This number should be sufficient to wipe out the disputes of evil people, since the majority are peace-loving). . . .

The various political phenomena described above have made it easier for Israel's harshest critics to argue that there is an intrinsic contradiction in a democratic Jewish state, but this contention could not be more mistaken. There is no inherent flaw in a state aspiring to be both Jewish and democratic, just as there is no reason for the state to be formed beside Israel not to be both Palestinian and democratic. Even when there are serious deviations, when certain Israeli decisions or actions are not democratic, this is not due to the fact that Israel is a Jewish state, or that it is the state of the Jews. It is simply because Israel has strayed from the path of democracy.

Since Israel was established to solve the problem of the Jews, and would otherwise not have become an independent state, it is fully justified in defining a pro-Jewish immigration policy. From the moment a person becomes an Israeli citizen, the principles of democracy demand that he or she be accorded equal rights. The Jewish character of the state stems from the fact that it has a Jewish majority. This is what dictates Israel's link to the Jewish world and its immigration policies, but it does not, and should not, prevent a non-Jewish Israeli from exercising any right or attaining any position in Israeli society. The reason that Arab citizens in Israel do not feel that they have equal rights is due to policies enacted by the Jewish majority, but these policies are not an inevitable result of Israel's identity as a Jewish state. We must work on correcting undemocratic policies, but this does not require us to renounce the special Jewish character of Israel.

The second problem that the Zionist visionaries did not foresee was the demographic issue of the large group of Christian and Muslim Arabs living in Palestine. Herzl did not refer to the number of Arabs in Palestine, and did not regard them as a security risk, a national or a demographic problem. The demographic question surfaced even before security or national issues. The right and left wings of the Zionist camp concurred that the Jewish state should be established only after attaining a Jewish majority in Palestine, since the state should be democratic. If the majority of the citizens were Arabs, the Jewish minority would not be able to prevail upon them to establish a Jewish state. There were other ideas proposed, but these remained the views of a minority. For example, Chaim Arlosoroff (1899–1933) suggested in a famous letter to Weizmann that the Jews first establish a state by force and then wait for a Jewish majority to materialize.

The Zionist movement failed in its efforts to guarantee a Jewish majority in Palestine. This was the background for the argument between Ben-Gurion's pragmatism and Jabotinsky's tenaciousness over the issue of partitioning western Palestine. Ben-Gurion supported the establishment of two states west of the Jordan River— one Jewish and one Arab—while Jabotinsky preferred to wait until a Jewish state with a Jewish majority could be declared. Just as Jabotinsky fiercely opposed the Peel Plan in 1937, Menachem Begin opposed the United Nations partition plan ten years later. Ben-Gurion accepted both of these plans, though they fell short of his dreams. These compromise decisions were not only motivated by Ben-Gurion's wish to attain sovereignty as soon as possible, but also by his belief that only a Jewish state could enable mass immigration. The opposite route had failed: a Jewish state could not be founded on mass immigration, since this immigration never materialized.

On the eve of the First Aliyah, in 1880, some 24,000 Jews were living in western Palestine among approximately 525,000 Arabs— a proportion of 1 to 22. In 1915, there were already 90,000 Jews, but still five times as many Arabs. In 1947, there were twice as many Arabs as Jews living in this area: approximately 630,000 Jews and 1,300,000 Arabs.

The partition plan that the United Nations proposed in its Resolution 181 on November 29, 1947, included two states: a Jewish state with about 630,000 Jews and 500,000 Arabs, and an Arab state with some 800,000 Arabs. The Arab rejection of the UN plan turned out to be the biggest mistake of its generation. If the Arab world had adopted the partition plan, the tiny Jewish state would have faced a very difficult demographic problem.

In the end, the War of Independence created a much more comfortable situation for the Jewish state, which was able to expand its sovereignty beyond the borders of the UN plan to include an area in which 850,000 Arabs had lived up until 1948. If all of these Arabs had remained, the Jewish population would have been faced with ruling over an Arab majority. But this did not happen, as only 150,000 Arabs remained in the area that became the Jewish state, together with 650,000 Jews. Of the 700,000 Arabs who left this area, some were driven off by Israeli soldiers and some decided to flee on their own accord, hoping to return with victorious Arab armies, as promised by the mufti of Jerusalem, Hajj Amin al-Husseini (1893–1974). They moved to Gaza and the West Bank, Jordan, Lebanon, Syria, Iraq, and elsewhere, and this refugee problem became one of the most sensitive issues in the Arab-Jewish conflict.

The refugee issue has some very practical aspects to be settled as part of the final status negotiations between Israel and the Palestinian Authority. There is also the historical argument, with the Palestinians claiming that nearly all of the refugees were driven away by Israel, while Israel says that only a minority were expelled and most left of their own volition. The truth probably lies somewhere in between. That is, about 350,000 were forcibly evicted and about 350,000 fled on their own.

After the War of Independence, the demographic issue ceased to be an immediate problem, but it was still a question that very much concerned the Israeli leadership. This leadership granted Israeli citizenship to all Arab residents but severely restricted their movement and freedom to act under the military government. The relatively small number of Israeli Arabs, together with the large waves of Jewish immigration from Europe, North Africa, Iraq, and Yemen, ensured a stable Jewish majority for the Jewish state.

The demographic issue appeared again on the national agenda after Israel conquered Gaza and the West Bank in 1967. Those opposed to a Palestinian state and advocating the annexation of the territories won in the Six-Day War must be very optimistic regarding future immigration to Israel, since there are already some 3.5 million Arabs in western Palestine versus 5 million Jews. (Approximately 1 million Arabs are citizens of Israel and 2.5 million more live in the West Bank and Gaza Strip.) For many years, more Arab babies have been born west of the Jordan River than Jewish babies. The natural increase among the Arabs could create an Arab majority before too long. Only a repartitioning of Palestine would ensure that the State of Israel maintains a Jewish majority.

The Arab-Israeli problem is also intensifying within the pre-1967 borders in light of the large number of Israeli Arabs and the demands of their young leadership. In the past, their demands focused on improving living conditions; more recently, however, they seek to achieve a fuller integration into the life of the state. Their demands include new symbols, such as a national anthem that Arabs could accept, and a revised definition of Israel as a state belonging to all of its citizens, and not a Jewish state.

Israel is a Jewish state. This is its entitlement to exist. Israel is also a Jewish state because most of its citizens are Jewish and choose to live in a Jewish culture (even if this culture is defined differently by various segments of the population). Notwithstanding, Israel is also a state belonging to all of its citizens, since it is a democratic state that must extend equal rights to all. Any attempt to undermine any one of these foundations would undermine the existence of this special state.

The Arab-Jewish problem soon became the primary obstacle

to realizing the Zionist dream, and it remains today a burden preventing its fulfillment. The establishment of a Palestinian state beside the State of Israel is likely to solve the core of the demographic issue and facilitate the completion of the peace process between Israel and its neighbors, thus decreasing the threats to Israel's survival. Yet the relations with the Arab and Druze minorities in Israel will continue to demand our attention in the future, and peace with the Arab world will not necessarily make these internal Israeli issues any simpler.

Israel is a fantastic success story, regardless of the vision that gave birth to it. It brought forth great energies from the Jewish people and provided the challenge of creating something from scratch. The Zionist movement made deserts bloom after thousands of years, drained swamps that stood for hundreds of years, and brought to life an area that provides a livelihood for many people and has raised the standard of living for the region. A fascinating laboratory of ideas and forms of settlement was created here, with a chance to contribute in the future to the rehabilitation of one of the most neglected parts of the world.

This is a democratic state that did not stop being so even in the most difficult days of war, even in the darkest days of internal strife—when a prime minister was assassinated. Its democracy has regional implications, the first and foremost being its influence on Palestinian democracy.

Important works of art and literature have been created, and Hebrew has been revived as a living, modern language—a feat Herzl never dared to dream of. Beautiful and significant Jewish sources serve as the basis for an entire culture, mainly secular, which draws its inspiration from the unique process of returning home, from the old-new scenery, and from the ancient Jewish wellspring.

The Israeli success story is reinforced by the state's economic success and its place in the top 10 percent of the world economy, its success in agriculture and assistance to Third World countries, its rapid industrialization, and its transition from traditional industry to high-tech. Israel's military power and its unusual ingenuity—demonstrated, for example, in the destruction of the Arab air forces in the Six-Day War and the rescue of the Entebbe hostages in 1976—have made the country a focus of attention in the world press second only to the United States and Russia.

Fifty years after it was established, and one hundred years after it was conceived as an almost esoteric notion, Israel's population is greater than such countries as Denmark, Norway, and Finland. Israel has the same number of residents as Switzerland, and its standard of living is higher than some member nations in the European Community, approaching that of Great Britain. Israel is an established fact. It is at once fascinating, divided, problematic, and intriguing. It has managed to forge a special relationship with the United States, and the world does not fail to take notice of this. Despite Israel's fine economic condition, it receives the highest amount of U.S. civilian and military aid of any country in the world—in both absolute and relative terms—without this engendering any significant opposition in America. The alliance with Israel is taken for granted by most of the American leadership in both major parties. Israel's perceived ability to influence decisionmakers in the United States has created a myth about Israel that reinforces its might in the eyes of many countries in the world.

Israel is a country whose citizens feel part of a mission. The primary mission is to ensure its existence, and the fierce disagreement between the left and right involves the desire to mold the character of this existence. Divisions of opinion shape Israel: right and left, hawks and doves, religious and secular, Jews and Arabs. The feeling of being part of a mission will not necessarily last forever, and may pass as solutions are found for various problems. But this "mission" explains why immigration to Israel is called *aliyah* ("going up") while emigration is termed *yeridah* ("going down") and is considered to be a turning of one's back on the collective.

Israel's great success lies in its ability to be a common denominator for world Jewry. The issue of Israel is frequently a valid excuse for Jewish gatherings. Discussing the problems of Israel is a good way to bring together Jews who do not normally meet in a synagogue or *mikveh* (ritual bath). Concern for Israel, pride in Israel, the need to collect money for Israel, visits to Israel—together, all of these things create an important agenda for encouraging Jewish involvement in the Diaspora when other agendas become irrelevant.

Despite all of these positive things, Israel—like the Jewish *yishuv* or settlement in Palestine before the establishment of the state—is the fallback option, not the first choice, for most immigrants. Recent historiography has been kind to the pioneers, highlighting their role in forming the Jewish state. But the number of immigrants who were motivated by true Zionist fervor was small. The Bilu group, which arrived in the First Aliyah, before Herzl became a Zionist, included only about a dozen members. David Ben-Gurion used to say that 90 percent of the Second Aliyah immigrants eventually returned to their countries of origin.

Many of the Jews arrived in Palestine because they had nowhere else to go, especially after they became refugees in Eastern Europe and the United States closed its gates. This applies to the two largest waves of immigration prior to 1948: the Fourth Aliyah, which followed the draconian U.S. Immigration Law of 1924, and the Fifth Aliyah, which fled Germany and was unable to reach America due to the stiff immigration restrictions still in effect. Many of the Holocaust survivors who were transferred to displaced-persons camps in Germany preferred to travel to the United States rather than be absorbed in Israel. Against this backdrop, David Ben-Gurion decided to transfer entire Jewish communities from Arab countries to Israel. He did not do this out of fear for the survival of these communities, but because he wanted to maintain the Jewish majority in Israel and understood that Jewish immigrants were not arriving of their own accord.

What Ben-Gurion did with the Jews of Yemen, Iraq, Morocco, Tunisia, Libya, and Algeria was what Herzl had hoped to do with the Jews of Europe, but without the economic foundation Herzl called "the Jewish Company." With the barest of financial means, Ben-Gurion brought whole communities to Israel, distributed them in tent cities and rough wooden barracks throughout the land and along the borders, and thus sought to establish the Jewish spirit in Israel while securing the frontier. This was a bold beginning and farsighted approach, but one that exacted a steep social cost. The social structure was seriously damaged and the attempt to integrate these communities into the Israeli melting pot was not very successful. The location of the outlying development towns kept some of these Jews from taking advantages of opportunities available only in the center of the country.

The implications of these social costs have found expression in Israeli society since the 1970s, as the ethnic divide became a real stumbling block in the way of social integration. Just as some may compare the relative economic and social success of Eastern European Jews who immigrated to the United States with that of those who came to Israel, many Jews from Arab countries—especially from North Africa—view those who moved to France as much more successful than those who immigrated to Israel.

When the gates of the Soviet Union were opened in the 1970s and in 1989, the émigrés preferred to relocate to America. Israel exerted great efforts to prevent the United States from according refugee status to Soviet Jews so that they would come to Israel instead. This was one of the rare disputes between Israel and the American Jewish establishment, which did not understand how Israelis—across the political spectrum—could try to deny the freedom of choice to other Jews and, in effect, force them to come to Israel. There is no doubt that only a very small percentage of

Jews from the former Soviet Union would have immigrated to Israel had the gates of America been open to them.

Most of the Jews who fled Iran in 1979, after the Khomeini revolution, also preferred America. And with the end of white rule in South Africa, most of the Jews who decided to leave that country chose Australia and Canada over Israel. On the other hand, Jews and would-be Jews from the Third World are anxious to come to Israel and be recognized as Jewish immigrants, as in the case of the Beta Israel tribes of Ethiopia (commonly known by the vulgar Amharic term *falasha*, "exiles").

Israel is viewed by much of world Jewry as "the poor man's America," a second-best option. Herzl anticipated this. In *The Jewish State* he wrote: "If today there were any friendly country offering benefits, even if much fewer than those promised in the future Jewish state, a great stream of Jews would head off for this country. The poorest, those with nothing to lose, [however,] would naturally be drawn to it. . . ."

For the Israeli leadership, this is an unacceptable affront. David Ben-Gurion could not understand what Zionism could mean—after the establishment of the state—without *aliyah*. Yitzhak Rabin (1922–1995) did not hesitate to call *yordim*—those who leave the State of Israel—"the residue of weaklings." President Ezer Weizman (born 1924) incurred the wrath of many Diaspora Jews when he told a gathering at his official residence several years ago that the proper thing for them to do is simply to immigrate to Israel.

Israel, more than fifty years after its establishment, is not able to attract Jews who are doing well, and Jews who are not doing well prefer to immigrate to other places. Those who do immigrate to Israel are primarily those who did not manage to gain entry to the United States or another Western nation, or are penniless immigrants who greatly improve their standard of living upon arriving in Israel. In addition, there are some immigrants (though relatively few) who are motivated by Zionist or religious ideology or a combination of the two. After the waves of large-scale immigration that Israel brought from Arab lands, or which Israel prevented from reaching Western nations, it seems that the distribution of Jews in the world is stabilizing.

Some 500,000 Israelis have left the state since 1948. Of these about 80 percent have emigrated to the United States and the rest have moved to Canada, France, Great Britain, Germany, and Australia.

The State of Israel is the amazing fulfillment of a vision but one that turned out to be very different from the original vision. If one follows Herzl's analysis, it is reasonable to expect that the prophet of the Jewish state would have abandoned his efforts to gain a concession to establish a Jewish state in Palestine had he known what was to transpire in the decades following the First Zionist Congress. That is, it is likely that he would have focused instead on lobbying for a promise to absorb the Jews of Eastern Europe in America.

If Herzl had known that America would be different from other places of exile, and that—contrary to his theory—it would not become anti-Semitic, he would have preferred to try to direct Jews to the United States, where they could freely assimilate and pursue the kind of life that he, Dreyfus, and many others so desired. For him, the establishment of a Jewish state was an act of frustration pursued only after failing to assimilate in modern culture, a sort of forced retreat. The American Jewish experience is precisely what he had hoped for European Jewry. Even if Herzl would be very proud of Israel's many achievements, he would nevertheless have to admit that his outlook had favored a different solution.

The same could not be said of Ben-Gurion and his contemporaries. For them, the establishment of a Jewish state in Palestine was the only possible and desirable outcome for Jews and Jewish life, and for this they were willing to pay any price.

Ben-Gurion was part of a national movement whose faith included a belief that the assimilation of Jews is nearly as tragic as their annihilation. An Israel with a strong army, a developed economy, and some five million Jews, and whose authors—writing in the revived language of Hebrew—are awarded the Nobel Prize, represents a complete realization of this dream, or even surpasses it.

Israel at the beginning of the twenty-first century is not a "normal state," nor is it the most secure place for Jews, but it is the most secure place for being Jewish. From this perspective, it goes a long way toward fulfilling Ahad Ha'am's somewhat nebulous vision of a Jewish spiritual center.

Jews may continue to thrive in the secular world of the twenty-first century, but this does not guarantee a Jewish future. In order for the Jewish people to continue to exist, young Jews must actively prefer marriage partners who will join them in maintaining Jewish family values. The best venues for this preference exist among Orthodox Jews in the Diaspora and among all Jews in Israel, where potential Jewish spouses—religious and secular—are readily available. In Israel, it is possible to develop a Jewish future in a secular world.

Israel, then, is the solution for the continuation of secular Jewish life, and since most of world Jewry is not religious, it is reasonable to conclude that Israel is the solution for Jewish life. Even if it is not a sufficient solution, and if it still needs many improvements, this fact has become self-evident in recent years. When Israel completes the circle of peace, it could indeed become the solution for Jews and Jewish life.

Herzl at the beginning of the twenty-first century would have chosen America over Israel. In the United States he might have become a television broadcaster, a Broadway playwright, or a Hollywood screenwriter. He might have reported in gossip columns on the glamorous parties he attended and contributed small sums to the United Jewish Appeal, though preferring vacations in the Bahamas to the long trip to Israel.

He would have made that choice not only because his uncircumcised son would have faced difficulties growing up in Israeli society, but because he would not have viewed it as a safe place for Jews. Israel did not become the European island in the heart of the Middle East, a haven of peace and quiet for the Jews, with no vestiges of anti-Semitism. A country where survival is the primary issue on the national agenda would not have attracted Herzl. As someone who clearly advocated maintaining only a professional army, compulsory military service for three years would have seemed too heavy a burden for his children, and the dangers of war and terrorism would not have endeared Israel to him.

The Gordian knot between religion and state would have made him shudder. The last thing he would have wanted to do was to move to a place that imposed religious law and limited his activities on Saturdays. The enormous political influence of the ultra-Orthodox would have been enough to dissuade him from considering immigration to Israel. He addressed this issue plainly enough in *The Jewish State:*

> Indeed, will we have a theocracy in the end? No! Our faith does unite us, but science makes us free. Therefore, we will not allow the theocratic tendencies of our rabbinical leaders to surface. We'll know how to keep them in their synagogues, just as we keep our standing army in its military barracks. The army and the rabbis will be greatly respected, as is required and appropriate to their honored positions. But they must not interfere in the affairs of state—with all due respect toward them—lest they bring about domestic and external difficulties.

Even the Hebrew language may have deterred Herzl from making *aliyah.*

> You see, we are not able to converse with one another in Hebrew. Who among us knows Hebrew well enough to be able to buy a train ticket in this language? . . . Every person will maintain his

own language, which is the precious homeland of his thoughts. Switzerland is a good example of the possibility of maintaining linguistic federalism. We will also remain there what we are now, just as we will never stop loving—with sadness and nostalgia— the native lands from which we were expelled.

Herzl, a brokenhearted man who felt burdened by the fact of his Jewish birth, viewed the transfer to a Jewish state as an expulsion from the European garden of Eden, not as the fulfillment of an age-old dream. Yet he created a vision for people like my grandfather.

It was a historic paradox, both amazing and sad—that assimilating Central European intellectuals like Herzl and Nordau should invent political Zionism out of desperation, but without ever considering the possibility that they personally would immigrate to Palestine. Young Eastern European Jews of the next generation looked toward them as the venerated leaders of a messianic movement, identifying intensely with the Zionist dream as a solution for their distress, which was quite different from the assimilation problems being addressed by Herzl.

Jabotinsky, Ben-Gurion, Berl Katznelson (1887–1944) and others sought to escape the pogroms and poverty. They wanted to build a different life and believed that they could make a completely new start in Palestine. They did not think of themselves as exiles from Europe, but rather as Jews escaping the exile. In no way did they wish to reproduce the European model of Jewish life in Palestine. They wanted to forget the language of the exile, along with its customs, its forms of livelihood, and even its rabbinic sensibilities. Instead they looked to reconnect with David and Solomon, Judah the Maccabee and Bar Kochba.

Herzl wanted to form a little Europe in Palestine, a sort of small shrine to what the Jews would have to leave behind. But he sparked a fire in Eastern Europe, providing an unintentional vision for enthusiastic young people. My grandfather was wrong to consider

Herzl a man who betrayed his principles when he raised the Uganda Plan. He betrayed my grandfather's dream, not his own.

Herzl was able to be the hero of the Second Aliyah and of those who came afterward mainly due to the fact that he died so young. Thus, he was able to remain a consensual leader, a messiah in retrospect. Otherwise, the internal conflict he encountered prior to his death would have reduced him to the leader of an angry faction, no longer the esteemed and accepted prophet of the modern Jewish state.

It is hard to imagine how Herzl's vision could be further from the reality that was eventually created. Zionism's uniqueness lies in the very fact of it being realized, but it would be a mistake to portray its realization as a fulfillment of the original plan. Herzl did not invent the Zionist idea. Moses Hess (1812–1875), Zvi Kalischer (1795–1874), and Leo Pinsker all preceded him. Even the term *Zionism* was coined by Nathan Birnbaum (1864–1937), not by Herzl. Herzl proposed a very detailed program and carried out a "pyrotechnic" public-relations campaign that succeeded in reaching the far corners of the Jewish world. The Zionist fires that ultimately were kindled were very different from his initial spark.

It was the combination of Herzl's special personality, the lavish Zionist congresses, and a detailed program that excited the Jewish world at a time when it was frantically searching for solutions for its physical and spiritual distress.

Herzl recognized a very problematic situation in Europe and hoped to implement his plan in Uganda, Sharm al-Sheikh, or Palestine within a few years. His pursuit of European leaders, his efforts at the sultan's court, the pathetic meeting that did or did not occur with the German kaiser, were all aimed at attaining an immediate solution for Jews in distress, and, as such, were complete failures.

Herzl was more a visionary of the Holocaust than of the Jewish state. Of course, he was unable to predict the extent of the atrocity, yet he discerned the earthquake about to overtake European Jewry long before others. He sought to extricate the Jews of Europe quickly and in an orderly fashion. His main concern was to get the Jews to a place of safe refuge. The precise location of this refuge was of far less importance to him.

Already during Herzl's lifetime, but especially after his death, the Zionist movement was focused on Palestine. The ones who, to a large extent, continued Herzl's primary concern of arranging an exodus from Europe were the "Territorialists." At various stages, people like Dov Ber Borochov and Nahman Syrkin (1868–1924) joined them. On the other side were the Zionei Zion—Zionists who would consider no destination for the European exodus but Palestine.

One of the reasons Herzl failed was the difficulty in warning against an earthquake that had not yet occurred. It is very hard to persuade people to leave their homes and familiar surroundings and go to an unknown place. The price of emigration is high, as each group of immigrants is almost certain to become a transitional generation of "wanderers in the desert," with only the next generation fully assimilated into its new society.

Herzl failed since his successors in the Zionist movement preferred to concentrate their efforts on the Palestine option, often choosing to temporarily prevent emigration from Europe in order to better prepare for the absorption of those who would come in the future. On the eve of the Holocaust, the non-European world was already closed to the Jews. They were trapped, as hunted animals, in the countries where they lived, and few were able to escape.

Israel's role in the twenty-first century, besides the obligation of any country to promote the welfare of its citizens, is to ensure Jewish continuity. This is a role that cannot be assigned to Israel without Israel taking the role upon itself as part of the Zionist movement. Israel will need to fill a central role in preserving the existence of the Jewish people, whether through continued immigration or through a much closer relationship with world Jewry and greater involvement in their activities.

Israel is much more the result of the practical Zionism of Ben-Gurion than the political Zionism of Herzl and even the "synthetic" Zionism of Weizmann. It is a campaign against harsh terrain and parched land, in opposition to its Arab residents and the Arab world, and often against the entire world. The story of the difficulties encountered in fulfilling Zionism is not just the story of the Arab uprisings of the 1920s and thirties, or the White Papers of the British Mandatory government, which restricted Jewish migration and land acquisition. This story also includes the Arab boycott and the harsh United Nations resolutions, the most infamous being the 1975 resolution that described Zionism as a racist movement. Nothing would have been more likely to break Herzl's heart than the portrayal of his movement as racist.

The Zionism of Ben-Gurion dreamed of massive immigration, motivated by conviction. He did not give up on the Jews of America and Europe, Australia and South Africa. On this point, it was Herzl who was the more practical.

Very few Jews immigrated out of nationalist, Zionist idealism for Palestine during the early waves of *aliyah*. Since the establishment of the state, tens of thousands of Jews have moved to Israel from North America and other Western countries, but a significant percentage of these immigrants have returned to their countries of origin, and their overall number is very small. From this perspective, Herzl was right.

Israel today is the result of multiple waves of immigration, but it is also a unique entity in its own right. The fact that almost all of the Australians would not be living in Australia were they not the descendants of penal-colony deportees does not detract anything from the Australian success story or make it less attractive for immigrants. Similarly, the fact that immigrants do not arrive in Israel out of Zionism does not mean that it is not a success story.

Israel can still become a state that attracts not only poor Jews (and those who are even ready to convert to Judaism in order to raise their standard of living) but also people like Theodor Herzl. In the twenty-first century, Israel should prepare itself for the Herzls of the world and become attractive enough so that someone who has the option of immigrating to North America would seriously consider settling in Israel instead.

# CHAPTER 3

# Israel and the Diaspora

One winter day in December 1993, Shimon Peres, then foreign minister, asked me to appear in his place at a world conference of the Women's International Zionist Organization (WIZO) in Tel Aviv. Being his faithful deputy, I of course agreed. But that was not the only reason. Except for a few brief visits, I have never lived in the Diaspora, so I always welcome the opportunity to meet with Diaspora Jews who provide a window to a world that fascinates me so.

After my introductory remarks on Israel's foreign relations, the floor was open to questions. One of the representatives asked me, "How important is the financial assistance Israel receives from the Jewish world?" I explained to her my longstanding view, one that was especially reinforced when I served as deputy finance minister: the Israel Bonds campaign, once extremely important, is now completely unnecessary. Moreover, it exacts a heavy price from Israel, considering the staff involved in managing the program and the high rate of interest Israel pays on the bonds it sells.

The United Jewish Appeal is very important to the Jewish federations in the United States, where funds are channeled directly into social welfare programs, educational programs, and programs for the preservation of Jewish identity. But the relatively small sums transferred each year to the State of Israel by the UJA and the Keren HaYesod is marginal for Israel, comprising less than one-half of one percent of our annual budget. Of course, the treasury is always happy to receive money, and without this money we would need to raise taxes or streamline other budget items to finance the programs (mostly social welfare) now covered by the UJA. Still, these funds would be better used for the welfare of the Jewish world and for Jewish continuity worldwide.

Israel is a well-established state ranked in the top 10 percent of the world's nations in per capita GNP. It is in better economic shape than most of the countries in which fund-raising for Israel takes place. If, occasionally, large waves of immigration like those from Ethiopia or the former Soviet Union present themselves, then Israel could appropriately enlist the Jewish people at large to aid in financing the initial absorption of the new immigrants. But there is no need to direct UJA money to the Israeli social-welfare system on a regular basis. It is of far greater importance for world Jewry to invest this money in Jewish education in the Diaspora and in trips to Israel for young Jews.

When I finished explaining my view on this question, the WIZO women were stunned and literally speechless. They felt insulted and angry, and their response was soon to follow. Several of them told me that they felt as if their work of a lifetime suddenly meant nothing, that all their efforts for Israel had been for naught.

I tried to explain that Jewish fund-raising for Israel had indeed served a vital role during the state's early years, in both the economic and the military spheres, but we now live in a different era. Today these funds create a benefactor-recipient relationship between the Diaspora and Israel for which there is no objective justification. This only reinforces the impression in the Jewish world that Israel is still a weak and poor nation that cannot survive without the money of its Jewish siblings.

The leadership of world Jewry is mainly connected to the neediest segments of the Israeli population in the framework of Project Renewal (investing in poor neighborhoods) and similar programs. The majority of Israelis do not fall within their scope of interest.

I tried to impress upon the WIZO audience that something in this relationship is unhealthy. What was appropriate in the 1950s is no longer valid on the eve of the twenty-first century. But the establishment is comfortable with its old familiar procedures. A poor Israel fighting for its survival and sacrificing its sons in war every ten years is a much better fund-raising theme than the local Jewish community's old-age home. Those representing Israel at lavish UJA dinners are often willing to pay the price of this distorted portrayal of Israel in exchange for their plane tickets. Some have even made these junkets an integral part of their lives. It is a comfortable arrangement for Israel, even if the UJA allocations amount to less than $300 million, since it leaves the Jewish world with the impression that it is contributing and maintaining a connection with Israel.

This unrealistic relationship distorts reality and teaches Israel to feel dependent even though there is no justification for Israel to be dependent. More important, young Jews in the world will never view Israel as a potential second home as long as the state is portrayed as an undeveloped country of deserts and camels, dependent on the assistance of the developed world.

The real Israel—developed, modern, culturally rich and fascinating—is a well-kept secret for the more than 80 percent of world Jewry who have never visited it. If Israel continues to be depicted as a needy state, as it is at UJA dinners, two things will happen: first, Israel, perceived as a failure after fifty years of existence, will become less and less attractive to world Jewry; and, second, major donors—who *are* familiar with the real Israel—will eventually stop contributing to the UJA, thereby removing support that is desperately needed locally.

My explanations did not help. These good ladies, who devote such great efforts for Israel, felt betrayed. They tried to convince me that there are many poor people in Israel who need the help of world Jewry; they did not accept my contention that this is Israel's responsibility and not theirs. They explained to me that even if Israel does not need the assistance, it is important to continue fund-raising for Israel since this is the way the Jews of the world express their connection with Israel. If Israel were to reject their helping hand, this connection would be broken.

I told them about a friend of mine, an affluent man whose aunt in Long Island would send him packages from America twice a year. This started back in Israel's early days of austerity, when secondhand clothes, coffee, chocolate, and powdered milk were prized items. In the 1970s, when his aunt, at a very old age, was still sending these packages, my friend paid her a visit and asked her to stop sending them. He tried to explain to her, gently, that, despite the fact that he lived in Israel, he was considerably more wealthy than she. She looked at him with surprise and said, "That's very nice. But you can never know . . ."

This anachronistic relationship was comfortable for my friend's aunt, but for the relations between Israel and the Diaspora there is a price to be paid for "care packages" from America. "Do you also think that the WIZO women should stop their work for Israel?" I was asked. "Not at all," I responded. "You represent a voluntary organization and if you wish to assist day-care centers and other activities in Israel, this will only strengthen the connection between us. If an American Jew wants to contribute to a museum, hospital, or ideological movement, this assistance should be welcomed. By the same token, if an Israeli wishes to support a New York orchestra, why not? But the funds collected under the national and institutional frameworks should be directed toward programs aimed at promoting Jewish continuity rather than financing social-welfare programs in Israel."

My comments traveled quickly via the unofficial Jewish network to the various communities and were interpreted by many as an Israeli rejection of the Jewish Diaspora. Instead of understanding my words as an expression of an Israeli leader's commitment to Jewish continuity, they were portrayed as a sign of indifference to the Jewish world. There were those who exploited this interpretation of my comments to declare that if Israel was no longer interested in their money, they would no longer contribute to the UJA.

Some declared that without Israel as a fund-raising standard, it would be impossible to raise funds for the local community. Others went a step further and admitted that there is indeed no reason for the Jewish Diaspora to continue to finance Israeli social-welfare programs. But, they argued, if U.S. Jews themselves stopped contributing to Israel, they would no longer be in a position to ask their government to grant Israel $3 billion in annual assistance. This is a specious argument, since the U.S. government is certainly aware of Israel's economic situation, and U.S. assistance is based on American strategic interests, not on the sentimental perception of an impoverished Israel.

I was astonished by the waves my comments created in the Jewish world. I admit that initially I regretted the whole episode, since it was something totally unplanned. If I had not stood in for Peres at the WIZO meeting and had not been asked this particular question, I would have kept my views on the subject to myself. It was not as if I had convened a press conference to tell the world what I thought about the UJA.

However, I later came to view the episode as a special opportunity to promote dialogue with Jews from various parts of the world about the future of Israel-Diaspora relations and the possibilities for secular Jewish life in the twenty-first century. I have found many to be deeply concerned and ready to discuss these issues, but hardly any have offered answers. From my tentative start a few years ago, the question of Israel-Diaspora relations has developed, from a side interest of concern and curiosity, to emerge as one of the central issues of my public life. I find myself more and more in contact with Jewish communities outside Israel, speaking with people of all ages, struggling to understand the issues and striving to find solutions.

What characterized the fifty years that preceded Israel's formation was the debate over whether it was necessary to establish a Jewish state. The ultra-Orthodox opposed the establishment of a Jewish state as a brazen attempt to meddle with the designs of Heaven. They preferred to wait for the Messiah. The Bundists (the Bund was an extremist Jewish socialist party) viewed Zionist activities as an escape from the real challenge of joining ranks with the working masses in Eastern Europe to win their social liberation. The territorialists were prepared to accept a more readily available location than Palestine for the Jewish state.

When the Nazis came to power in Germany, the Zionist movement strengthened. During World War II, Zionism became a movement supported by the majority of Jews in the United States and in the European lands not conquered by the Nazis. While critics of Herzl's Zionism charged that it, in effect, gave credence to the anti-Semitic premise that the Jews constituted a foreign element in the national makeup of European peoples, the Holocaust of European Jewry proved that Herzl was right. (Of course, Herzl, even in his worst nightmares, never imagined an anti-Semitic episode as cataclysmic as the Holocaust.) It was thus a sad paradox that a phenomenon such as Nazism, which Zionism failed to prevent, was responsible for creating a consensus for Zionism.

The establishment of Israel was not a central event in the life of the modern Diaspora. In retrospect, it is clear that the two events that had the largest impact on the Jews of the Diaspora were the Holocaust and the Six-Day War. The establishment of Israel in

1948 came at a time when Jews were still trying to cope with the magnitude of the Holocaust; perhaps this is why it was not recognized as a momentous event. But while 1948 was not a turning point for the Jews of America or Europe, the State of Israel soon became a new and problematic player in the Jewish system. For two thousand years the Land of Israel had not been home to an important Jewish community, and suddenly a new entity was created, which, despite its small size, declared itself a home for all Jews.

Issues raised in the debate over Zionism became more acute with the establishment of the state. In one sense, Israel created a new common denominator for the Jewish communities in the world. Since its inception, most of the world's Jews have shared a concern for Israel's survival and a hope for its success. At the same time, the establishment of the state brought another line of questioning to the fore: Could Israel claim a preeminent role among Jewish communities? Could Israel contend that it is the natural place for every Jew? Could it assert that whoever lives in Israel is doing the right thing, while Jews who remain in the Diaspora are in error? Is Israel already the Jewish spiritual center? Will Israel determine Jewish law—for example, in deciding who is or is not a Jew? Or is America in fact the center of Jewish spirituality?

There was an additional concern, especially in the years immediately following the establishment of the state, that anti-Semites would exploit Israel's self-proclaimed identity as the Jewish homeland and call for Diaspora Jews to leave their countries for Israel. If a country's Jewish citizens were ready to view Israel as their true home, they might be perceived as having divided loyalties. Some might say that these Jews could no longer be trusted because of their sympathies for another country.

One of the organizations that was worried about the establishment of the state, though it still supported the UN partition plan, was the American Jewish Committee. This organization, which at the time was considered the voice of American Jewry and enjoyed the greatest access to the American government, represented the non-Zionists in the Jewish Agency. Central figures in this organization expressed concern that the establishment of Israel would create serious problems for American Jews. It was very important for them that Israel be recognized as a state that only represents its resident citizens and makes no claim to represent the entire Jewish people.

Three of the organization's leaders were invited to visit Israel in May 1948 by Ben-Gurion. They told the prime minister that Israel cannot portray itself as a state of the Jewish people or as its spokesman, and should not act to encourage *aliyah* from the United States. The American Jewish Committee leaders explained that a call for the emigration of U.S. Jews would raise the specter of dual loyalty. They asked Ben-Gurion to cease encouraging young American Jews to move to Israel, warning him that if he continued to do so, they would be forced to reconsider their support of Israel. In their view, the question of *aliyah* was an internal matter for American Jews, and Israel's calls for immigration constituted outside intervention in their affairs and was an attempt to stir up Jewish nationalism in America.

Judge Joseph Proskauer (1877–1971), one of the leaders of the American Jewish Committee, wrote a letter to Ben-Gurion reiterating this view in October 1949, after Ben-Gurion called for young American Jews to immigrate to Israel in an appearance before the UJA. Proskauer stated that he would not be able to urge Americans to contribute to someone who encourages such an un-American act as the emigration of American Jews to Israel.

Those were difficult years for Israel. Ben-Gurion desperately needed the assistance of American Jews and could not allow a serious breach to develop. He responded to the American Jewish Committee by saying that his intention in the speech was to call for "selective" *aliyah* from America. That is, he tried to explain, his call to the young people of America was directed at specific individuals and not the mass of American Jewry.

The American Jewish Congress, the historical rival of the American Jewish Committee, accused the Committee of extorting the government of Israel. Nonetheless, the Committee endeavored to confirm that American Jewry should not be depicted as an exiled community destined to return home to Israel. On the contrary, they contended, it was the powerful Jewish presence in America that enabled Israel to exist—through philanthropic support and influence on behalf of Israel's security.

Contradictory responses from Israel's leaders led Jacob Blaustein (1892–1970), an oil billionaire who served as head of the American Jewish Committee, to demand an official commitment from Ben-Gurion regarding the dividing lines between Israel and the Jewish world on the issue of *aliyah*. In August 1950, Ben-Gurion invited Blaustein to Israel, where they met in tough and intensive negotiations. In the end, on August 23, they exchanged formal statements. This exchange became the working basis of the relationship between Israel and the Jews of the United States. No one has ever explicitly modified or abrogated these understandings.

Ben-Gurion did not submit these statements for cabinet approval, nor did he make them an official Israeli document. Similarly, Blaustein did not represent all U.S. Jews, yet the exchange of statements, which came to be known as the "Ben-Gurion–Blaustein Agreement," was regarded by both sides as a valid and binding document for a period of many years.

A look at the two statements immediately reveals that Blaustein was "boss." He commended Israel's achievements, cited its democracy as an American value, and noted that the existence of Israel boosted Jewish morale after the Holocaust. But Israel, Blaustein noted, also has "a responsibility in terms of not affecting adversely the sensibilities of Jews who are citizens of other states by what it says or does." (See Appendix A for the full text of the Ben-Gurion–Blaustein statements.) Blaustein added:

American Jews vigorously repudiate any suggestion or implication that they are in exile. American Jews—young and old alike, Zionists and non-Zionists alike—are profoundly attached to America. America welcomed their immigrant parents in their need. Under America's free institutions, they and their children have achieved that sense of security unknown for long centuries of travail. American Jews have truly become Americans. . . . To American Jews, America is home. . . . A world in which it would be possible for Jews to be driven by persecution from America would not be a safe world for Israel either. . . . Harm has been done to the morale and to some extent to the sense of security of the American Jewish community through unwise and unwarranted statements and appeals which ignore the feelings and aspirations of American Jewry. Even greater harm has been done to the State of Israel itself by weakening the readiness of American Jews to do their full share in the rebuilding of Israel, which faces such enormous political, social and economic problems.

Ben-Gurion made it clear in his own statement that "The State of Israel represents and speaks only on behalf of its own citizens and in no way presumes to represent or speak in the name of Jews who are citizens of any other country." The prime minister emphasized that

> We, the people of Israel, have no desire and no intention to interfere in any way with the internal affairs of Jewish communities abroad. . . . Our success or failure depends on a large measure on our cooperation with, and on the strength of, the great Jewish community of the United States, and, we, therefore, are anxious that nothing should be said or done which could in the slightest degree undermine the sense of security and stability of American Jewry.

Ben-Gurion's remarks regarding *aliyah* are particularly interesting and curious:

Let me say a word about immigration. We should like to see American Jews come and take part in our effort. We need their technical knowledge, their unrivalled experience, their spirit of enterprise, their bold vision, their "know-how." We need engineers, chemists, builders, work managers and technicians. The tasks which face us in this country are eminently such as would appeal to the American genius for technical development and social progress. But the decision as to whether they wish to come—permanently or temporarily—rests with the free discretion of each American Jew himself. It is entirely a matter of his own volition. We need *halutzim*, pioneers, too. *Halutzim* have come to us—and we believe more will come, not only from those countries where the Jews are oppressed and in "exile" but also from countries where the Jews live a life of freedom and are equal in status to all other citizens in their country. But the essence of *halutziut* [pioneering] is free choice. They will come from among those who believe that their aspirations as human beings and as Jews can best be fulfilled by life and work in Israel.

At this critical juncture in forging the relations between Israel and the Diaspora, at a time when Ben-Gurion was actively involved in trying to bring entire Jewish communities from the Arab world to Israel in order to achieve the critical mass he dreamed of, he was forced to give in to Blaustein on two essential points. First, he acknowledged that the U.S. Jewish community, the largest in the world, was not in exile but was to be viewed as a "big sister" to Israel. Speaking thus, he depicted the exile as a place where Jews are persecuted, not simply a place where Jews live outside of their homeland. Second, Ben-Gurion capitulated on the call to young American Jews to come to Israel, even though they represented the largest and most professional reservoir of Jews.

During the years that followed, there were several "violations" of the Ben-Gurion–Blaustein agreement by both sides, including by Ben-Gurion himself. For example, on October 2, 1956, Ben-Gurion responded to criticism expressed by Blaustein, then no longer chairman of the American Jewish Committee, by reaffirming his commitment to the statements they exchanged in 1950. Ben-Gurion stressed that, from his point of view, to be a Zionist means to live in Israel and personally build an independent Jewish life. But, he continued, he understood that Zionists have the right to interpret Zionism in their own way, just as Jews can attribute different meaning to their own Jewishness. Such a response and his public pronouncements over the next few years continued to exacerbate the situation.

In December 1960, Blaustein sent an angry letter to Ben-Gurion in which he enumerated several additional violations of their agreement. These violations created an atmosphere of anger and confusion similar to that which preceded the drafting of the agreement ten years earlier. "American, Canadian and English Jewries are up in arms about these violations," wrote Blaustein, "and I think I should tell you that some are charging me with having been naive in even having accepted the August 1950 Statement as bona fide. . . ."

Some of the violations to which I refer are as follows:

1.  Israel's notes addressed to the United States, Britain, and other governments regarding the swastika daubing in those countries last winter. . . . Israel should have confined itself to discussing [the issue] with the Jewish communities in those countries. . . .

2.  General Moshe Dayan's incomprehensible March 9, 1960, statement in Canada that "his government should not only represent the people of Israel, but the interests of all Jews."

3.  And Foreign Minister Golda Meir's reply to the delegation of the Anglo-Jewish Association which resulted in the startling headlines in the *Jewish National Post* (April 15, 1960): "Israel will continue to speak for Jewry."

Blaustein concluded his letter (marked "Personal and Confidential") with the following words: "Out of my closeness to you, I feel I can venture to say that you cannot expect diplomatic and financial cooperation even from friends, including me, when understandings with them, and principles dear to them, are violated or ignored."

The American Jewish Committee issued a memorandum in December 1960 charging that, after discussions with Golda Meir and other Israelis (but not Ben-Gurion), it was clear that the Israelis were convinced that Israel is solely authorized to speak in the name of the Jewish nation. The memorandum is therefore harshly critical of Ben-Gurion's speech before the Twenty-fifth Zionist Congress, in which he said that Jews living outside of Israel are hindering Jewish fulfillment. Ben-Gurion also said in this address that Diaspora Jews in the free and prosperous countries of the world lived under the threat of the "kiss of death" of a slow but steady assimilation process.

The American Jewish Committee also did not hesitate to criticize the Law of Return, claiming that the automatic granting of citizenship to all Jews creates the impression that Jews living outside of Israel are people without a home, or that Israel is their only natural home.

Ben-Gurion did not challenge these harsh criticisms, preferring to avoid a confrontation with American Jewry. Moreover, Ben-Gurion met again with Jacob Blaustein on April 23, 1961, during a private visit by Blaustein to Israel, at which time the two reaffirmed their full commitment to the original statements of 1950. However, they also agreed that there was room for differences of opinion between Jews living in Israel and those in the Diaspora regarding the question of what it means to be a Jew. Ben-Gurion also promised to see that his ministers would fully respect the spirit and content of the original understandings.

When Levi Eshkol (1895–1969) became prime minister in 1963,

he reaffirmed Israel's commitment to the Ben-Gurion–Blaustein agreements, as did Prime Minister Golda Meir (1898–1978) in a letter to Blaustein himself in 1970. Yet while the official commitment was indeed maintained, the Six-Day War made it obsolete, changing in an instant the relationship between Israel and the Diaspora.

## The Six-Day War

The days of waiting in May 1967, and the fears of a war that would exact a terrible price from Israel, were traumatic for world Jewry, especially in the Free World, where information flowed quickly. Arthur Hertzberg believes that American Jews tried in 1967 to make up for what they failed to do for their brethren in Europe during the 1940s.

Not only did the rich increase their contributions. Hardworking middle-class people cashed in their savings and contributed money to Israel during these difficult and worrisome days. During 1967, American Jews contributed $600 million, a record amount in real terms. Some 10,000 Jews sought to come to Israel. Never before, or since, has there been such identification with Israel by American Jews.

Jews who were prominent as "doves" on Vietnam became "hawks" in the cause of the Six-Day War. "American Jews identified with the most successful army in the world," writes Hertzberg. "At a time when the U.S. was stuck deep in the quagmire of Vietnam, Israel came and proved to the world that the Jews are a breed of heroic warriors."

In Western Europe, support for Israel became a civic religion after 1967. Fund-raising for Israel became fashionable and prestigious, lending additional power to affluent contributors who became the prominent members of the Jewish community. In this way, the Six-Day War strengthened the financial elite among the Jews in Europe. The great distinction that Israel enjoyed after the war helped Diaspora communities mobilize and provided a common focus. Israel convincingly demonstrated its potential as a place of refuge in time of need.

During this time, Zionism completed the process of becoming a consensus movement. The State of Israel proved that it was not a mere episode, but a powerful phenomenon. A feeling of self-confidence returned to many Jews living in the West, who now worried less about charges of divided loyalties. Many Jews "came out of the closet," consciously choosing to emphasize their Jewishness and their identification with Israel.

The Six-Day War, with its days of fearful waiting and mighty victory—which ended up saddling Israeli society with the onerous issue of the conquered territories—served as a wake-up call for the Jewish people, bringing an entire generation back into contact with their Jewish identity, and with Israel.

In Eastern Europe, the situation was different. The Jews were indeed very excited about the victories of the Israel Defense Forces, and there was also a greater interest in visiting Israel, and even in *aliyah,* but emigration from the Soviet Union and most of the states of Eastern Europe was still impossible. The entire Communist Bloc, with the sole exception of Romania, broke off diplomatic relations with Israel, and the attitude toward Jews generally deteriorated. Jews in Eastern Europe were further distanced from positions of power under the pretext that they had divided loyalties. While the Six-Day War thus had negative implications for many Jews in Eastern Europe, it did contribute to the strengthening of the underground Jewish movements that in the 1970s began to demand the right to emigrate to Israel.

Since 1967, Israel's presence has been strongly felt among the Jews of the world. In the United States, Israel has become a rationale for Jewish gatherings. It has been easier for Jewish members of Congress, and especially Jewish senators, to convene meetings on issues related to Israel than to meet as Jews. Unlike the days of Blaustein and Ben-Gurion, a new situation has developed in which

Israel's impact on the nature of the American Jewish leadership is quite significant. The importance of an American Jewish leader is largely dependent on the importance ascribed to him or her by the American government, and the American government regards as important those Jewish leaders who have access to the Israeli leadership.

American Jewish institutions have, to a large extent, completed their mission of struggling for the rights of American Jews. Speaking on behalf of Israel has accorded them a new goal, which provides a source of pride and bolsters a sense of Jewish unity. AIPAC became a powerful Jewish entity in the early 1970s, as Jews were glad to contribute to an organization whose true goal was to defend and support Israeli interests in America.

The UJA was able to collect more money, both for local Jewish communities and for Israel, thanks to this heightened identification with Israel. There was nothing more stirring for American Jewish audiences in those days than to hear an Israeli soldier recount his acts of gallantry in broken English as they wiped away their tears. These were golden days for the top army brass who traveled to America and presented the new Israel to their Jewish brethren. This was the finest hour for the Israel Bonds program.

The Conference of Presidents of Major Jewish Organizations grew stronger during this period, when it was suddenly required to defend Israel at the United Nations and elsewhere against depictions of Israel as an occupier and exploiter. This combination of pride in a great victory and the need to defend Israel against its critics produced a new generation of pro-Israeli American leadership. This generation drew its strength from Israel and assisted Israel. It was an entirely new relationship, unprecedented in Jewish history.

A threatening change occurred in 1973. It did not erase the huge impression left by the Six-Day War, nor did it turn the hearts of Jews in the Free World against Israel. But this time it was a different Israel, returned to victim status. Instead of a grand victory,

Israel survived by the skin of its teeth, having come perilously close to defeat.

## The Yom Kippur War

During the Yom Kippur War, when Israel found itself exposed to much greater danger than in 1967 and the number of casualties was four times as high, fewer volunteers arrived in Israel from the United States; American Jewry was more passive. In Europe, Israel began to be perceived after 1973 as racist, on the one hand, and weak, on the other.

The energy crisis that erupted against the backdrop of the war pushed Western Europe closer to the Arab world and further from Israel, making many Jews feel uncomfortable. In the eyes of some Jews, Israel became more a source of consternation than pride. They found themselves on the defensive, faced with having to justify Israel's positions. Some disassociated themselves from Israel specifically to avoid such explanations.

Israelis were now no longer the only targets of Palestinian terror. Beginning in 1976, acts of terrorism were perpetrated against Jewish targets in France. Identification with Israel became a security risk and a financial burden for Jews throughout the world, and they began to initiate measures to defend themselves. A wave of anti-Jewish terror swept the Jews of Europe in 1980 following the fall of the Shah of Iran and another rise in oil prices. Acts of terror occurred in Germany, Belgium, France, and Austria. A terrorist attack in Rome followed the world-wide condemnation of Israel for allowing the slaughter of Muslims by Lebanese Christians in the Sabra and Shatila refugee camps in 1982. In 1986, similar terrorism was directed against Jews in Turkey. Argentina, as mentioned above, was the site of two terrible terrorist incidents in the early 1990s—one against the Israeli Embassy and one aimed at Jewish community institutions—presumably to avenge Israeli actions against Hezbollah leaders in Lebanon.

Israel's policies affect Diaspora Jews in many areas. For example, Menachem Begin's decision to expose the contacts between the American ambassador to the United Nations, Andrew Young, and the PLO in 1979 led to the dismissal of this important leader and triggered a serious deterioration in the relations between the black community in America and American Jews, who were automatically identified with the Israeli decision. Black-Jewish relations were already strained at this time for very different reasons, and the prime minister of Israel did not take this into account, focusing singularly on what he thought to be crucial for Israel: preventing further U.S. contacts with the PLO.

On the other hand, when the World Jewish Congress decided to expose the Nazi past of Austrian president Kurt Waldheim, it led, almost automatically, to the recall of the Israeli ambassador from Vienna. Israel cannot afford to separate its policies from such actions taken by world Jewry—even when these actions are not in Israel's direct interest.

## Who Is a Jew?

The issue that connects Israel to the Diaspora more than any other is "Who is a Jew?" The way that Israel defines Jewishness has a direct impact on Jewish communities around the world. Recognizing someone as a Jew only in terms of an Orthodox interpretation of Jewish law *(halachah)* turns many of those considered Jewish by Conservative or Reform criteria into non-Jews when they arrive in Israel. Each time Israel's religious parties seek to modify the Law of Return's definition of "Who is a Jew?" most of the organized Jewish community in the United States and elsewhere rally to prevent the amendment.

The importance world Jewry ascribes to how Israeli authorities define a Jew gives Israel centrality in the Jewish world even before it becomes the largest Jewish community in the world. The debate has focused mainly on the issue of conversion, since, according to the Law of Return, Israel considers anyone a Jew "who was born to a Jewish mother or who converted, and is not a member of another religion."

Since this definition entered the law in 1970, Israel's religious parties have sought to add the words "according to *halachah*" after the reference to conversion. They believe that this would guarantee that only Orthodox conversions would be considered kosher and would prevent the other streams in Judaism from gaining ground in Israel via the "back door," through the recognition of their converts.

For American Jews, the phrase "according to *halachah*" has come to epitomize the struggle against Orthodox hegemony in Israel. Central figures in world Jewry, and especially in North America, have stated that they would have nothing more to do with Israel if it failed to recognize the Jewishness of their grandchildren born to mothers converted by Reform rabbis.

The "Who is a Jew?" issue came before the Knesset several times. Each time, whether they were part of the government coalition or in opposition, the Likud supported the addition of "according to *halachah*," while the Labor Party opposed it; in this way, the former pleases the Orthodox faction and the latter pleases the Conservative and Reform Jewish movements.

Following the 1988 elections, the ultra-Orthodox Agudat Yisrael Party announced that the "according to *halachah*" amendment would be a condition for its participation in any government. The election results found the two main blocs in a deadlock. The Likud won forty-one seats, while Labor received forty. Either party could have formed a government coalition with the support of the religious parties.

At that time, the ultra-Orthodox parties were leaning toward joining a Labor government headed by Shimon Peres, rather than a Likud government led by Yitzhak Shamir. However, the Lubavitch *rebbe* demanded that they insist on the *"halachah"* issue. (The ultra-Orthodox had been willing at one point to settle for having the issue being brought before Labor's Central Committee for debate.)

The temptation for the Labor Party leaders was great, especially in light of prospects for convening an international conference based on the London agreement reached by Peres and Jordan's King Hussein. The national unity government headed by Yitzhak Shamir opposed this agreement, but a new Labor-led coalition would be in a position to implement it.

From this moment, Israel became inundated with delegations of American Jews who met with Likud and Labor leaders involved in the coalition negotiations. The American guests were very distraught. Some of their contentions were undoubtedly correct, while some were a bit exaggerated. An example of the latter was the argument that the "according to *halachah*" amendment would cause Israel to view all Reform Jews as non-Jews.

The Labor Party was persuaded not to initiate an internal debate on this issue. Shamir also realized that he could not afford such a difficult confrontation with American Jews and decided to return to the "national unity" concept, a formula for government paralysis. The government that was ultimately formed was pulled in every possible direction, achieved nothing, and disintegrated after a year and a half. This was a government that was formed—indirectly, but indisputably—by the Jews of the United States. Never before or since have U.S. Jews influenced Israeli politics so profoundly.

The Israeli peace camp has often complained that the non-Orthodox community in America has been lax in supporting peace initiatives, even after the Labor Party paid an enormous price for deferring to their sensibilities on the "Who is a Jew?" issue. Labor's unwillingness to support the *"halachah"* amendment has kept it from becoming law, though a majority of Likud members were ready to support it.

The Labor Party could have secured a majority coalition on several occasions—certainly in 1988—if it had acceded to the demands of the religious parties on this issue. This government could have enabled the Oslo process to begin in 1988, preventing the unnecessary bloodshed of the Intifada (the prolonged uprising of Arabs in the West Bank and Gaza Strip that erupted in late 1987) and moving the Middle East so much sooner in the direction the peace camp advocated.

The leaders of the Labor Party and Meretz chose to forgo the reins of government since the concerns of American Jewry were important to them and they did not want a confrontation. Yet the same Jews who convinced the Labor Party to reject a chance to form a government, when later approached on the issue of the peace process, were always quick to say that they would not interfere in the internal affairs of the State of Israel and would support the policies of the elected government.

The same people who supported the peace process enthusiastically in private conversations (and who had shown even more passion in preventing the formation of a Labor-led government over the conversion issue), later lent their names to newspaper advertisements and letters to the U.S. Congress and the White House in support of policies that froze the peace process. When asked to explain this behavior, they responded: "We simply support the government of Israel, whether it is right or wrong, and we do not intervene in the internal debates that take place in Israel."

It seems that the Jews of the United States were loath to admit, even to themselves, how deeply they intervened in the internal affairs of Israel when it came to an issue they felt directly affected them.

## The 1995 Conversion Bill

A similar question arose around the Conversion Bill in 1995. Since someone who undergoes a Conservative or Reform conversion outside of Israel is registered as a Jew in Israel, the Reform movement in Israel asked the High Court of Justice to apply the same standards to someone who converts under similar auspices in Israel. That is, why should someone's Conservative or Reform conversion not be recognized as valid for registration purposes just because it took place in the Jewish state? The High Court acknowledged that there was a problem with this double standard but postponed any decision for six months in order to give the Knesset an opportunity to clarify the situation via legislation.

When the ultra-Orthodox Shas Party left Yitzhak Rabin's coalition in 1993, it became a minority government dependent on the support of Hadash and the Democratic Arab Party. After the assassination of Rabin in 1995, Shas expressed its readiness to join the government led by Shimon Peres if the Labor Party would support legislation against recognizing Conservative and Reform conversions conducted in Israel. This legislation was called the "Conversion Bill." The Labor Party rejected this demand and, as a result, no religious parties joined the coalition. Several months later, Peres decided to call early elections. After Benjamin Netanyahu's victory, the Likud signed a coalition agreement with the religious parties, promising to support the Conversion Bill.

The number of non-Orthodox conversions conducted in Israel has been small. For most of Israel's history, this issue has not been on the agenda. Indeed, the Labor Party was sorely tempted to accept the Conversion Bill and thus win wide support in the Knesset for its top agenda items, which included—and still include—aspirations for attaining peace accords with Syria and the Palestinians. The decision to reject the demands of the religious parties derived from our clear understanding of the implications for Conservative and Reform Jews in the United States if Israel passed special legislation invalidating their conversions. This was again a case where the relations between Israel and the Diaspora had a direct impact on internal Israeli politics and affected Israel's most crucial interests.

In light of these implications, can American Jewry contend that it does not intervene in Israel's internal affairs? Significant intervention is evident in the very fact that delegations were sent to lobby against the *"halachah"* amendment to the Law of Return and against the Conversion Bill. The truth of the matter is that changes in Israeli policy affect American Jewry, their relations with the U.S. administration, their relations with other communities, as well as their security and status. After all, the days of the Intifada were not the same as the days of the Oslo signing. The days of the Rabin-Clinton friendship were not the same as the days of the Netanyahu-Clinton confrontation. The days of the Entebbe operation and heroic rescue of the Air France plane were not the same as the days of Sabra and Shatila.

Organized American Jewry has actually undergone a long transition process regarding Israel and its policies. In the 1950s and sixties, things were clear! They were the "uncle in America" and Israel was the poor relation whose very existence was uncertain. The Ben-Gurion–Blaustein agreement, even if it was not fully implemented, provided the guidelines: Jews had found a home in America and owed it their sole allegiance. American Jewry did not consider itself a potential reservoir of *aliyah.* Israel, on the other hand, was an independent Jewish community that required the assistance of its American Jewry. American Jews would provide this assistance as long as Israel did not claim to speak on their behalf. Likewise, since American Jews did not serve in the IDF and did not bear the price of Israeli's policies, their support for Israel, their "little sister," must not be conditional on particular policies. It was also clear that Israel and its leaders would not think of interfering in the internal affairs of the American Jewish community.

This relationship was comfortable for both sides and remained unchanged until the Six-Day War. The balance changed after the war. On one hand, the needy little sister became a macho Jew. On the other hand, the conquest of the territories made it more difficult to maintain a consensus regarding Israeli government policy. Some American Jews began to question the policy of continuing to rule the territories until a negotiating partner was found.

In the spring of 1973, Breira ("Alternative") was formed by a group of Jewish intellectuals, most of whom were affiliated with B'nai B'rith's Hillel branches at various American universities. The original goal of the group was to facilitate an open dialogue between Israel and the Diaspora. But after the Yom Kippur War, in October 1973, Breira became a platform for promoting mutual recognition between Israel and the Palestinians.

Israel viewed this organization as a serious problem, constituting unacceptable interference in its affairs. The organized Jewish community in the United States rejected Breira. Even the liberal Jewish leader Arthur Hertzberg (born 1921), president of the American Jewish Congress, refused to participate in a public forum together with a Breira representative. The Jewish community's ostracism of the organization began to take its toll. B'nai B'rith decided to distance itself from Breira, and many young Hillel rabbis left the group, which was eventually disbanded in 1977.

The American Jewish left, supporters of the Israeli Peace Now movement, formed an American counterpart of that organization after the invasion of Lebanon in 1982. During the years of right-wing coalitions in Israel, this group led rallies, demonstrated, and provided assistance to Peace Now in Israel.

On the other side, the right-wing organization Americans for a Secure Israel was established. During the period of Rabin's government, and especially after the signing of the Oslo accords, it became very vocal, along with other organizations, such as For Israel and the Zionist Organization of America. Their goal was to prevent the implementation of the accords, block American aid to the Palestinian Authority, and to "reveal the true face" of the Arabs.

Today, even if no one ever declared the Ben-Gurion–Blaustein agreement null and void or proposed an alternative arrangement, no one feels obligated any longer by this exchange of statements in August 1950. Israel does not refrain from calling on American Jews to immigrate to Israel, and quite a few *aliyah* emissaries are deployed across the United States. But the number of Jews who have moved in the opposite direction—from Israel to America—is about four times the number of American Jews who have come to live in Israel. Blaustein's great concern about Zionist propaganda in America simply had no basis in reality.

Israel sees itself as the state of the Jewish people and often speaks on behalf of world Jewry. No one criticizes Israeli leaders nowadays when they condemn expressions of anti-Semitism in the Diaspora. On the contrary, Israeli leaders are taken to task for their silence if they hesitate to speak out.

Lip service is still paid to the principle of nonintervention in Israel's affairs. Many Jews adopt this line and quote Ben-Gurion and Golda Meir as the ones who "taught" them to support every elected Israeli government. In practice, however, intervention in Israel's "internal affairs" is considerable. Today more than ever, American Jews give their support to political organizations advocating various approaches to the Arab-Israeli conflict, on both sides of the political map.

In 1990, American Jews financed the public movement that led to a change in Israel's election laws, including a change to the direct election of the prime minister. This shift was intended to "prevent religious blackmail" and allow the prime minister a stronger hand in forming a government. When it later became evident that the new system actually exposed the prime minister more than ever to extortive ultra-Orthodox demands, it was again American Jewry who funded a campaign to restore the previous system of parliamentary election of the prime minister.

American Jews contribute to Israeli political parties, and since primaries were inaugurated in the early 1990s, American supporters have been asked to finance their candidates. A number of affluent Jews from America have founded institutes in Israel that deal with such issues as parliamentary democracy, free-market economics, religious pluralism, the peace process, and relations between Arabs and Jews in Israel. These issues represent the central problems facing Israeli society, and the intensive intervention by American Jews in these issues is something quite new.

The established Jewish organizations continue to officially adhere to a policy of nonintervention. This is true of the Conference of Presidents and other older organizations. But it is no secret that an organization like the American Jewish Congress traditionally favors a moderate political stance, while AIPAC—headed by a right-wing group—advocates a more hawkish direction. AIPAC's hawkish stance has, in fact, become its raison d'être.

As mentioned above, AIPAC was originally formed as the Washington branch of the American Zionist Movement, only later becoming the "American Israel Public Affairs Committee." It is not the Israel lobby in the United States, nor is it registered as a foreign agent. Rather, it is an American organization that aims to improve relations between Israel and the United States.

Its story includes both real and imagined victories, but the myth surrounding AIPAC is one of ongoing success. It is considered the strongest lobbying group in Washington and is accused of keeping a "black book" on legislators unfriendly to Israel, whom it then targets for removal when they face reelection. AIPAC is also accused of suggesting to legislators—in not so subtle ways—that they will lose the financial support of Jewish constituents if their voting is not consistent with AIPAC's agenda. On the other hand, legislators favored by the organization are honored and, even more important, receive financial backing for their reelection bids.

AIPAC has helped Israel on some very important matters over the past generation. Beyond its assistance in securing Israel's annual congressional allocation, it has successfully lobbied against arms sales to countries that are in a state of war with Israel, has pressured for emigration rights for Soviet Jews, and has even worked for economic assistance to Romania, a country that did allow its Jews to emigrate.

The 1970s and eighties were AIPAC's golden years. Many organizations in the world tried to copy its success, but none of them came close. Many countries in the world sought closer ties with Israel because of AIPAC's power. There is no doubt that some countries renewed diplomatic relations with Israel in the belief that they would enjoy better relations with the United States through the influence of AIPAC.

AIPAC began as a group devoted to lobbying Congress, but it expanded its scope to include the American administration. It succeeded in raising funds to implement its plans, developed a research branch, brought delegations of American legislators to Israel at its expense, and opened a network of branches across the United States in order to lobby representatives in their home districts.

Dividing lines were never clearly defined between the activities of AIPAC and those of the Israeli Embassy in Washington. In many cases, especially when the embassy appeared to be weak, AIPAC served as a type of super-embassy. In the eyes of Congress and the White House, AIPAC was viewed as an authentic representative of Israeli interests, and it was understood by them that AIPAC would not take any step that was not coordinated with the government of Israel. In reality, however, this was not necessarily the case.

AIPAC is an independent organization whose interests include those of its founders, its policymakers, its employees, and its fund-raisers. It is an organization that can only exist and grow stronger as a fighting opposition. (Despite the fact that AIPAC has always included people with "dovish" views on both American and Israeli issues, and some of its leaders have been identified with the Democratic Party, it is essentially regarded as an organization close to the Republican Party.) Today it wages a campaign against Congress, tomorrow against the administration, and perhaps the next day against both. There have been quite a few occasions when Israeli interests—and those of American Jewry—called for closer relations with the United States but AIPAC went in a different direction. The very organization that is supposed to promote good relations between the two countries becomes almost irrelevant when these relations are not stormy.

AIPAC was much more relevant when Yitzhak Shamir was prime minister, even though it failed to win $10 billion in loan guarantees for Israel. AIPAC was much less relevant during Yitzhak Rabin's term as prime minister, when Israel easily received this guarantee. Part of the organization's aura is due to its struggle on important issues, even if its results are not achieved. For example, the Jackson-Vanik Amendment (to pressure the Soviet Union to allow increased Jewish emigration) and the fight against the sale of AWACS planes to Saudi Arabia did not succeed, but the fighting spirit of these efforts bolstered the myth of AIPAC, justified its existence, and enabled it to broaden its base of support.

AIPAC sometimes feels it needs to outdo Israel in its fighting spirit and has occasionally led legislative initiatives that have entangled Israel in impossible situations. I was involved in one of these situations as director general of the Foreign Ministry. In this official capacity, I held talks several times a year with Undersecretary of State Michael Armacost and Assistant Secretary of State Richard Murphy. During one of these meetings in 1987, I raised a subject of great importance to Israel, a request for American backing of Israel's efforts to attain membership in the Economic and Social Council of the UN (ECOSOC). Israel had never been accepted as a member of this economic organization on account of Arab pressure.

Armacost and Murphy were very cognizant of the subject and immediately responded with a request that Israel withdraw its candidacy. I was stunned by this response and asked why Israel should be prevented from membership in a council to which it could greatly contribute as well as derive benefits. Murphy explained that AIPAC had managed to persuade Congress to pass a resolution requiring the United States to withdraw from any international organization that expels Israel or refuses to accept it as a member. Israel's chances of acceptance in ECOSOC then stood at about 50 percent. The departure of the United States from ECOSOC in the wake of another rejection of Israel would be a death knell for the council. Since it was important for the United States to remain in ECOSOC, Murphy asked that Israel withdraw its candidacy.

I did not need to ponder long on this question. I had brought a long "shopping list" to Washington that included high priority items like direct flights from the Soviet Union to Israel, so I agreed to withdraw Israel's ECOSOC candidacy for the time being. Later I met with AIPAC officials and was admonished for giving in so easily on the ECOSOC issue. I told them: "You did not consult with us about pushing a resolution through Congress linking American membership in international organizations to Israeli membership. Naturally, it seemed to you that the more you strengthened this link the better. But were it not for that resolution, Israel would have submitted its candidacy to the council—with American support—and it is quite likely we would have joined. I was compelled to withdraw my request due to a linkage that you created. You believe that I should have pulled the United States out of ECOSOC. But I ask what price Israel would have had to pay for such damage to American interests." I can't say that I persuaded anyone that day. AIPAC believes it is in their interest to send Israel to the battlefield in America.

When Israel asked the United States to lend assistance to cooperative projects in the Middle East and to finance the activities of the Palestinian Authority under the framework of the UN's "Donors' Conference" (established for humanitarian relief and development assistance in October 1993), AIPAC felt that it would be awkward for it to become involved in lobbying members of Congress for such purposes. During these years, most of the AIPAC officials went about their work on the issue of Palestinian aid as if frozen by the sight of a ghost. I think it is safe to say that Netanyahu's victory in 1996 was greeted with a sigh of relief by many of them. The Likud enabled AIPAC to resume its traditional role, together with other segments of the American Jewish establishment: that of defending Israel and its policies against a world of double standards and hypocrisy, and struggling against the Palestinians. The victory of Barak in 1999 put AIPAC again in an inconvenient situation to which the organization had to adapt.

The fact that AIPAC's existence is justified only when there is a souring of the relations it is supposed to promote is not the only paradox in the complicated relations between Israel and the Jews of the United States. The fact that Israel's existence strengthens the Diaspora is probably the biggest paradox. American Jews feel a closer connection to their Jewishness as a result of Israel's prominent role. In *Jewish Power*, J. J. Goldberg argues that "The celebration of Israel's existence has become a central issue for organized American Jewry."

Diaspora Jews are aware that they have a homeland that will always be ready to accept them as lovely swans rather than ugly ducklings, and this helps them feel more secure about living outside of this homeland. Knowing that Israel exists as a second home for all Jews, provides even those considering *aliyah* with a feeling that they do not need to rush—Israel will always welcome them with open arms. The fact that Jews received their own "Ireland" or "Italy" in 1948 enables them to feel in America and elsewhere like other immigrants who left the "old country" behind. While they sometimes still feel nostalgic for the "old country," they view it as a past they have no intention of returning to. Israel bestows upon Jews worldwide a sense of equality unknown to them before the establishment of the state.

It is a curious situation. Instead of the Jewish state serving as a magnet to attract the world's Jews, it has actually contributed to the normalization of Jewish life in the Diaspora, enabling Jews living outside of Israel to feel more at home. Alan M. Dershowitz presents this as a paradox, but it is only a paradox for some of the Zionists. Indeed, Ben-Gurion could not accept a situation in which Jews who lived a comfortable life in the Diaspora did not immigrate to Israel. The best place for every Jew was in Israel, he believed. Herzl, on the other hand, envisioned the Jewish state as a refuge for the poor masses and was not at all sure that more prosperous Jews would follow. In the view of Ahad Ha'am, it was logical that Israel should be the spiritual center that enabled the continued existence of the Diaspora.

Dershowitz writes about the inherent contradiction between Israel and the Diaspora: while Diaspora Jews seek to prove to themselves and to others that Jews can be an integral part of the society in which they live, and that they can succeed in lowering the level of hostility toward them, the Israeli establishment has an interest in drawing attention to examples of unrelenting anti-Semitism, as evidence that Jews cannot really integrate successfully into non-Jewish society.

I think that this is a very superficial analysis. The Holocaust did raise the level of Jewish anxiety over anti-Semitism, and Israelis were taught to view Israel as the only place in the world where anti-Semitism could not exist. They were also taught to regard any anti-Semitic expression as a potential danger for the local Jews. Israelis do often feel that Diaspora Jews, like the Jews of Europe prior to World War II, turn a blind eye to the storm brewing around them.

At the same time, the Jews in Israel are very proud of the achievements of their Diaspora brethren and have no desire to see them fail. The Israeli Zionist establishment that calls for the Jews of the world to immigrate to Israel believes that successful Diaspora Jews could make even a greater contribution if they lived in Israel. One would have to be very cynical to think that Israeli leaders across the political spectrum and throughout the generations hoped to witness a disaster in the Diaspora that would trigger *aliyah* to Israel. But it certainly would be correct to say that this leadership has viewed Israel as a place of refuge for Jews in the event of such a disaster.

The Israeli establishment's call for prosperous Jews to immigrate to Israel will continue to echo without producing results. Israel's leadership in the twenty-first century needs to rewrite its speeches. Fifty years ago, when Ben-Gurion told young Jews that their place was in Israel, he only managed to aggravate Jacob Blaustein. Today, no one makes a fuss over such oratory. Whoever wishes to engage in a real dialogue between Israel and the Diaspora must reexamine the relationship and modify the message.

During the new century, there will no longer be Jews in distress—no dramatic rescue missions for entire communities and no need for hunger strikes at embassies demanding "Let my people go." Israel will live in peace with its neighbors and will no longer send army officers to tell war stories to UJA donors. Israel's economic condition will be strong.

The Jews of America will integrate even more into American society and will likely assimilate more with non-Jews. The majority of remaining family ties between Jews in Israel and Jews in America will be those involving Israeli émigrés. Israel will still be a focus of identity for world Jewry and continue to be a factor that helps make Diaspora life easier, although the connection between Israel and the Diaspora will be very different from what it was in the twentieth century. If it does not change, and if we use the same institutions and same arguments, then the ties are liable to weaken, with serious implications for Jewish continuity.

## The Distribution of Jews in the World

The distribution of Jews in the world at the beginning of the twenty-first century is nothing like that of a century ago. Instead of Russia and Poland, the United States and Israel have become the largest Jewish communities in the world. After the Holocaust, and due to emigration from the former Soviet Union, the number of Jews in Europe is at its lowest point in several centuries. The Arab world is almost empty of Jews—with the exception of Morocco, where 6,500 Jews continue to reside. Canada, Argentina, Brazil,

Australia, and South Africa have emerged as important Jewish centers.

For the first time in Jewish history, there are no Jews in distress. In recent years, we worked to obtain freedom for Soviet Jews and the Jews of Syria. We responded to the cries of Argentina's Jews, and we tried to reach the Jews of Eastern Europe. We provided a homeland for Yemenite Jews and rescued Ethiopian Jews. All of this activity has ended. There are no Jews today who are prohibited from emigrating from their countries.

In today's Jewish world, as the rate of intermarriage rises each year, Israel is the only Jewish community with a positive rate of natural increase. The twin trends of negative fertility and intermarriage will reduce the size of the Jewish Diaspora in the twenty-first century, though it is hard to predict by how much. The references to 12 or 13 million Jews in the world today already seem exaggerated. If we count only Jews who are defined as such by Jewish law (halachah), we arrive at a figure closer to 10 million. In the United States, for example, only 4.1 million of the 5.6 million Jews are offspring of two Jewish parents. The proportion is probably similar in Western Europe, while in Eastern Europe, even fewer Jews are descended from two Jewish parents.

Jews in the twenty-first century will apparently migrate much less than they did in the twentieth century. We can expect to see continued emigration from Russia and Ukraine in the direction of Israel, the United States, Canada, and Germany, as well as emigration from South Africa to Australia and Canada. The bottom line is that Israel will become the largest Jewish community in the world in the first quarter of the twenty-first century, while the U.S. Jewish community will shrink considerably and the number of Jews in Europe will continue to decline drastically.

At the end of the nineteenth century, the connection between the Jews of the world was very different. A Jew could move through the Jewish world speaking Jewish languages (Yiddish and Ladino).

Today, only very few Jews know these languages. In the twenty-first century, Yiddish will hardly be spoken and Ladino will not be used at all. Family connections linked the Jews of various Jewish communities. Those who departed Europe in the large wave of immigration between 1881 and 1914 left sisters and brothers behind. There were families in which some children emigrated to the United States, others went to Israel, and some chose to remain in Europe.

The children of the immigrants maintained contacts with their cousins in other lands. In the third and fourth generations, these family connections are mostly lost. My generation in Israel always had an "uncle in America." My children's generation do not have relatives in America. It used to be that the first thing we looked to do when landing in another country was to call our relatives. This phenomenon is disappearing, and we are becoming strangers abroad.

Jewish communities of second-generation children of immigrants can look to the older communities of fourth- and fifth-generation Jews to understand what can be expected to happen to their own communities. What is happening in Canada and Australia, and to a large extent in South Africa, is not only a result of successful and dedicated leadership, but also (and mainly) due to the fact that these communities are comprised mostly of first- and second-generation Jews. The more the community is distanced in time from the immigrant generation, the higher the rate of intermarriage, while Jewish education declines and connections with other Jewish communities in the world are lost.

Never has the definition of a Jew been so complicated as it is today. The Gordian knot between the Jewish people and the Jewish religion raises many questions. The natural inclination of many Jews in the world to continue to be Jews sometimes comes into conflict with their concurrent desire to identify with their home nation. The meaning of secular Jewishness is an issue of concern to

Jews everywhere and influences their daily lives. The Jewish ghetto, to a large extent, prevented assimilation, even when ghetto dwellers regularly traveled outside the ghetto.

The ghetto was, first and foremost, a meeting place for Jews that offered the religious services the Jews required: synagogues, schools, ritual baths, kosher food, burial societies, and so on. Thus, in a world of non-Jews, they created for themselves a type of island where they knew and married one another.

As the demand for accessible religious services declines, and the walking distance from the synagogue becomes irrelevant—since Jews either drive to the synagogue or do not bother to go at all—Jewish living patterns become dispersed and Jewish neighborhoods disappear. Assimilation mounts and marriage between Jews becomes purely optional when Jews study in public schools and universities with non-Jews, work with non-Jews, and meet few other Jews in their neighborhoods.

It is no coincidence that the 350,000 ultra-Orthodox Jews living in the Diaspora are the only group outside of Israel that is virtually unaffected by assimilation and has a positive rate of natural increase. These Jews are the only ones to have maintained a self-imposed ghetto and thus do not struggle with the question of Jewish continuity. This is the group that will multiply itself over and over during the next decades.

While the Jewish world is undergoing this enormous transformation, Jewish institutions are slow to change and refuse to be abolished. The Jewish leadership today is amazingly similar to that of twenty years ago, despite the major changes that have occurred in the Jewish world during this period.

I recently met with the new president of B'nai B'rith, a dynamic and impressive attorney named Richard Heideman. he told me that his election at age fifty-one had created a sensation. It turned out that he was the youngest president in the organization's 150-year history. In a country where Bill Clinton was elected president at age forty-six, I thought to myself, only in a Jewish organization would the election of a fifty-one-year-old president create such a fuss.

The new distribution of Jews in the world, the opening of the gates of the former Soviet Union, and the fact that there are no longer Jews in distress, together create a situation requiring new organizational behavior. Yet organizations are inherently conservative and resist change mightily. The question is whether the Jewish people can allow itself such organizational weakness in the face of challenges so unlike those the organizations were originally intended to address.

# CHAPTER 4

# What to Do?

## Ideal Solutions and Practical Solutions

Throughout most of Jewish history, the question of what to do to maintain Jewish community and continuity was seldom on the agenda. In order merely to survive, Jews were forced to react to changing events. The historical dilemma for many Jews was the choice between renouncing their religion and being expelled, or even killed. After the expulsion from Spain, Jewish communities spread throughout the world, existing as autonomous local enclaves grateful for the privilege to maintain communal life. The distances between these communities, and the difficulties involved in traveling between them, led to the development of all sorts of local customs and prayers. Under the circumstances, it was impossible for the Jewish world to make collective decisions.

It is no longer impossible. I believe that we can secure the existence of the Jewish people in the twenty-first century. I am not satisfied with the view that fate is best left to inertia. I believe we have the tools and resources to make changes that will unite the Jewish people—comprised mainly of its two largest communities—into one Jewish world. What we require of these communities are institutional changes and innovative approaches to what seem ostensibly internal matters.

The highest priority should be given to building bridges. In 1998, an informal American-Israeli Jewish Forum was established by Professor Steve Cohen and myself. It consists of about twenty people from each country, including Israeli ministers and members of the Knesset, and members of both the United States Senate and House of Representatives. There are also businessmen and academics from both countries. The Forum's first task is to prepare a declaration of interdependency that will replace the old consensus of nonintervention with a new blueprint for a common course of action.

One of the most critical issues on the agenda is the question of how to define a secular Jew. If we were able to make some progress on this sensitive issue, we would perhaps be able to slow the rapid pace of assimilation. The development of a "secular conversion" procedure would encourage non-Jewish spouses (who do not follow another religion) to join the Jewish people. This sort of practical solution, though controversial, would enable these spouses to register as Jews at the local federation and be recognized as Jews in Israel.

A "birthright" program in Israel for every Jew who reaches the age of seventeen could become the major project of the Jewish world. If the new joint forum of the two communities (which would constitute the basis for a future world Jewish parliament) were to adopt this idea of organized visits to Israel by Jewish teenagers as one of its central activities, it could also create a range of preparatory and follow-up projects. The young people returning from their "birthright visit" could be offered a number of ways to become involved in maintaining the links between the American and Israeli Jewish communities. Even though I view the visits by Americans to Israel as having special significance, I have no doubt that trips by young Israelis to Jewish communities in the United States and other countries would be part of the future effort to unite the Jewish world.

Other solutions I mention in this chapter—a Jewish television network, Internet chat rooms, videoconferences, and more—are intended to take advantage of advanced technologies in order to build a virtual Jewish world. These technologies could also be used to help advance the efforts of international Jewry in assisting the Third World in fields such as medicine, agriculture, management, and so on.

The purpose of this chapter is to raise a variety of ideas. Some are new and some have already been proposed. There is no magical remedy offered in any one of the proposals, but taken together, they could very well help to achieve the changes we need. I do not propose a complete theory or set of instructions, but raise issues derived mainly from an on-going dialogue between Israelis and Jews around the world. I am convinced that the institutionalization of this dialogue would produce other practical ideas and win priority for their implementation.

Worldwide Jewish organizations like B'nai B'rith and the World Zionist Organization have been in existence only since the nineteenth century. More of these collective organizations were established in the twentieth century. There are now more possibilities for discussing the future of the Jewish people than ever before, but some still question whether there is reason to conduct such a discussion.

The ultra-Orthodox—some 500,000 in Israel and 350,000 in the Diaspora—are, of course, not happy with their minority status within the Jewish People. Yet they put their trust in God and believe in Jewish exclusivity. They see themselves as the true Jews, knowing that there have been Hellenizers of various sorts throughout Jewish history. They believe that only their version of Judaism will survive in the long run, with their rate of natural increase ensuring sufficient numbers until the coming of the Messiah, who will change everything.

On the other hand, at least three million of the world's thirteen million Jews carry on their lives without any connection to Jewish culture or community, yet they still regard themselves as Jews. Many of them are also defined as such by Jewish law *(halachah)*. These Jews are certainly not awaiting proclamations or promises from any Jewish figure, Messiah or otherwise, and are not interested in becoming any more Jewish than they currently are. Being Jewish for them is part of their personal biography, like their place of residence, entailing no special obligations.

The rest of the Jewish world—the majority, some nine million—maintain their Jewishness mainly through affinity and culture, with varying measures of religious tradition. It is worth noting, however, that they include a moderate Orthodox minority that lives an intensively Jewish life, has raised its level of natural increase (compared with thirty years ago), and is continually expanding its educational institutions.

A growing subset of Jews involves those who have intermarried or whose children have intermarried without abandoning their Jewish identity. This group is especially sensitive to concerns over the Jewish future of their children and grandchildren, as well as the future of the entire Jewish people in the next generation. Much of the literature dealing with the potential disappearance of American Jews was written by those personally affected by the issue of intermarriage, people like Alan Dershowitz, whose son intermarried. There is a growing feeling that something must be done.

For several decades, it was clear to Israel that what needed to be done was to persuade the Jewish people to immigrate to Israel, and to explain that there was no future in the Diaspora, regardless of whether the Jews lived in lands of plenty or lands of poverty. The poor Diaspora was at times convinced, but not the affluent one. American Jews believed that all they needed to do to maintain a connection to their community and to contribute money to Israel was to be good Americans.

It is now becoming apparent to both sides that the status quo is their greatest enemy. The perpetuation of the current situation will likely create more uncertainty over the future of the Jewish people. More than ever, there is a need to act today to face this uncertain future. More than ever, it is also possible to act today, as the Jewish people is concentrated in two main communities and the means of communication between the two communities are rapid and easily accessible. The question remains: What are the correct steps to be taken to prevent the twenty-first century from witnessing the fatal dwindling of the Jewish people?

In some respects, this is an attempt to "fit a square peg into a round hole," since the "surest" way to remain Jewish is to return to the pre-Emancipation era of the eighteenth century. But this option is neither realistic nor desirable. The ultra-Orthodox Jews are not the "true Jews." They are Jews who are running from reality and avoiding the need to adjust to it. They create for themselves a real or imagined ghetto, live in a different century, and do not even bother to investigate whether it is possible to be a religious Jew in the context of modern technology.

The ultra-Orthodox are the Karaites of the twenty-first century. Just as the Karaites stop with the Written Law (rejecting the later compilations of the Oral Law), the ultra-Orthodox come to a halt in the Eastern Europe of the eighteenth century. They view the everyday use of the Hebrew language as blasphemy and regard the establishment of Israel as a disaster, or at best a mistake. The ultra-Orthodox cannot function without the help of non-Jews, or secular Jews, to run the modern systems that they refrain from maintaining on the Sabbath and Jewish holidays. Their interpretation of Judaism is quite limited and, in my opinion, distorted and surrealistic. Any trend in this direction is similar in my eyes to the assimilation process: it constitutes a real departure from the Jewish people.

The second way to "guarantee" that our grandchildren will be

Jews is to make sure that they live in Israel, where the large and homogeneous Jewish community makes intermarriage a marginal phenomenon. Though Jewish education in Israel remains largely superficial and many would argue that the state lacks an appropriately Jewish character, Israel still offers an alternative to the religious ghetto. It enables one to live a secular life without giving up the ready accessibility of potential Jewish partners.

Israel is an option for a considerable portion of the Jewish people, though not for the majority (for the time being). Whoever speaks of *aliyah* as the way to ensure Jewish continuity is speaking of a phenomenon that is simply not about to occur; to do so is, in effect, to give up on the majority of the Jewish people today. I do not allow myself any illusions about mass *aliyah*, even if I wholeheartedly join in the call for Jews to immigrate to Israel.

The third option is more complicated. It represents an attempt to successfully realize both the emancipation and auto-emancipation processes. The auto-emancipation community in Israel and the emancipation community living in the United States and a few other countries would create a Jewish umbrella community offering membership to any Jew in the world who wishes to join. For members of this framework it would be a source of pride, strengthening their self-definition and adding a unique aspect to their lives—like belonging to a "good family." This framework should not impose itself on its members; but it must enable them to meet with one another and create opportunities for meeting potential mates. At the same time, it should offer solutions for mixed marriages in order to encourage a strong Jewish connection in the children of these marriages, even if these children are not considered Jews according to strict interpretations of *halachah*. The intention is to create a Jewish world in which its members move freely about, especially between Israel and the United States. This Jewish world would be able to deal with the many issues of modern Jewish life while avoiding the extremes of ultra-Orthodoxy and assimilation.

Our ability to assess the future is so limited that statistical trends are almost always misleading. But it is clear that something sad is happening in the Jewish world if its 1965 intermarriage rate of just 9 percent has skyrocketed to 52 percent by 1990, while there is also a negative rate of natural increase throughout the Jewish world outside Israel.

If the "Jewish parents' committee" does not attempt to influence the direction of things, if the ultra-Orthodox continue to wait for the Messiah, and if everyone else says that it is impossible to work against the inevitable unfolding of events, then the dire predictions for Jewish continuity will come true. In this scenario, Israel, the ultra-Orthodox, and some modern Orthodox Jews will be all that remains at the end of the twenty-first century, together with many others "of Jewish origin" who will not be part of any Jewish community and whose connection to things Jewish and Israel will be completely negligible.

The "Jewish parents' committee" can take advantage of another interesting trend that exists in the Diaspora today: a concern about assimilation and the threat to Jewish continuity, accompanied by a search for ways to strengthen Jewish education and the connection to Israel. There are hundreds of Jewish charitable funds in the United States devoted to Jewish education and Jewish continuity. There is strong interest in Judaism, particularly among many of the 185,000 or so converts in the United States. It appears that the core of deeply connected Jews is strengthening its connection and looking for answers. The question is: What can be done?

There are two central schools of thought among those who believe that there is an answer to this question, and this duality is reflected in the allocation of resources. For example, Morton Mandel, whose family sponsors one of the most important Jewish charitable funds in America, prefers to direct his efforts toward the committed core group. He invests considerable resources in training educators and in ongoing courses for future leaders of American and Israeli Jewry. Mandel believes that the higher the quality of this core group, the greater the chances for a wider circle of Jews to preserve their Jewish character. The "core" school argues that the attempt to attract less-committed Jews is very costly and may not be realistic. Moreover, while engaging in this almost hopeless attempt, we could lose the core of committed Jews who, without sufficient investment, would not be able to reach the same level of education and interest required for the future leadership of the Jewish people.

The "universal" school, on the other hand represented by philanthropists like Charles Bronfman and Michael Steinhardt, seeks to stop the flight from the Jewish home and try to reach every young Jew through an educational program, visits to Israel, and similar initiatives. They feel that time is working against the Jewish interest, and the funds that they have established are not directed primarily toward the usual group of active Jews. Instead, they aim to lend a hand to those who may not have an especially strong Jewish connection and might otherwise be lost to the Jewish people.

I believe that it is unnecessary to choose between these two schools of thought. In the current and unprecedented circumstances of the Jewish people, we must act on both fronts at the same time. On the one hand, we must develop a cadre of Jewish thinkers and scholars who can assume a public role in the Diaspora. It should be clearly recognized that one of the most serious problems in Jewish America today is the lack of personal or group leadership capable of making decisions. The likes of Abba Hillel Silver and Arthur Hertzberg have not emerged from the Jewish economic elite—the lay leadership—or from among the professionals who directly manage American Jewish institutions. There are thinkers and scholars who develop programs for Jewish studies and Jewish thought on many campuses, but they have not found their place in the Jewish leadership. Strengthening the leadership, convincing the convinced, and educating the educated are therefore essential.

On the other hand, we cannot allow ourselves even one day of neglecting the universal aspect. It is very difficult to return once you have lost a strong Jewish connection. It is very rare for someone with a scant Jewish background, who marries a non-Jew and raises non-Jewish children to suddenly show up at the Jewish community center. The decision to leave is more easily made than the decision to join. There are good-sized Jewish communities in the United States where the proportion of unaffiliated Jews reaches 70 percent. While many of the unaffiliated may still identify as Jews, they are certainly on the way toward a complete departure.

In New Delhi, there is a large digital clock that warns the public of the danger of overpopulation, with the number of India's residents growing each second on the display. A clock like this could be installed in every Jewish community to show the continual erosion in the number of its members. This would say, to those who care, that we are facing a decrease of frightening proportions and if we want to stop it, or at least slow its pace, we cannot be content with solutions directed only toward the core of committed Jews, nor can we afford to wait. Those who leave will not return.

The ideas commonly suggested to solve the problem of shrinking Jewish numbers include some that are simply slogans and some that are undesirable or impossible to implement. Raising the rate of natural increase among the Jews of the world is neither possible or desirable. A smaller number of children in the family usually allows for greater opportunities, for greater equality for women and for a more favorable economic situation. Ben-Gurion's effort to encourage a higher birthrate in the 1950s by promising to reward women (with 100 lirot—about $100) who gave birth to ten children was a cruel and misguided policy. The poorest of families were thus called upon to sink further into poverty by bringing more children into the world. Even if this were a correct policy, it is hard to believe that repeating the call for a higher birthrate would lead to a greater number of children in most Jewish homes.

The picture of Jews from lands of prosperity immigrating to Israel is attractive, certainly, but not practical. In an open world, more Israelis will emigrate to the United States than American Jews to Israel—unless dramatic changes occur in both countries. Compared to the 80,000 American Jews who have immigrated to Israel, many of whom eventually returned, some 350,000 Israelis have taken the opposite route since the founding of the state.

The two central pillars of the Jewish world today are the United States and Israel, and neither should adopt an arrogant approach toward the other. Israel's pretentious claim to be the spiritual center for American Jewry is very far from being realized. American Jews are better educated than their Israeli counterparts, and there is more evidence of Jewish creativity today in the United States than in Israel. The existence of the various streams of Judaism allows for much greater religious creativity than does the Orthodox monopoly in Israel.

However, Israel cannot accept the contention of many American Jews that their continued presence in the United States is required in order to ensure the political and financial support crucial to Israel. If it were up to us, we would much prefer to see this wealth of human talent and potential here in Israel. The many proposals for promoting Jewish continuity need to start from a premise of equality between the major Jewish centers, even after Israel becomes, in a few years, the largest community of Jews in the world.

Israel cannot ignore the story of American Jewry. In Israeli history books, this community is depicted as a marginal group of Jews who mistakenly arrived at the wrong destination. The history of this large Jewish community—especially during the past 120 years—is very interesting, is essential for an understanding of the Jewish world, and deserves to be a part of Israel's educational curriculum no less than the British White Papers and the forced conscription of Russian Jews into the czar's army.

The United States, for its part, long ago gave up on Blaustein's demand that Israel refrain from speaking on behalf of the Jewish people as a whole. This demand seems particularly ironic now, as it echoes the demands of some Israeli Arabs that the state should represent only its resident citizens and not claim to be the state of all the Jews.

If we aim to lower the walls dividing the Jewish world and allow as many Jews as possible to move, visit, work, and study in more than one place, Israel must undertake a painful analysis and make two basic changes: cancel the laws mandating religious marriage in Israel and end the Orthodox hegemony. These are two changes that we Israelis owe to ourselves. They also constitute the two greatest barriers between Israel and most of the Jewish world.

It is inconceivable that in the twenty-first century a Muslim and a Christian living in the same Galilee village may not get married because the Jewish state allows only for same-faith marriages by religious authorities! Instead, couples wishing to wed should be registered by a civil marriage registrar and divorced in a similar way. Whoever so wishes, could choose to add a religious ceremony. (This would apply equally, of course, to Israelis of all religions.)

Israel should also recognize the other streams of Judaism and treat them the same way it does the Orthodox community. That is, if the state continues to support organized religion, it should provide the same support for all streams, in proportion to their relative numbers. If, however, Israel decides to adopt the American system of separation of church and state, then none of the streams should receive government funding.

The latter approach has been discussed for many years but can only be achieved if the large streams within Zionism, together with religious movements like Meimad (which calls for religious values within a democratic framework), act in concert to oppose Orthodox contentions that this essential change would cause a fatal rift in the Jewish people. In fact, this rift is not the potential dispute between extreme Orthodox elements and the rest of the Jewish world but an existing one between Israel and the vast majority of American Jews over the persistent questions of "Who is a Jew?" and "Who is a rabbi?" and "Who is an authentic convert?" The rift already exists in the strong feelings of many American Jews that they are not regarded as legitimate Jews in Israel.

The threat of genealogical lists and the registration of those married under non-Orthodox auspices, for purposes of identifying "illegitimate" offspring *(mamzerim),* has already become a fact of Israeli life. As a result of the many Israelis choosing to marry abroad rather than in Orthodox ceremonies at home, separate lists are maintained in Israel. Practically speaking, I do not foresee any real problem making the changes suggested above, though they will surely spark heated protests by the Orthodox establishment in Israel. These changes represent an opportunity to expand, rather than decrease, the ranks of the Jewish people. The Zionist movement surely has no interest in pushing away people who regard and conduct themselves as Jews simply because they—or their mothers—were converted by the Conservative or Reform movements. (I will discuss further, below, the possibility of conversion outside of the existing religious frameworks.)

The completion of the peace process is another essential requirement for realizing the Zionist vision. Peace is not only vital for the citizens of Israel, it is also important for world Jewry, as it will enable them to regard Israel at least as a second home. The fact that Israel is the least secure place for Jews is, as previously noted, a painful failure of Zionism that stands in complete contradiction to Herzl's dream of normalization. Many Jews in the world place their concerns for personal security above any contemplation of living in Israel or even visiting. Israel's military victories bolstered Jewish prestige but did not bring in new Jewish immigrants. Israel's rule over millions of Palestinians made it hard for many Jews to identify with Israel, even as security threats frightened them. If Israel can become a Jewish and normal state at peace with its neighbors, free to invest its energies in developing its economy and culture, both Jewish and general, it will be a natural place for Jews to turn.

By attaining these two goals—completion of the peace process (including peace with the Palestinians, Syria, and Lebanon) and religious pluralism (with an end to religious control of marriage registration) —Israel can contribute to fashioning a new image for the Jewish people in the twenty-first century. These goals will not be easy to achieve. There are those in Israel who are fearful of religious or political change, preferring the status quo. They are more comfortable with Israel as a ghetto in the world, as an island surrounded by enemies. They do not believe in the inherent equality of all people—neither between Jews and Jews nor between Jews and non-Jews. They always put "peace" in quotation marks since they do not believe that any compromise could possibly lead to it. The other side always seems to be looking to take something from them while deceitfully failing to carry through its part of the bargain. The notion of religious pluralism for them is almost tantamount to converting to Christianity. Religious pluralism, like peace, is considered a risky change. It may be possible to see how such change begins, but its dangerous denouement seems to lurk like a storm on the horizon.

The struggle to effect these two crucial changes cannot wait another fifty years. For our own sake, we cannot permit this delay. We cannot continue alienating such a large part of the Jewish people. For this two-pronged objective, we will need every assistance of the enlightened forces in the Jewish world. They cannot stand idly by and simply cheer, or take a neutral stance, since this is clearly their battle, too. An Israel that is becoming more controlled by the ultra-Orthodox, more cloistered, and ever more denounced by the world is a nightmare for the continuity of the Jewish people.

## Jewishness Based on Self-Definition and "Secular Conversion"

It does not make sense that in the twenty-first century, when most of the Jews in the world are not religious, that they will continue to leave the "Who is a Jew?" question to religious authorities. Of course, there is a big difference between the relative openness of the various streams in Judaism, but all of them share an exclusive outlook, all are careful regarding the scope of conversion, and all of them insist that the transition to the Jewish people be made only through a religious process.

All too often, conversion involves a white lie. Most people convert in order to marry a Jewish partner. Yet they must convince a rabbi that they wish to convert out of religious conviction and that they will faithfully abide by some form of Jewish law *(mitzvot),* while both the rabbis and most of the converts involved know full well that this will not be the case. Thus, many who wish to remain honest with themselves often prefer not to convert, even if they do personally identify with the Jewish people and the Jewish culture.

If Judaism were only a religion, there would be no room for disputing the rabbinical monopoly on conversion; there would remain only the contention between the different religious denominations. But since being Jewish is also "something else," there is no reason why rabbis should also convert people to this "something else" as part of a rabbinical monopoly. Judaism is also about a people, a culture, an existence.

Many Jews—maybe even the majority—are atheists or agnostics, but nobody calls their Jewishness into doubt. Why is someone like me entitled to be a Jewish agnostic, while this is not permitted of a Jewish convert? Why does a non-Jewish atheist or agnostic need to go to a rabbi in order to become a Jewish atheist or agnostic?

According to an assessment by sociologist Sidney Goldstein (reported by J. J. Goldberg in *Jewish Power*), there are some eight million people living in Jewish homes in the United States today. This number includes spouses, children, and parents of Jews or converts. Thus, more than two million of these people are non-Jewish members of Jewish households who do not choose to convert. It is reasonable to assume that they identify with Jewish culture—and many raise their children as Jews—but they do not choose to join the Jewish people through a religious procedure.

In Israel today, there are hundreds of thousands of people, most of them relatives of immigrants from the former Soviet Union, who do not opt for religious conversion, though they live as Jews. Unfortunately, a tragic situation arises when an immigrant soldier is killed while serving in the armed forces of the Jewish state but cannot be buried in a Jewish cemetery since it turns out that his mother is not recognized as a Jew.

Relatives of Jews and those wishing to be recognized as Jews should be granted the right to join the Jewish people as a result of their own self-definition. I can envisage a situation in which someone who is not Jewish and is not affiliated with another religion turns to the Jewish community where he or she lives and asks to be registered as a member of the community. The community might request references by members of the Jewish community, and examine the person about his or her motivations, identification with the Jewish people, and knowledge of Jewish history. If the community is convinced of the person's genuine motives, it would register the new Jew in its ranks without any religious ceremony.

If the new member wishes to have a Reform wedding, the Reform movement would require that he or she undergo Reform conversion. The same would apply to the Conservative and Orthodox movements. Each new Jew would decide whether or not to undertake a religious conversion. Yet, from the perspective of the Jewish community, they would already be recognized as Jews by reason of self-definition.

## New Jewish Organization

The connection between Israel and the Jewish community in America and other smaller Jewish communities must be institutionalized and continuous. It is shocking to consider that no joint institution has ever been established for the two largest Jewish communities in the world. Despite a full agenda to discuss, representatives of these two communities, each numbering about 5 million, meet only when UJA delegations visit Israel or when Israelis appear at an Israel Bonds dinner.

Perhaps a real Israeli-American Committee was never formed because Israel preferred to see American Jewry as a transient community in exile, while the sensitivity of American Jews to charges of dual loyalties made them hesitant about holding regularized meetings with Israelis. Anyone who reads the statements exchanged by Ben-Gurion and Blaustein can understand the failure to establish a joint institution, but—especially today—there can be no excuse for this.

The common agenda includes the question of Jewish education in Israel and the Diaspora, issues pertaining to the security of Jewish communities, and joint efforts against Holocaust deniers like the former president of Croatia, Franjo Tudjman. There are issues related to American assistance to Israel and the peace process, as well as questions of a religious nature, including conversion. Besides dealing with matters like the assets of Holocaust victims, this new Israeli-American Jewish forum would also discuss such issues as Israel's approach to leaders of America's minority communities—for example, Jesse Jackson and Louis Farrakhan.

The absence of this sort of joint conference table has allowed for a situation where the two sides have surprised each other over the decades, each side often failing even to seek the other's reactions afterwards. There is no reason to continue to conduct this awkward relationship simply because it was convenient to the leaders of the two communities fifty years ago.

The more I think about the strange relationship we have inherited, and which we so dutifully continue, the more difficult it is for me to believe that to this very day we are still maintaining a virtual world that is almost entirely disconnected from reality, and that we are prepared to pay the heavy price of unrealistic relations. It seems to me like a family in which two brothers are living in separate rooms and are forbidden by their parents to meet except under parental supervision.

Israeli leaders continue to call on American Jews to immigrate to Israel as if we were still living at the beginning of the twentieth century, failing to understand that American Jewry has never viewed the United States as a temporary place of refuge. In political speeches referring to the "ingathering of the exiles," the Jews of the United States are lumped together with the remaining Jews in Syria and Romania. This in itself reflects the artificial nature of the relationship between Israeli and American Jews. This artificial relationship is also manifested in the institutions that were all very relevant once but have now become mostly irrelevant or even debilitating.

Israel Bonds is a classic example of an organization that no longer has a role to play but still continues to function due to organizational inertia. In September 1950, Ben-Gurion convened a meeting of fifty Jews from the United States and other communities to propose forming a new institution devoted solely to raising capital for Israel. A group led by Harry Montor (1905–1982), an active Reform rabbi who had been dismissed from UJA management, took up this challenge and established the Israel Bonds organization in America in 1951.

The organization was founded as a new framework for purchasing Israeli government bonds, providing long-term loans at low interest rates. At that time, Israel needed large loans to finance the absorption of mass immigration and the construction of infrastructure. As a young state that had yet to prove its ability to repay loans, its only ready source of capital was the Jewish world.

The Israel Bonds organization was a success story. Managed as a separate American company, it attained a considerable amount of capital for Israel and provided many Jews with a feeling of partnership in building the young Jewish state. The purchase of Israel Bonds was not charity, though there was an element of contribution involved, considering the low interest paid on these bonds. Many of those who bought Israel Bonds would acquire new ones when they matured or contribute the proceeds to the UJA. Some cashed their bonds in for El Al tickets and thus strengthened their connection with Israel. Senior Israeli officials would don tuxedos and describe Israel's many needs at lavish Israel Bonds dinners. In sum, everyone was happy: American Jewry could take pride in an important institution that activated many supporters of Israel, while Israel enjoyed comfortable loans and Israeli lecturers had another address besides the UJA for their American tours.

The problem began when the number of American Jews investing in Israel Bonds dropped significantly. This presented the organization with a difficult choice: to disband due to lack of support or raise the interest rate on the bonds. Of course, they chose the latter. By this time—the late 1970s and early eighties—Israel had a respectable record of repaying its debts and was no longer dependent on Israel Bonds for credit. In fact, Israel was paying a higher rate on some Israel Bonds than it would have paid to commercial banks for the same capital. As a result, the Israel Bonds organization entered a new period of growth as American pension funds and trade unions eagerly purchased these bonds. The new buyers had discovered a gold mine: high interest on their investment, together with a very low risk of default.

When I encountered this Israel Bonds phenomenon, while serving as deputy finance minister in the late 1980s, I tried to understand why the government of Israel should continue to pay millions of dollars to maintain such an organization with its hundreds of employees. It did not make sense for Israel to pay a higher rate for these bonds than it would at the nearest bank. Government officials warned me that no one had succeeded in stopping this juggernaut and that I would fare no better. They were right. The leaders of Israel Bonds raised a cry, contending that the current availability of comfortable loans might only be temporary and that their organization was a crucial security net for rainy days. The Israel Bonds network, they argued, also still serves as an excellent bridge between Israel and the Diaspora, linking thousands of families throughout the world. The organization's leaders further volunteered that they had slightly lowered the interest rates. This anachronistic organization continues to thrive today, despite the fact that no one besides its own leaders and activists are able to justify its existence.

The Israel Bonds organization merely perpetuates the same old worn-out dialogue in which the Israelis describe their country's needs and the American donors ask about the Israelis' war experiences and whether their children are already serving in the army. The Americans are later told that the least they can do, considering the fact that their own children do not risk their lives defending the Jewish state, is to strengthen Israel through the purchase of bonds. I found myself in this artificial situation in the mid-1980s—which is when I decided to stop speaking at Israel Bonds dinners.

The case of the Jewish National Fund (JNF) is even more pathetic and severe. Up until the establishment of the state, it was one of the clearest expressions of the Zionist struggle: it collected money from the Jews of the world in order to purchase lands in Palestine for Jewish settlement. Despite the fact that the decision to establish the Jewish National Fund was approved at the Fifth Zionist Congress in 1901, it did not belong to the political Zionist outlook but rather was the brainchild of Hovevei Zion. Professor Zvi Herman Shapira (1840–1898) proposed this idea at the Kattowitz conference of Hovevei Zion in 1884 and worked to see it become a reality. Dr. M. Bodenheimer (1865–1940) presented Shapira's plan at the First Zionist Congress, telling the delegates: "Professor Shapira would like to establish a fund through an annual collection. This fund would not be touched until it reached a sum of ten million pounds sterling. Two-thirds of the interest on the fund would be solely devoted to the purchase of lands. It would be forbidden to sell these lands, only lease them for a period of forty-nine years. A Jewish plebiscite would be required to approve spending that exceeds the fund's annual interest."

The JNF acquired some 8 percent of the lands in western Palestine by the time Israel was established in 1948. This land acquisition was arduous, and often illegal. The sale of lands by rich Arab owners exacerbated the confrontation between Jewish settlers and the Arab tenant farmers working these lands. But the JNF land purchases enabled the Jewish settlement of important areas in what is now Israel. The JNF is an integral part of the Israeli ethos—overcoming great obstacles to acquire lands and draining swamps on these lands to replant the forests that had disappeared over the years. In Palestine, the JNF symbolized a refusal to accept the terrible neglect of the land and even a struggle against nature itself; for many Jews throughout the world, the fund came to express an identification with the "redemption of land" and renewed settlement in the land of Israel.

The JNF's great success derived from the popular appeal of the symbol it created. The blue box found its way into many homes, where it was sometimes the only connection with the Zionist enterprise and Judaism. When Woody Allen, for example, spoke about his Jewish roots, he told how he had collected contributions in his blue JNF box. (The blue box, by the way, has recently been called back from retirement by the JNF after years of serving only as a museum piece.)

It would have seemed natural for the JNF to transfer its land registry to the government of the new State of Israel in 1948 and announce that it would disband as an institution, while offering the assistance of its talented personnel in continuing this work under government auspices. But this did not happen. The continuation of the JNF was a convenient way for the government to avoid the transfer of lands to Arabs and (after 1967) to acquire lands in the West Bank under a different guise.

The "redemption of lands" by this Jewish fund took on a very different appearance after the period of struggle between Arabs and Jews resulted in a sovereign Jewish state that controlled the contested lands. Moreover, the JNF—with its clumsy management structure that provides representation to various political parties—became a state-funded contractor that competes under preferential conditions against private contractors in Israel. Thus, for example, the JNF paves bypass roads in the West Bank.

The JNF's fund-raising in the Diaspora these days amounts to no more than several tens of millions of dollars, which makes it difficult to justify maintaining the very expensive JNF operations abroad. On the other hand, the Jewish world views the JNF as another fund-raising appeal that perpetuates the relations of donor and emissary collecting for a needy Israel.

In his 1981 film *In Search of Identity*, Amos Gitai photographs an elderly Jewish woman walking in the streets of New York in the late 1970s with a blue box, seeking contributions for Israel. The interviewer asks the woman: "Why are you collecting the money?" She responds: "So that they can build synagogues, schools. It's very important." Viewing such a scene, we must ask ourselves: What have we done to Israel's image in the United States, how we have managed to so distort the perception of the young Jewish state for generations of Americans, and how we have made it completely impossible to conduct a dialogue between equals?

What kind of dialogue can develop between someone rattling a cup and someone dropping coins into it? Who would possibly think to establish the JNF today, when a state exists with its own large mechanisms for dealing with land (including the Israel Lands Authority and the Lands Registry Office). But who today would consider disbanding the JNF with all its considerable administration, chairmen, presidents, emissaries, information officers, and Israeli lecturers? Who can assess the price we have paid for perpetuating the image of "poor Israel" through the continued use of the blue box long after there was any need for it?

The United Jewish Appeal (UJA) has demonstrated more ability to change with the times than most of the other Jewish organizations. The organization of Jewish federations in the United States initiated the UJA in 1939, combining the efforts of the United Palestine Appeal and the Joint Distribution Committee, which had been working to provide aid to Jewish refugees throughout the world since World War I. The merger was only implemented in practice in 1945, after World War II.

It was a good arrangement for all concerned. The Joint Distribution Committee has since been assured consistent funding without having to mount a separate fund-raising campaign. The local federations could count on widespread contributions and were no longer dependent on an affluent few. This enabled them to plan their local budgets with confidence and engage in long-range development, while the engine for fund-raising was collecting money for Israel on the eve of its establishment and afterwards. Initially, some 70 percent of the money collected was transferred to Israel, but recently this division has been reversed; now 70 percent of the annual proceeds—about one billion dollars—remains for local use. The UJA became a well-oiled machine for collection and recently formed a union with the Council of Jewish Federations (CJF).

It is difficult to predict how this merger of the UJA and CJF—known now collectively as the United Jewish Communities (UJC)—will develop. It will almost certainly lead to a decrease in the amount of funds transferred to Israel. But it is not clear whether this focus on local activities will win the hearts—and pocketbooks—of American Jewry. Without the Israel motif, will the new organization still be able to raise a billion dollars annually?

In any case, this is not a framework for Israeli-American dialogue. Even more than the Israel Bonds, the UJA, by definition, was built on the premise of a needy Israel, which required contributions to fund the absorption of immigrants, improve its standard of living, and deal with security problems. The type of dialogue that developed between Israeli speakers at fund-raising events and

UJA donors, or between UJA delegations visiting Israel's poor neighborhoods, was never a dialogue between equals and cannot become such now.

The Jewish Agency was supposed to be the natural address for the exchange of ideas at the highest levels between Israelis and Diaspora Jews. The two organizations—the World Zionist Organization (WZO) and the Jewish Agency—were created in historical contexts very unlike the situation we find at the beginning of the twenty-first century.

The WZO, established along with the First Zionist Congress, was the only successful attempt to form a worldwide, democratic, Jewish organization. The WZO is an organization of members whose dues—if only a symbolic amount—entitle them to participate in democratic elections held throughout the Jewish world. The debates within the WZO's institutions have been very heated, and fateful decisions have been made. The political struggle between the various movements created great tensions, especially during the 1930s, in the wake of Chaim Arlosoroff's murder and the departure of Ze'ev Jabotinsky from the Zionist movement.

In 1929, the Jewish Agency for Palestine was established, in accordance with the British Mandate, to represent the Jewish world before the British authorities and coordinate the creation of the national home with these authorities. In practice, the Jewish Agency combined elected members of the WZO with affluent and prominent Jewish figures who were not necessarily Zionists sharing the goal of *aliyah* but who were willing to help the Jewish effort in Palestine. The founding convention of the Jewish Agency, festively held in Zurich, was quite promising. Half of the participants were representatives of the WZO and the other half represented twenty-six different countries. Among the prominent non-Zionists in attendance were Professor Albert Einstein (1879–1955); the French statesman Léon Blum (1872–1950), who was elected prime minister seven years later; and Louis Marshall (1856–1929), the chairman of the American Jewish Committee. Marshall was appointed to head the new organization.

The Jewish Agency, however, failed to live up to initial expectations and did not fill the role Weizmann intended for it. This was due to the sudden death of Marshall only days after the founding convention, as well as the economic depression that followed the Wall Street crash later that year, which impoverished many of the rich partners in this new enterprise. For many years, the Jewish Agency was synonymous with the WZO and was, in effect, the "state" in the making. It was the central body that functioned as the government of the Jewish settlement in the land of Israel (the *yishuv*), joined by the Histadrut (General Federation of Hebrew Workers) and the Va'ad Haleumi (National Council of Palestinian Jewry).

After the establishment of the state, few functions were left for the Jewish Agency. Elections in the Jewish world had also lost their significance after World War II, with most of the representatives being appointed by their communities. In Israel, representation was determined according to the Knesset elections. In 1971, a census of members was taken and about one million Jews throughout the world declared that they consider themselves part of the WZO. But this was no longer an organization of members as it was characterized from its inception through the late 1930s.

It seems logical that the WZO continued to exist after the founding of Israel, as millions of Jews were then living in distress and hoping to immigrate to Israel. The continuation of the Jewish Agency, however, was much more artificial. It was the scaffolding that helped in establishing a state but should have been removed when this task was accomplished. Instead it lingered, the way organizations tend to do, but also because it was difficult to separate the Jewish Agency from the WZO. Before the founding of the state, the Jewish Agency was directed by the foremost leaders of the Jewish community in Palestine. After 1948, however, many of these

figures were elected to the Knesset and filled senior positions in
government ministries. Their places were taken mainly by old-
timers relegated to the back benches of the new Israeli political
system, or sometimes by young politicians at the beginning of
their political careers.

Two functions remained in the hands of the Jewish Agency.
First, it was the only formal channel for receiving contributions
from world Jewry—money from the UJA and Keren HaYesod. Second, the Jewish Agency was also a sort of ministry of immigration
and absorption. The funds that arrived were mainly devoted to the
large-scale immigration operations, absorption of the new immigrants in transit camps or agricultural settlements. Jewish Agency
officials were the first ones to meet the new immigrants and
accompanied them during their initial period in Israel. This work
involved thousands of dedicated and professional people who
were partners in the state's great successes during its early years. In
the shadow of this success, however, feelings of discrimination
were engendered among many of the new immigrants that fes-
tered over the ensuing decades and continue to rankle Israeli society to this very day.

The WZO functioned as the elected body, while the Jewish
Agency acted as the executive body. Over the years, the Jewish
Agency regarded itself as a mechanism parallel to the state. The
status and salary of Jewish Agency department heads were identical to those of cabinet ministers. Thus, for example, the chairman
of the Jewish Agency/WZO received the same salary as the prime
minister of Israel.

In 1952 a law was passed concerning the status of the World
Zionist Organization, and in 1954 the government of Israel signed
a pact with the WZO that included the following statement: "The
State of Israel recognizes the World Zionist Organization as the
authorized agency that will continue to work in the State of Israel
to develop the country and its settlements, to absorb immigrants

from the Diaspora and to coordinate the activities in Israel of Jewish institutions and associations working in these fields."

With the establishment of the Ministry of Absorption in 1968, the overlapping functions of the Jewish Agency and WZO became even more conspicuous. The Jewish Agency then decided to try again to include non-Zionists. According to an agreement signed in August 1970, the highest authority in the Jewish Agency became the "Assembly," 50 percent of whose members were elected by the WZO, 30 percent by UJA representatives (that is, American millionaires), and 20 percent by the Foundation Fund (Keren HaYesod), the fundraising body in other countries of the world. The trustees of the Jewish Agency, appointed according to the same formula, have managed the affairs of the agency over the past three decades. The Jewish Agency's budget and widespread activities make it the largest Jewish institution in the world. From Israel's perspective, it is the largest nongovernmental organization that provides social and welfare services to the public. Cooperation between the government of Israel and the Jewish Agency/WZO, anchored in the pact signed in 1954, is monitored by a "coordinating institution" comprising members of the Israeli government and directors of the Jewish Agency/WZO.

Behind this complicated fabric of institutions, laws, pacts, and coordinating committees lies a much simpler reality. The WZO still sees itself as a world movement arguing the justice of the Zionist cause, sending *aliyah* emissaries to large Jewish communities, facilitating Jewish education in the Diaspora and assisting settlement in Israel.

The government of Israel views the WZO as a tool for settlement activity beyond the Green Line (the 1967 border) since the Jewish Agency is not permitted to engage in this activity. The Jewish Agency, on the other hand, is still an unrivaled tool for channeling funds collected in the Jewish world, providing Israel with reserves that are not included in the government budget. The sums that reach Israel via the Jewish Agency must indeed be used for activities in which the government is not involved, but it is clear to all that these are activities the government would have to finance itself were it not for this Jewish Agency funding.

The mission of the WZO ended when the struggle for emigration concluded. With the gates of emigration now open to world Jewry, there is no further justification for the WZO's continued existence. The tremendous success story of the Zionist movement is reason to disband the organization that led to the establishment of the State of Israel. The WZO's activities have decreased considerably, its contribution to encouraging *aliyah* from developed states is less than marginal, and its budget has become symbolic.

The elections for the Zionist congress held every four years have been replaced in most of the Jewish communities in the world by the appointment of representatives acceptable to the various parties. The Zionist parties in the Jewish world are generally very pale copies of the affiliated parties in Israel. The debates between these Diaspora parties in the Zionist congress have no significance in the Jewish world. It is not a Jewish parliament, and not even a Zionist parliament, since it represents very few people. Rather, it is a phenomenon that offers only nostalgic value.

Avraham Burg, in his former capacity as chairman of the Jewish Agency/WZO, proposed that a final Zionist congress be held to mark the hundredth anniversary of the Zionist movement in 1997. The WZO would then be disbanded. But Burg's proposal was rejected. As in many other cases, the organization proved to be stronger than its leader. Yet, as the WZO receives its budget from the Jewish Agency and the Jewish Agency has been trimming the WZO's budget in recent years, it is certainly possible that a lack of funds may yet spell an end to the WZO in the near future.

The Jewish Agency has become a leaner and more efficient organization in recent years, managed by the two major parties in Israel, Labor and Likud. It proved its professionalism in helping to absorb the masses of immigrants from the former Soviet Union in

the early 1990s, but its extragovernmental status cannot be justified except for it being the legal channel for transferring funds
from abroad. The Jewish Agency's professional administration and
knowledge could well serve the Ministry of Absorption or other
governmental bodies. There is no reason to maintain such a complex political mechanism in order to carry out bureaucratic tasks.
With its primary focus on internal reforms and the allocation of
the funds it receives, the Jewish Agency is certainly not a framework for real dialogue between Israel and the Diaspora.

The "coordinating institution" between the government and
the Jewish Agency/WZO is more titular than substantive. It is one
of the ministerial committees that include a number of ministers,
the Jewish Agency chairman, and other agency representatives.
The prime minister is the chairman of this committee, and, as in
all governments, this ensures that it will be infrequently convened,
and then only ceremoniously. Ostensibly, it should be the highest
framework for Israel-Diaspora dialogue, but it is practically inac-
tive, and when it does meet, Diaspora representatives rarely participate. Its agenda is set in advance, its resolutions a foregone
conclusion. If this committee convenes once or twice a year, it is
out of a feeling of obligation, and it continues to exist primarily on
paper.

On first glance, there is nothing so terrible about this. The
world is full of organizations whose time has passed, with overlapping mandates and large bureaucracies, but which find countless
tenuous purposes for self-justification. No one today would propose forming the JNF, the Jewish Agency, the WZO, or Israel Bonds;
they exist today only because they are already established. There
are many institutions in Israel and the world that we would not
reinvent today. Nonetheless, suggestions to disband them fall on
deaf ears.

The main obstacle is that the numerous organizations involved
in the relationship between Israel and the Diaspora have, over several decades, created the illusion that there is full and constant rap-

prochement between the Jews in America, Israel, and elsewhere in the world. This false impression is one of the reasons that no discussion of the sort I propose is really being conducted and no regular and organized forum exists for raising the very serious topics on our common agenda. We speak to one another through the media, have chance meetings, and share a feeling that we lack a real framework for Israel-Diaspora communication. The debates between the various party coalitions in the WZO chapters abroad have long been rather pathetic, dealing with issues that have already been resolved in Israel—and which represent, anyway, only a tiny percentage of the Jewish people. It is a virtual world whose danger lies in the fact that it has replaced and kept out the real world for several decades.

A true joint forum should be established at once. Perhaps it would supplant the institutions mentioned above, or at least some of them. Perhaps these institutions will continue for another fifty years, explaining why they are vital and irreplaceable, and blaming the new forum for duplicating existing channels. But such an annoyance would be a price worth paying. It is important that central Jewish figures who have something to say, and who represent large segments of the Jewish people, should finally sit together. A new forum could address the issues that are not discussed today—or are treated in the most superficial, conventional ways—in order to work out a consensus and work toward peaceful cooperation.

The democratic way is the preferable option since it is the most representative and legitimate; any other approach would raise questions. One may sometimes regret the decision of the voters but must still respect it. During its dynamic years, the Zionist movement proved that it is possible to maintain this kind of democratic forum. The question remains whether it is possible to repeat this attempt, which succeeded before the establishment of the state.

In 1993, Rabbi Asher (Dick) Hirsch proposed the establishment of a democratic Jewish parliament. He was dissatisfied with existing institutions and particularly uncomfortable with the nonrepresentative nature of the Jewish Agency. Professor Daniel Elazar, on the other hand, regards the Jewish Agency as an institution with the potential to play a central role in the life of the Jewish people. He has suggested that the Jewish Agency's current management be expanded to include the World Jewish Congress and other organizations. According to Elazar's plan, the large organizations would form the secretariat of this world Jewish association, while all of the organizations would participate in its council.

In late 1993, Dr. Michael Livne presented a detailed plan for a democratic organization to replace the Zionist congress. According to this plan, a new and democratic organization would be established for Israel and the Diaspora that would provide an alternative to the type of relationship in effect between Diaspora fund-raisers and the WZO. Elections would be held once every four years, with the right to vote granted to anyone who pays the modest membership dues. The supreme executive body would comprise 6,000 members and meet once during every four-year term. The directors of this organization—fifty in number—would meet every four months. A group of fourteen managing directors would meet in Israel and include only residents of Israel.

Dr. Arik Carmon has also proposed establishing a second body, like a senate, that would include influential Jews from Israel and the Diaspora and serve in a strictly advisory capacity.

These and other proposals all derive from a feeling that there is no real meeting today between representatives of the world's different Jewish communities and that there is a need to create a new forum for this type of meeting. None of these proposals, even the most modest of them, have yet to be realized. The existing institutions seem strong on the surface and unyielding to change. But the truth is that most of them are quite weak today and painfully aware that they no longer represent what they did decades ago. They still claim to represent the Jewish people, American Jewry, the major Jewish organizations, and so on; but know better than any-

one else how far from reality these claims are. The real dilemma—
with which I am also struggling—is whether to invest efforts in
forming a democratic world Jewish organization or to direct these
efforts toward establishing an organization that would reflect the
current configuration of the Jewish people and put off the lofty
goal of democracy.

In 1994, I proposed forming a House of Israel (Beit Yisrael)
organization that would conduct elections throughout the Jewish
world after enlisting at least one million members from Israel and
the Diaspora. This new framework would discard the artificial
distinction between Zionists and non-Zionists and grant equal
standing to the two major centers of the Jewish world. It would
meet on a regular basis several times a year in both New York and
Israel to discuss an agenda prepared in advance. The House of
Israel would have resources at its disposal—collected from the
Diaspora and Israel—that would empower it to exert influence on
a range of issues, including Jewish education. The "birthright"
project (described at length below) would be one of its central
missions.

Critics of my proposal have raised several arguments. First,
they note that the Jews in the Diaspora live in a voluntary society
and that it would be impossible to conduct general democratic
elections in this type of society since many of the central activists
simply would refrain from competing against each other. Thus,
the new organization would lose some of its best potential leadership.

A second argument is that certain well-organized groups,
despite the fact that they comprise only a minority in the Jewish
world, would gain control of a democratic, international, Jewish
organization. The silent majority would remain silent. They would
not bother to pay the fee that entitles voting rights and would have
no voice in electing representatives to the new organization.

Yet another argument put forward in response to my House of
Israel proposal notes that Israel comprises a political system that

enables the majority—even a bare majority—to make decisions. The Jewish world, on the other hand, is not a political system, and its mode of decision-making is generally one of consensus. Since there are no means of enforcing decisions, an attempt to form a real parliament would not succeed.

While there is a measure of logic in each of these contentions, I am not willing to give up on the notion of establishing a new democratic Jewish framework, such as the American-Israeli Jewish Forum, and letting it decide future election procedures.

The American-Israeli nucleus can eventually expand to include the remaining 20 percent of the Jewish world in the new organization. It is important that we define procedures to prevent the founding group from holding on indefinitely to the reins of leadership. Thus, even if we initially decide not to hold democratic elections, it is essential to set term limits and encourage organizational flexibility that would facilitate significant dialogue. The success of the new venture will be measured primarily by the quality of this dialogue and not by the number of delegates attending gala congresses or by the efficiency demonstrated in organizing such mass events. A forum of one to two hundred people will meet annually, while a smaller forum will convene four times a year. The organization's administrative staff will be located in Jerusalem and New York.

I know. Yes, it is certainly possible that the existing organizations will continue to function and that the new venture will just be another in a series of Jewish organizations that initially generate interest and enthusiasm but become anachronistic and less relevant twenty or thirty years later. I have no patent against the "Iron Law of Oligarchy" described by Robert Michels ("Who says organization, says oligarchy."), but should this prevent the formation of a new framework? If it were possible, I would recommend determining in advance that this new framework be disbanded—legally and organizationally—twenty years from the day of its inauguration. A new version of the organization could then be fashioned, if so desired. But perhaps it is unfeasible to make such a determination at this point, and I would not want to burden the Forum with impractical commitments when it is just getting off the ground.

## The Birthright

Is there a magical solution for Jewish continuity? Is there a single proposal upon which we can focus in order to guarantee to the "Jewish parents' committee" that their children will not drop out? It is difficult to believe that such a solution exists. But it is equally hard to witness our financial and spiritual resources spread over multiple solutions while the hemorrhaging continues unstaunched.

Jewish education, of course, is a key element. In recent years, there have been several encouraging developments in this field, though not of a revolutionary nature. Concerted efforts have been devoted to establishing Jewish day schools in the Diaspora. Yet while some local success has been achieved in this direction, only 5 percent of Jewish children in the United States attend such schools.

Families affiliated with the local Jewish federation generally send their children to part-time religious schools until they reach the age of bar/bat mitzvah. This framework provides a very superficial dose of Jewish learning, preparing the children for their bar/bat mitzvah ceremonies in the synagogue, which mark the end of Jewish education for the vast majority of American Jews. Most Jewish youngsters do not enjoy religious schools, look forward to being done with this burden, and quickly forget most of the little they have learned.

Many parents who wish to provide a good Jewish education to their children are nevertheless hesitant about sending them to a Jewish day school. They are concerned that this would distance their children from their immediate surroundings, keep them from learning other secular subjects, and make it more difficult for their children to integrate into non-Jewish society, which is the key to their future success.

Secular Jewish studies have flourished in Israel in recent years, with a growing number of programs for studying Torah and Talmud as academic subjects. More and more people are showing an interest in learning about their Jewish heritage and are happy to do so without having to accept any predetermined religious conclusions. At the same time, however, there has been a very significant decrease in the Jewish curriculum in Israel's secular state schools, especially in the field of the religious law. As a result, there is a growing gap between secular and religious youth in Israel. The lack of basic knowledge regarding Jewish ideas—developed over thousands of years of our people's history—never ceases to amaze and disappoint.

The problem, of course, is not the availability of learning materials. The knowledge is available. There are thousands of Jewish sites on the Internet that deal with the Bible, Mishnah, Talmud, and *geniza* scrolls. There is an enormous amount of information (including several encyclopedias on Judaism) on CD-ROMs, a Holocaust museum in Washington and Yad Vashem in Jerusalem, and numerous television series on Jewish topics. The ORT educational system, for example, developed a program in England for the study of Hebrew and preparation for bar/bat mitzvah via the Internet, primarily for remote communities. Still, the question remains how to attract young people to take advantage of Jewish Internet programs instead of watching their favorite TV series. Accessibility is essential, but not enough.

The same is true regarding visits to Israel. The secret is not in making these available, but in exploiting this availability. It has become clear to me beyond any doubt that a visit to Israel, especially during the teenage years, is directly connected to subsequent decisions on maintaining some type of Jewish framework and raising children as Jews. Researchers such as Gary Tobin, Annette Hochstein, Eric Cohen, Barry Chazan, David Mittleberg, and

Steven M. Cohen, who have studied the impact of visits by Jewish youth to Israel, conclude that nearly all of the participants have positive experiences. The special dynamics that develop among the teenagers, encounters with their Israeli peers, and counselors who share their knowledge and experience with the participants—all contribute to the success of these summer programs. This unique opportunity for young Jews to learn firsthand about their Jewish roots and modern-day Israel provides visiting teenagers with feelings of autonomy, identity, and purpose.

Of course, not all visits are identical or have the same impact. But teenage programs are usually successful when they explore more than one aspect of Israel, include encounters with Israelis, and are followed by organized efforts to maintain the group's connections. Charles Bronfman was one of the first to recognize the uniqueness of such visits and created the "Israel Experience," which has brought thousands of young Jews to Israel—mostly from North America—on subsidized summer programs.

Many similar programs were subsequently developed. One local federation calls its program "Passport to Israel," and another has a "Bar/Bat Mitzvah" program. Some federations bear a part of the program cost, often subsidizing from 30 to 50 percent of participants' expenses. In some communities, the federation contributes one-third and the synagogue one-third, while the teenager's parents pay the rest from a savings account opened for this purpose when the child was born.

The results observed over the past decade are rather enlightening. On the one hand, it is clear that teenagers who make this kind of visit, including those who were not closely involved in Jewish activities prior to the trip, are strongly influenced by it. The young Jews who participate in these programs tend to come back for subsequent visits; some register for study programs in Israel and even think about making Israel their home. On the other hand, only a very small percentage of the pool of Jewish teenagers participates in these programs. There are today some 90,000 Jewish children at each grade level in the Diaspora, and there are about 250 programs for visiting Israel that are generously subsidized by local federations of national organizations. But the number of Jewish youth who take advantage of these opportunities does not exceed 2 percent.

This is perhaps not so surprising in light of the fact that 74 percent of American Jews have never visited Israel. Nonetheless, the special efforts to attract Jewish youth to programs in Israel have yielded disappointing results. A large number of those who do participate in these trips are connected to Jewish educational institutions and youth movements. The overwhelming majority prefer to spend the summers with their non-Jewish friends, in camps, or on trips to other destinations. The researchers note that "most of the parents are not enthusiastic about their children traveling with youth groups to Israel." Some parents worry primarily about their children's security, while others are afraid that they might decide to settle in Israel.

It should be much easier to convince teenagers to take advantage of these relatively inexpensive programs than to persuade them to attend Jewish day schools or even to make use of the Jewish reference materials on the Internet. These programs have an amazing impact. Therefore, if it were possible to send the 90,000 or so Jewish youth who reach a certain "threshold" age each year to Israel, we would be making a huge difference in their lives and in the future of the Jewish people. A visit to Israel has proven to be the third most influential factor in preventing assimilation and is the one most relevant for most of Diaspora Jewry.

In order to persuade more young Jews to participate in Israel programs, the subsidies for these trips have been increased. As mentioned above, most American Jewish teenagers can receive a subsidy of about one-third of the program cost from their local federation. In most cases, the remaining two-thirds of the cost represents a hurdle; yet the greatest obstacle appears to be that a visit to Israel is not a major aspiration of the typical American Jewish teenager. There is a large gap between teenagers' expectations concerning Israeli programs and the actual impressions made on those who participate in them.

In 1994, I offered a proposal to the General Assembly of Jewish Federations that spoke of the "birthright" of every young Jew to visit Israel in an organized summer program. The birthright program would last several weeks and be entirely funded by the Jewish people. This birthright is not dependent on the young person's economic situation or connection to a Jewish community or particular stream of Judaism. Neither does it matter whether the young Jew has visited Israel previously or is defined as a Jew under the Law of Return or according to the Orthodox interpretation of *halachah*.

The young visitors would not be receiving a gift from us; rather, we would profit from their visit to Israel. Thus, the invitation would not involve performing any obligation whatsoever. There would be no requirement to work in the community in order to receive the plane ticket, or to repay the cost after the visit. From my point of view, there should not even be an obligation to participate in a course about Israel that would be offered prior to the visit. Simply come!

According to my proposal, every young Jew would receive a birthday card from the local federation on his or her seventeenth birthday with a coupon for travel and accommodations in Israel during the next summer vacation. I fixed on the age of seventeen because young people reach a high degree of independence by this age—one year before going off to college—but are still rather more impressionable than when they are older. It is also the last year that Diaspora teenagers can still meet with their Israeli counterparts, who enlist in the army at age eighteen. When Israelis finally enter the university several years later—in many cases after traveling the world for several months or more—they are no longer natural partners for eighteen-year-old American students. The coupon would be a personalized one and could not be transferred or saved for later use. It would offer a range of programs for each young Jew to select from. While all of the programs would include some segments on Jewish and Israeli history, each participant would be able to choose between offerings in music, computers, archeology, art, and so on. All of the programs would offer much more than the usual dose of Masada, Jerusalem, kibbutz, Bedouin tent, and camels in the Negev. Israeli teenagers would accompany each group for at least part of the visit.

The idea is to transform the visit to Israel from a small group of tourists to a "jamboree" of young Jews. It would be an annual gathering of the youth of world Jewry that would promote the development of long-term relationships between the participants, including those who come from the same areas of the world but did not have the opportunity to meet previously. The birthright program would enable the Jewish people—via Israel—to meet the widest possible variety of Jews and amass, over the years, a storehouse of information on the Jewish people and serve as a conduit for information exchange.

One of the project's central tasks would be to develop followup programs to these visits and offer additional options. After returning home from their Israel visit, the young Jews would be encouraged to maintain contact with Israel and their local Jewish community. They would be asked if they would like to receive more information on other Israel programs, opportunities for studying in Israel, updates on developments in their fields of interest, more resources on Jewish history and Judaism, and so on. Without effective follow-up, the visits to Israel will not realize their full potential and importance.

Once the program becomes a sort of second bar/bat mitzvah that each young Jew comes to expect on his or her seventeenth birthday, it would not be necessary to aggressively market the idea. It should become relatively easy to also reach Jewish teenagers whose families are not affiliated with a local federation, once they see that their friends are taking advantage of this birthright to visit

Israel. In this way, the local federations would also have a better chance of contacting and engaging families who have not been involved in the Jewish community.

I am assuming here that a coupon for free travel would be more difficult to refuse than a partially subsidized program. A teenager who finds a coupon for a free trip to Israel in the mailbox is likely to think twice before tossing it in the trash. His or her parents are also likely to seriously consider taking advantage of this one-time opportunity to send their child to Israel at no cost. If the program indeed succeeds, it would offer the advantage of universality—an ability to quickly encompass complete age groups of the Jewish people without losing precious time. It would not replace programs for training teachers and leaders, but it is the most effective idea that I can imagine for quickly and broadly dealing with the problem of the Jewish people's diminishing numbers.

Funding for the birthright program could, in my opinion, come from UJA and Keren HaYesod money that is currently allocated for social welfare programs in Israel. The government of Israel should—and could—finance these programs itself. Israel would contribute to the birthright program by its willingness to forgo this Diaspora funding of social welfare projects in Israel. In other areas, Israel would actually stand to benefit economically from the thousands of visiting teenagers. The flights to Israel could be via El Al, and the tourist services, food, and counselors would be funded as part of the program. Israel would need to build up a significant base of counselors, tour guides, coordinators for Israeli groups, and others. These resources would be called into action mainly during the summer, and to a lesser extent during the winter months, when teenagers from South America, Australia, and South Africa are on vacation.

One argument raised against my plan is that even if the amount of UJA money allocated for Israel today is less than 30 percent, most of the contributors feel that they are sending assistance to Israel. According to fund-raising experts, it is difficult to collect money for schools or nursing homes, and much easier to mount a fund drive for an Israel in need of economic and military assistance that is struggling to absorb penniless refugees. Moreover, if American Jews stop contributing to Israel, why should the United States continue to grant such generous aid to Israel? Another argument contends that if something is offered for free, then it is regarded as having little value. If the teenagers know that they are not obligated to do anything in return for the birthright program, then they will not take it seriously.

There are those who say that the problem is not one of funding or availability of Israel programs—these are just excuses. Young Jews are simply not interested in visiting Israel, and their parents are wary of such visits. Even if a coupon like this arrives at their home, they would put it aside and would not visit Israel.

A more extreme response argues that this whole idea mistakenly holds up Israel as a magical cure for assimilation, while in reality Israel offers no such cure. Israeli Jews who move abroad tend to assimilate just as quickly as American Jews, if not more quickly. Young Israelis have no "Jewish advantage" when compared with their Diaspora peers, and the encounter with Israel is liable to frustrate visiting Jewish teenagers and even drive them away rather than draw them closer to the Jewish people.

There is some truth in almost all of these arguments, but not enough to convince me that it would be better to shelve the birthright concept as just another concoction for Jewish continuity that stirs the imagination but cannot guarantee that our grandchildren will be Jewish.

It is already difficult to raise money today even though Israel is still the main focus of the fund drives. Even Jews who do not visit Israel know that its standard of living places it among the top 10 percent of the world's countries. As mentioned previously, Israel's standard of living is comparable to that of the United Kingdom. But England certainly does not seek to collect contributions from Americans of British ancestry, despite the fact that difficult conditions of poverty and unemployment exist in the U.K. There is similarly no logic in American Jews continuing to assist Israel to finance its social welfare system. It makes sense to collect money for special *aliyah* and absorption missions like Operation Moses and Operation Solomon for Ethiopian Jews, or Operation Exodus for Jews from the Soviet Union, but not for the ordinary needs of Israel.

Those who do not look beyond the "Israel card" and are not busy preparing alternative strategies for financing American Jewish activities are doing a grave injustice to this important fund-raising system, which could soon collapse if it continues to be based on this artificial focus on Israel. These fund-raising efforts need a new "card," and the birthright program could very well fit this need. The Jewish world, including Israel, could rally around this new national mission. This project, which has no time limits, could make a significant contribution to Jewish continuity and would bring economic benefits to Israel.

There is no direct connection between the contributions collected from American Jews and the economic assistance provided by the American government. The United States administration is very well informed about Israel's economy and it does not grant billions of dollars in aid each year because it thinks that Israel is a poor country. The security aid is a substitute for the fact that Israel is not a NATO member and is granted because of Israel's strategic importance, even after the end of the Cold War. America's economic assistance to Israel helps to finance debt payments to the United States—debts that are related to Israel's defense requirements. The governments of Israel and the United States have agreed to gradually decrease this economic assistance during the coming years. An increase in Jewish financial contributions to Israel will not bring about an increase in U.S. aid, just as a decrease will not lead to a reduction in aid. It is likely that peace with the Palestinians and Syrians will entail special American grants to cover redeployment costs and compensation payments. Allocation of these government funds will not be dependent on the continuation of American Jewish fund-raising for Israel or on the amount of Jewish contributions collected.

Is it true that people do not value something they receive for free? It depends on what is being offered. If someone on the street stuffs a pamphlet into your hand, it is indeed likely that you will not bother to look at it and will drop it in the nearest trash can—even if it has some monetary value. On the other hand, if you were to learn that a distant relative bequeathed a house to you, it is reasonable to assume that you would take this piece of news very seriously and begin to regard the property as your own. If someone were to contest the bequest, you might even find yourself arguing over "your new home" in court.

If the visit is exciting and fascinating, the teenager will regard it as if it were a trip paid for by his or her parents. If, unfortunately, the visit leaves the teenager with negative feelings, the question of who financed it becomes totally irrelevant. The idea of issuing coupons for the birthright program occurred to me after I learned how people take advantage of the coupons they receive from the supermarket, pharmacy, restaurants, and food and credit-card companies. Among regular coupon clippers are wealthy people who could allow themselves to pay the full price, but do not waive their coupon rights. Take the example of the couple who find themselves vacationing off-season in a place they never thought to visit, simply because they received a coupon for the trip when they purchased a new vacuum cleaner or because of frequent-flyer points that were about to expire. Many restaurant patrons have ordered that extra side-order of french fries simply because it was included in a free coupon offer. Thus, I assume that there is a good chance that most of the teenagers who receive the coupon in the mail will not simply throw it away without stopping to consider the opportunity.

The birthright program would be an opportunity to thoroughly test the contention that the relatively low numbers of Jewish visitors to Israel is due to deeply rooted resistance, rather than financial considerations. If it becomes clear that the percentage of Jewish youth arriving in Israel has not risen significantly within a few years of extending the birthright program to every Jewish home, then the idea would be a proven flop. It would then be necessary to try other ideas for rallying the Jewish world. From a financial aspect, the failure of the birthright program would have only marginal significance, since expenses would not be incurred for those who do not sign up for the visits.

The question of the content and nature of the Israel experience is another question altogether. I would rather not engage in an argument over values. Suffice it to say that there is an abundant body of research available indicating that a visit to Israel at this age and in this type of framework can make a real change in the Jewish consciousness of most visitors and transform their attitudes toward Israel. For some, Israel is not Jewish enough. For others, Israel is too religious. There are those who view Israel as a less successful version of America. Some are very concerned that extremists may gain control in Israel.

The Land of Israel is a unique phenomenon—for better or worse. It is interesting, unpredictable, and constantly in the headlines. Israel's Jewishness is expressed in many ways, from the Hebrew language to the closure of stores on Saturday. It is difficult for any visitor to remain indifferent to Israel. If some of the teenagers arriving from the Diaspora have a richer background in the Jewish heritage than their Israeli peers, then this would benefit the young Israelis they meet. The question is not one of ideology or values. Israel would become the focus of visits by young Jews not because it is necessarily "better," but because it is the cradle of Judaism and the only Jewish state in the world. This does not mean that the connection can have only one direction; if it is possible to find the funding, Israeli teenagers could be invited to tour the Jewish communities of the Diaspora, especially the United States. In any case, the first stage would still be the visit to Israel.

It took me about three years to convince my American friends to consider this idea seriously. Finally, in the summer of 1997, Michael Steinhardt and Charles Bronfman, Jewish businessmen who both sponsor funds related to Jewish continuity, joined together to adopt the birthright idea as a central initiative for the Jewish people. They have enlisted the support of a group of Jewish philanthropists, have opened offices in Israel and the United States, and received the support of the General Assembly of Jewish Federations in November 1998. The birthright idea has also won the blessing of, and financial assistance from, the government of Israel. The first group of 6,000 young Jews from all over the world came to Israel in January 2000.

As things now stand, the visits are financed by a combination of federation allocations (previously used to partially subsidize Israel visits), funds collected from major contributors, and a sum apportioned by the Israeli government. The birthright program is currently being offered to young Jews up to the age of twenty-five. It may indeed make sense to offer the program to a wider age group at first and only later focus on seventeen-year-olds. In any case, if the program takes off and the number of birthright participants reaches 50,000 per year, this will translate into a cost of about $200 million annually. Again, in my opinion, it would be wise to finance a program of this scope with the funds now being transferred to the Israeli social welfare system.

## Virtual Community of the Twenty-First Century

In addition to the two divergent trends already discussed—the assimilation of Diaspora Jews and the growing interest in Jewish subjects—the technological revolution is a third phenomenon that can be harnessed to help rebuild the Jewish world by bridging the distances separating its major constituents. Like the "global village" that CNN and similar networks have created, new technologies provide an opportunity to build a "Jewish global village." Using satellite technology, for example, a Jewish television network operating on an interactive basis could attract a wide following.

A network like this could serve as a common Jewish experience for the young generation, who would view the same programs and then be able to share impressions with young Jews in other corners of the world. In order to succeed, this network should not be limited to dry, "educational" programs that would drive away viewers. I can imagine the program listings including situation comedies, films on a variety of Jewish topics, educational programs that include panel discussions on current events in Israel or other issues of Jewish interest, and historical series like Abba Eban's *Heritage.* The satellite network would include Hebrew lessons for the Jews of the Diaspora and would offer room for creativity. It would be open to all Jewish denominations and allow for expression of the full spectrum of Israeli and Jewish opinion.

A network like this could be tremendously influential so long as it does not become the tool of any particular political or religious group. It would also be important to make sure that the network does not merely become another boring religious school that youngsters are anxious to skip past. Essentially, this television network should offer entertainment that could also interest non-Jews. Not every broadcast minute has to be replete with Jewish content.

The network would broadcast primarily in English, which is to a large extent the modern-day Yiddish and Ladino of the Jewish world. It is the principal language in the United States, Canada, Britain, South Africa, Australia, New Zealand, and Ireland; in Israel, and most of the other countries where Jews live, English is the second language. In addition to the English-language broadcasts, special hours would be devoted to programs in French, Spanish, and Russian, as well as regularly scheduled Hebrew lessons. This type of network could contribute to the development of a world Jewish community.

A Jewish television network could be a profitable venture,

deriving its revenues from commercials. Starting the network, however, could be an expensive proposition and would perhaps merit the investment of Jewish funds. I view the American-Israeli Jewish Forum as a platform for serious and constructive discussion of this idea, which would in turn be presented to the private sector or assisted with communal funds. A special authority would be established to manage the network in order to ensure maximal openness and objectivity.

In the near future, television and computer programs will both be accessed in every home via a single screen. The percentage of Jewish homes with computers is already very high. The Internet offers easy access to a huge wealth of Jewish information. Jewish television programming may be able to reach out to less-committed Jews, while the Internet can serve the core of committed Jews searching for more Jewish information.

One of the great advantages of the Internet is the possibility of creating communities of people who share common interests, regardless of their geographic location. The virtual communities of the Internet are very appropriate for the Jewish people, whose two major population centers are separated by the Atlantic Ocean. The ultra-Orthodox Jewish community was the first to understand the potential of the Internet—the Chabad movement, for example, has a well-established Internet presence.

The creation of secular, traditional, and religious Internet sites is a challenge of the highest order, with potential for widening access to Jewish information, discussions on Jewish thought and current events, and intellectual stimulation that could open new horizons for Jewish life. Facilitating incisive discussions between learned Jews and making these discussions a matter of prestige would not only help to strengthen and widen the core of committed Jews, but would also create a framework for Jewish research.

These forums could raise tantalizing ideas for less knowledgeable Jews and include everything from contests and quizzes on Jewish topics to tips on how to more effectively use the new communications technologies. Internet sites visited by relatively few users could generate ideas for a mass audience. A "chat room" discussion on illegal immigration during the British Mandate, for example, could lead to an idea for a blockbuster movie that might replace the flawed portrait given in the movie *Exodus*.

It is hard to understand today how this superficial and naïve film, based on the Leon Uris novel, generated such a huge swell of emotion that extended beyond the Jewish world and became a symbol for an entire generation. Even today, when I travel to far-flung destinations and meet with Jews, people still tell me that they know about Israel from the movie starring Paul Newman they saw forty years ago. While rankled by the fact that this *Exodus* image of Israel persists in the eyes of so many, I am constantly amazed at the universal power of the movie and television media. If it is a high-quality and reliable production, a film with such enormous popular appeal at the beginning of the twenty-first century could create a new Jewish identification. Ideas for such productions could grow out of Internet discussions and the Jewish television network could perhaps produce them.

Eli N. Evans is correct in arguing that the single home screen for television and computer applications should offer a Jewish presence that is attractive, creative, and high-quality. This is an opportunity that will be feasible in our century, precisely at a time when the assimilation rate is so high, when the old Jewish organizations are attracting fewer and fewer members, and when the number of Jews affiliated with their local federation is declining. This could be a golden era of Jewish creativity, one that could help fashion a new type of Jew, promote pride in Jewish identification, and result in face-to-face meetings between Jews with common interests who first meet on the information superhighway. The technological revolution—more than any other factor—could bring about a revolution in Jewish culture and education, creating a new Jewish society based on mutual cultural experiences.

Videoconferences will become commonplace, as every computer will be equipped with a camera that can transmit the image of its user. This will facilitate meetings between leaders and enable discussions to be held without waiting for a mutually convenient time and place to assemble. The American-Israeli Jewish Forum, for example, can be managed via such technologies, with annual meetings devoted to more general discussions and personal conversations in the corridor—something that is still hard to simulate in videoconferencing. Internet chat rooms will also become easier to maintain as they become more visual and less virtual.

The capability of creating a direct connection between Jewish communities in the United States, Israel, and the rest of the world will facilitate the welcome process of decentralization. Programs like Partnership 2000, the brainchild of Brian Lurie, a liberal rabbi and federation head, can maintain on-going communication via teleconferences, instead of depending only on actual visits. (Partnership 2000, administered by the Jewish Agency, is an interesting attempt to match Jewish communities in the United States with those in Israel—not just on the old basis of benefactor and recipient.)

In the twenty-first century, there are more and more people working from remote computer links. Even if telecommuting from home does not turn into a mass phenomenon, it is clear that Jews will comprise a significant proportion of those working in this mode, among them journalists, software developers, and other professionals in the fast-growing information industry. As the location of one's residence becomes less dependent on a particular workplace, a growing number of people will find it easier to move from one spot to another, equipped with their laptop computer and modem. Israelis invited to work in America or Europe will not necessarily be required to uproot their families from their homes in Israel. They will be able to spend part of their time abroad and draw a foreign salary, while still based in Israel. Jews from America and elsewhere will likewise be able to maintain their jobs abroad while spending part of their lives in Israel—without necessarily becoming new immigrants.

More flexible options will be available in the coming years, especially if we encourage this as Israelis and Jews. More and more Jews will be able to purchase a second home in Israel without having to sever professional ties or undergo the difficult experience of looking for a job in a new country. Israelis will also be able to live in two worlds and benefit from opportunities to study and work with professional colleagues abroad.

It is likewise hard to believe that aircraft flight times will not be drastically decreased. The eleven-hour flight from Tel Aviv to New York may not seem so bad compared to the long weeks required to sail from Europe to America a century ago. But it is reasonable to expect that in the twenty-first century—and not only toward the end of it—a flight from Israel to Western Europe will take one hour, to fly to the East Coast of the United States will take three hours, and the Tel Aviv–Los Angeles transit will require only four hours. This will happen as new developments make existing technologies economically feasible. In this situation, more and more Jews will move back and forth between the Diaspora and Israel. Dual citizenship, or residence in one country and citizenship in another, could eventually become characteristic of being Jewish.

Some of the ideas raised in recent years for providing Jewish life with new content can be realized during the next century with the help of the new technologies. For example, it will be possible to try to implement Avraham Burg's proposal for establishing an open university for the Jewish people, with teachers and students from all over the world. This type of university could take advantage of the brightest lecturers and researchers in the Jewish world and exploit the Internet and Jewish television network to deliver lectures and share information from any location in the world. Students would receive written materials via the Internet or other media, would be tested in the same way, and be awarded an academic degree after completing their studies. The great advantage of an open university of this sort is, first and foremost, its accessibility to young Jews even if they are not located near major Jewish centers. Another advantage lies in the possibility of creating a common base for a wide Jewish public, providing students with a world of common concepts before they begin pursuing their individual life paths.

## Cooperative Projects in the Jewish World and the Third World

The greater ease of mobility could also be exploited for cooperative Jewish projects in various communities in the world. Jewish volunteers from Israel, the United States, Europe, Australia, and elsewhere could work for a period of several months to a year in Jewish communities requiring help in education, youth organization, refurbishing of buildings, and other projects. In the former Soviet Union, for example, where Jews are showing increasing interest in their heritage, these volunteers could help build Jewish communities as well as encourage *aliyah* to Israel for those considering this option. There are major difficulties in important communities like Argentina, which experienced two serious terrorist attacks in the 1990s, and there is no doubt but that young Jewish volunteers could help the Argentine Jewish community in the field of education and other areas.

Such initiatives would naturally involve only a small part of the young generation of Jews in the world, but could definitely strengthen the core of committed Jews, provide a unique Jewish experience, and broaden circles of direct personal acquaintances that will be so important for the existence of the Jewish people in the twenty-first century. Someone would need to determine where assistance is especially needed, locate funding for the volunteer activities (including housing and living allowances), and serve as a liaison between the volunteers and the communities. This is another example of the need for a central Jewish "clearinghouse," or general assembly, like the House of Israel. This organization would have the most up-to-date information on the needs of the various communities in the Jewish world. It could maintain permanent missions in certain communities and organize special task forces in communities that encounter unexpected financial problems, incidents of anti-Semitism, a shortage of Jewish educators, and other sorts of difficulties.

The success of these volunteer projects would be dependent on a constant flow of reliable information on developments in the Jewish world and the availability of resources that would enable these activities. The recipient communities would need to feel that the assistance extended to them is indeed relevant. The idea is not to organize groups of young people who, as in the joke about the overzealous boy scout, force the old lady to cross the street in order to do a good deed. The success of this enterprise would also depend on the flexibility of the organization and its ability to rapidly deploy volunteers in urgent situations. This activity should not devolve into a meaningless routine in which prosperous communities continue to host young Jewish volunteers simply because a group of volunteers came last year, and the year before that, and so on—and no one can remember why anymore, since the main problems were solved long ago!

Another challenge, even more ambitious, is an attempt to establish a worldwide Jewish framework for assisting the Third World. In the twenty-first century, many Jews in Israel and the Diaspora will be in a situation to offer assistance to people in other parts of the world (even if there will always remain some poor people in their own cities). The population explosion in the Third World, together with harsh conditions of poverty and disease, make it the open sore of the new century. No immediate solution is in sight, and a growing feeling of disappointment and despair characterizes the attitude of the United States and Europe toward this problem.

The physical infrastructure is deteriorating in Africa and other regions, while funds previously directed to the Third World are now being channeled to Eastern Europe and other places. The huge population of the Third World is suffering terribly and its growing misery may even lead to an explosion that threatens the rest of the world, which prefers to ignore the situation.

Beginning in the 1960s, Israel developed important systems for assisting the Third World, especially in the fields of agriculture and medicine. Israel sends experts abroad and invites people from the Third World to participate in training courses in Israel. (Diplomatic relations with much of the Third World were cut off for about two decades before being renewed in the early 1990s, at which time the Foreign Ministry resumed Israel's international aid programs.) But Israel has the potential, in terms of human and financial resources, for much greater involvement. Israel can become one of the main providers of aid to the Third World, like the Scandinavian countries, which contribute principally by donating a fixed percentage of their national budgets.

Joint efforts in the developing world by Jewish experts from Israel and the Diaspora could become an important and on-going project that would provide an added sense of purpose. An awareness of mission characterizes Israel as long as it is an embattled nation; once Israel attains a comprehensive peace with its neighbors, we will need to decide where to direct this sense of mission and how to avoid feelings of frustration and lack of purpose. Intensive international activity could help to fill this need.

Joining forces with Jewish experts from the Diaspora in such fields as medicine, education, agriculture, and social work, we could advance several goals at the same time. We would be providing crucial assistance to countries in dire situations, fulfilling the need for a feeling of mission (and the Jewish aspiration to be "a light unto the nations"), and strengthening the ties between Israel and the Diaspora. The Jews of the Diaspora would also be helping Israel to play an important role in the world and to become a source of "good news."

It's worth noting that it would be a mistake to prevent non-Jews from participating in such special efforts, especially if they are successful. Even if it eventually becomes a multinational mission in the Third World, the alliance between Israel and Diaspora Jews will still play a pivotal role.

CHAPTER 5

# In Retrospect

The number of Jews has remained at approximately 13.1 million in the 1990s, the positive rate of natural increase in Israel offsetting the negative rate in the Diaspora. In 1948, the 630,000 Jews in Israel comprised 6 percent of the 11.5 million Jews in the world. Fifty years later, Israel's 4.8 million Jews accounted for 36 percent of world Jewry.

Jews can be found in almost every corner of the world. On a visit to Taipei, the capital of Taiwan, I met with the local Jewish community of about forty members. In my opening remarks, I mentioned that I had not yet visited their two synagogues—and I thought my sly reference to that old joke would be understood. But nobody even smiled. At the end of the meeting, however, one of the Jews approached me and asked if I was referring to the story about the Jew who builds two synagogues on a deserted island—including one that he vows never to set foot in. "Yes," I answered, "and I was surprised that no one laughed. I thought everyone was familiar with that joke!"

"Yes, indeed," the local Jew told me, "but they thought you were being serious, since there *are* two synagogues here—one built by the Chabad people, and the other established by those who want nothing to do with that missionary movement. . . ."

But the great majority of Jews at the beginning of the third millennium live in two large communities: North America and Israel. About 95 percent of world Jewry today live in one of ten communities: the United States, Israel, France, Canada, Russia, Britain, Argentina, Ukraine, Brazil, and South Africa. In the United States, there is a negative rate of natural increase and growing assimilation. The Jews in Argentina numbered 310,000 in the early 1960s, but only about 206,000 Jews live there today. Similarly, the number of Jews in Britain has dropped from 336,000 in 1977 to approximately 292,000 in 1995.

In many ways, however, the situation of Jews is more encouraging than ever. Israel is an amazing success story, and Diaspora Jews have attained unprecedented achievements while integrating into the societies where they live. Nonetheless, there are Jews on both sides of the Atlantic who are very concerned.

In his book *The Vanishing American Jew,* the prominent American attorney Alan Dershowitz expresses serious concern about the potential disappearance of American Jewry. He notes that returning to the ghetto and joining the ultra-Orthodox community could ensure Jewish continuity, but the ultra-Orthodox do not represent true Judaism in his eyes. He knows that immigration to Israel could ensure Jewish continuity, but he does not consider this a practical solution—unless, that is, an outbreak of serious anti-Semitism were to threaten the Diaspora. Israel is very problematic in Dershowitz's view. At least since Yitzhak Rabin's assassination, it appears to be torn between fanatics, immensely influenced by religious parties, and faced with questions of identity that will only intensify when Israel is living at peace with its neighbors. These questions of identity, according to Dershowitz, are no less difficult than those confronting American Jewry.

Toward the end of his book, Dershowitz holds forth universal values of Judaism—justice, altruism, study, intellectual pluralism, and *tikkun olam* ("fixing the world")—that characterize for him the basis for Jewish continuity in a world where Jews are neither religious nor anxious to immigrate to Israel.

Up until the nineteenth century, proposals for solving the problem of the Jews, or the problem of being Jewish, were not raised for discussion. Before the Emancipation, the basic assumption of most of the Jews in the world was that they must survive despite the harsh reality. They would bow their heads when necessary and look within their own communities for recognition. In the wake of the Emancipation, a range of solutions for the new plight of the Jews was proposed. From the mid-nineteenth century through the mid-twentieth century, these solutions included: Hibbat Zion, Zionism, territorialism, mass immigration to the New World, support for international movements, and others.

It appears that since the mid-twentieth century this fountain of ideas has dried up and we have returned to set patterns of thinking. Existing Jewish institutions have proven themselves incapable of changing, and new ones are not being established to replace them. The world's two principal Jewish communities wring their hands and conjecture, writing books about the anticipated disappearance of the Jewish people. We have returned to the stage of passivity, accepting the shrinkage of world Jewry as if it were a divine decree. It does not have to be so.

Our special vantage point at the beginning of the third millennium affords us a momentary advantage over our predecessors. At least we know what has happened in the meantime. For the moment—and only for the moment—we have the most far-reaching view of history. We can look back at the actions of our forefathers and see their results. This allows us to make a very different review than was possible when they wrote their works, delivered their speeches, and undertook their actions.

Other ancient peoples were destroyed by overpowering empires.

Our fate was different. We were exiled, dispersed, and permitted to live. Along the way, many of us disappeared. We are still on the lookout for the ten lost tribes, but they will not be found—they simply became the ancestors of non-Jewish civilizations that are now thousands of years old. Those who remained Jews did so because they remained part of a community. The community—whether of its own accord or because non-Jews compelled it—built its own world (or ghetto). It provided religious and educational services, and afforded rewards and advancement that compensated in many cases for the hatred and severe occupational restrictions the Jews suffered in most of their places of residence.

Throughout history there were Jews who filled important roles in royal courts, as advisors or physicians, but this was a relatively negligible phenomenon. Jews who sought to live outside of Jewish communities did not succeed in preserving their Jewish identity over generations. The Jews who lived as Marranos in Spain led dual lives, although they were eventually fully assimilated as Christians. Jews who wished to attain central positions in non-Jewish society would convert to Christianity or Islam. Conversion was quite commonplace during the Middle Ages and long afterwards—even though we have been brought up on stories of Rabbi Amnon and other Jews who preferred exile or death to conversion.

The Emancipation movement took the Jews by surprise, and the Jews in turn surprised the world by exploiting it so quickly. This movement had no Jewish motive behind it and was certainly not the result of a Jewish struggle for equality. Prior to the Emancipation, the Jews had come to terms with their situation, moved from place to place when necessary, establishing communities practically everywhere.

The Emancipation was part of the liberal outlook that blossomed toward the end of the eighteenth century. The American constitution in 1787 was the first in the world to prohibit religious and racial discrimination, and the French Revolution in 1789 called for granting full and equal rights to the groups in society that had formerly been disenfranchised. It was Napoleon Bonaparte who disseminated the message of the Emancipation throughout Europe and many countries followed France's lead: Holland in 1796, Belgium in 1832, the German states in the 1830s, and Denmark in 1848.

A "golden age" is so designated only in retrospect. As it unfolds, it is usually seen as a natural part of historic development, and only later does it appear magnificent in comparison to the more troubled periods that precede and follow it. This applies to the "golden age" of Spanish Jewry under Muslim rule in the tenth century. In Europe, a "golden age" can be identified as the period between the beginning of the Emancipation in the late eighteenth century and the outbreak of anti-Semitism in the last quarter of the nineteenth century. Despite the difficulties still faced by very many Jews during this hundred years, it was the best century—relatively speaking, a golden age—for European Jewry.

If there is a "Jewish genius," it burst out in its widest sense during the Emancipation. Previously, almost all Jewish energies were focused in two directions: in sheer survival, and in succeeding within the Jewish framework. Emancipation created the false impression that survival was guaranteed and allowed for energies to thrust out from the walls of the Jewish ghetto. The European intellectual community was suddenly enriched by a pent-up reservoir of several million literate Jews, residing in the center of the continent, their lives characterized by a centuries-old tradition of study. The Jews comprised the best-prepared group in Europe for the Emancipation, which occurred at an especially appropriate moment for them.

A look at the great explosion of Jewish creative energies unleashed by the Emancipation shows how "hungry" the Jews were. These masters of survival, so detested for their different appearance and customs, and who were denied basic rights for so long, eagerly dashed toward what they perceived to be the open embrace of the world. All of them were of course born as Jews. Some reached the pinnacle of success in their fields of endeavor as Jews and died as Jews. Others were baptized in childhood by their parents, who expected it would be easier for them to grow up as Christians. Some got themselves baptized in their social ascent, out of concern—sometimes justified, sometimes not—that their path would be blocked if they did not take that extra step toward assimilation. A small number of these even became anti-Semites.

Some were proud of their Jewishness and even boasted of their Jewish ancestry after converting to Christianity. Most preferred not to bring attention to the fact that they were Jews, and some chose to change their names. They rose to the highest echelons of European society and played a prominent role in the cultural and scientific life of nineteenth-century Europe. If in previous centuries they excelled at home, it seemed that in the nineteenth century they conquered the world.

Here is an alphabetical list of some Jews who burst upon the world stage in this period:

SARAH BERNHARDT (1844–1923), called "the divine Sarah" by Victor Hugo, was a famous actress in France's Comédie Française and Odéon.

ISAAC-ADOLPHE CRÉMIEUX (1796–1880) was one of the leaders of the radical left branch of the French Chamber of Deputies. As minister of justice, he led the effort to cancel the death penalty for political transgressions and abolish slavery in French colonies.

BENJAMIN DISRAELI (1804–1881) served six years as prime minister of Britain. He acquired the Suez Canal for his country and initiated the Berlin Conference that forced the Russians to surrender their Balkan conquests.

ÉMILE DURKHEIM (1858–1917), one of the first sociologists in Europe, was a French university professor famous for noting the connection between loss of social identity and suicide.

PAUL EHRLICH (1854–1915), a winner of the Nobel Prize for medicine, was a chemist and pioneer in the fields of hematology and chemotherapy. His medical research included studies on blood, tissues, and tissue regeneration.

SIGMUND FREUD (1856–1939) was the father of psychoanalysis. Freud's work on the subconscious opened a new frontier for understanding human behavior. He lived in Vienna.

HEINRICH HEINE (1797–1856) was one of Germany's greatest poets.

FERDINAND LASSALLE (1825–1864) was one of the fathers of socialism and the founder of the Socialist Party in Germany. He was an advocate of the unification of Germany and died in a duel related to a romantic affair.

CESARE LOMBROSO (1836–1909), an Italian physician, was one of the pioneers in the field of criminology. He was a professor of forensic medicine, psychiatry, and criminal anthropology at universities in Pavia and Turin.

LUIGI LUZZATTI (1841–1927) was a professor of constitutional law at the University of Padua in Italy. He was also an expert in economics who served three times as finance minister and reduced his country's national debt. He was later elected prime minister.

GUSTAV MAHLER (1860–1911), the great composer, conducted the orchestra of the Vienna Opera for ten years.

KARL HEINRICH MARX (1818–1883) was the father of Marxism, whose communist ideal and Socialist International organization changed the face of the world.

FELIX MENDELSSOHN-BARTHOLDY (1809–1847), the great German composer, conductor, and pianist, was the most renowned musician in Europe during the 1840s. He was converted in childhood to Christianity. His grandfather, Moses, the philosopher and essayist who translated the Bible into German, is regarded as the Jew who most symbolized the Emancipation.

SIR MOSES HAIM MONTEFIORE (1784–1885), the Italian-born financier, lived in England, where he was appointed sheriff of London. In addition, he was active in a wide range of Jewish philanthropies and journeyed seven times to the Holy Land.

JACQUES OFFENBACH, born Ya'akov Avrasht (1819–1880), was a prominent French musician and composer. The son of a cantor, he composed ninety operettas.

CAMILLE JACOB PISSARRO (1830–1903) was a leading Impressionist painter in France and one of the greatest artists of the nineteenth century.

RACHEL, or Alisa Rachel Felix (1820–1858) was considered the greatest French actress of her generation.

ARTHUR SCHNITZLER (1862–1931) was a renowned novelist and playwright, as well as a physician. His psychological dramas portrayed bourgeois Viennese life at the turn of the century.

LUDWIK LEJZER ZAMENHOF (1859–1917), who lived in Warsaw, was the father of the Esperanto language.

The Emancipation opened the door and the Jews hurried through to take advantage of the new opportunities. Their successes engendered hatred. This hatred was initially expressed in a benign manner: in 1843, the German theologian and historian Bruno Bauer published an article titled "The Jewish Question" in which he called into question the right of the Jews to fill some of the positions they had begun to attain. But this new prejudice against, and hatred of, the Jews evinced after the Emancipation could not be escaped by religious conversion. The fact that some Jews—converted or not—were rising to the pinnacle of European society after only a few decades gave birth to a different type of enmity toward Jews, one based on racial grounds.

The term *anti-Semitism* appeared for the first time in 1879, at the peak of the Emancipation, when a German journalist named Wilhelm Barr called for adopting a policy of discrimination against the Jews. This new attitude, which drew support from those nostalgic for the old hatred of Jews, offered the Jews only one solution—to keep their distance. It is not a coincidence that the writer Nathan Birnbaum coined the term *Zionism* in 1890, only eleven years after the first mention of *anti-Semitism*. Here the close link between the Emancipation, anti-Semitism, and Zionism becomes evident.

Both Moses Hess and Theodor Herzl considered the option of conversion during the early stages of their thinking. Hess believed at first that the hatred of Jews would wane only after they disappeared as Jews. The young Herzl felt the same way fifty years later. But both arrived at the conclusion that conversion would not help and turned to the notion of a Jewish state.

Baron Maurice de Hirsch also came to the conclusion that the Jews should be removed from Europe. He established agricultural colonies in Brazil and Argentina for European Jews, under the assumption that their intelligence and superior qualities would be less conspicuous—sparing them the hatred and resentment of their neighbors—if they were farmers.

Others believed that the idea of congregating the Jews in one place, especially in a Jewish state, would exacerbate anti-Semitism even more. For example, Adolf (Aharon) Yelinick, one of the greatest Jewish sermonizers of the day, told Leo Pinsker in 1865 that the Jews should focus on emancipation and oppose auto-emancipation because a Jewish state would make the Jews of the West, who regarded the West as their home, appear to be transients in the eyes of their neighbors.

This was a concern that troubled the opponents of Zionism from the moment that the notion of building a Jewish state in the Land of Israel became a respectable idea. This was also Blaustein's concern in 1950. As the Israeli historian Anita Shapira has noted, Zionism did not wage a battle against anti-Semitism, but rather came to terms with it and accepted its basic premise of the Jews as a foreign body in the national framework of Europe. For Herzl and Nordau, Zionism was a tragic admission of the failure of the Emancipation. It was like saying, "Okay, if we're not wanted here, then the hell with it, we'll leave!"

They were not able to find a positive message for Zionism, and subsequent generations were also unsuccessful in this attempt. Ahad Ha'am's central complaint after witnessing the First Zionist Congress addressed this negative message directly. In an article titled "The Congress and Its Creator," he wrote:

> This Zionism views the Jews as separate people, compelled to unite by their common enemy, but does not see Judaism as a single block that also aspires to exist in unity in the absence of any external coercion. This is its principal deficiency, which is evident in all of its activities.

Zionism came into the world linked with, and dependent on, anti-Semitism. The visionary of the Jewish state admitted this and in *The Jewish State* himself wondered what would happen if the Jews, once in their own state, found themselves without any enemy. His answer was: Don't worry, this will never happen . . .

In my review of these issues—and in an attempt to understand why the Holocaust of European Jews occurred, and whether it could have been prevented or diminished—I encountered a wider range of solutions than I expected to find. We were taught about three schools of Zionism: Herzl's political Zionism versus Ben-Gurion's practical Zionism versus the synthetic Zionism of Chaim Weizmann.

- Political Zionism focused on attaining international legitimacy and did not ascribe great importance to secondary activities under way in Palestine. Ze'ev Jabotinsky was a prominent advocate of this Herzlian approach to Zionism.

- Practical Zionism held that independent Jewish sovereignty would be achieved only by creating facts on the ground ("acre by acre, goat by goat").

- Weizmann's synthetic Zionism sought to pursue international backing while at the same time advancing the practical interests of Jewish settlement in Palestine.

Another distinction was conventionally made between Hibbat Zion, a movement that believed in the possibility of a popular return to the Land of Israel, and Zionism, which set forth a real plan for this return. In time, the name Hibbat Zion came to be used—mistakenly—to refer to any approach that supported the idea of a Jewish state in principle and from afar but did not address the issue of immigration to Israel on a practical level.

I believe, however, that the most meaningful distinction is between Zionism and Palestine-oriented Jewish nationalism. The

Zionists (Herzl, Wolffsohn, Ahad Ha'am, and others) felt that they were being driven out of Europe. They undoubtedly preferred their lives in Europe but understood that anti-Semitism had made life for them there impossible. The Jewish nationalists, on the other hand (among them David Ben-Gurion, Ze'ev Jabotinsky, and even Chaim Weizmann), sought to flee Europe of their own accord in order to establish a separate national entity in what they considered the only logical place for such an entity—Palestine. They were part of the nationalist awakening of the nineteenth century and would not have chosen to remain in Europe even if they had felt welcome there.

Herzl, having identified the severity of anti-Semitism, believed that the Jews should not remain in Europe and offered a detailed plan for their orderly relocation to a place where they could live autonomous lives in their own state, a place where they would no longer have to suffer from anti-Semitism. When he wrote *The Jewish State,* he was indifferent as to the location—Argentina was as likely a choice for him as Palestine. He was interested in finding a place where Jews could freely immigrate, without arbitrary interference. He concluded that Jewish sovereignty was the only way to guarantee that the gates would remain open to Jewish immigrants.

The Hibbat Zion movement joined ranks almost immediately with Herzl. This movement was formed in the wake of the 1881 pogroms in Russia, even before the publication (in 1882) of Pinsker's essay *Auto-Emancipation.* Its members established an extensive network of Jews across Europe who shared an interest in creating a large Jewish settlement in Palestine. Herzl won their overwhelming support, but from the start they were supporting quite a different idea than the one Herzl had envisioned. At the First Zionist Congress—an event that could easily have turned into a farce but instead became a great public-relations success—Herzl was already considered the leader of a movement seeking to build a Jewish state in Palestine. Yet in his opening remarks, he still mentioned Argentina and Palestine in the same breath: "We shall never

be able, nor shall we desire, to speak of these attempts at colonization in Palestine and in Argentina otherwise than with genuine
gratitude."

The leadership of the Zionist movement at the end of the nineteenth century sought to establish a state immediately, and preferred that it be in Palestine. Ahad Ha'am's criticism of Zionism
was actually consistent with Herzl's original thinking. Ahad Ha'am
was looking, first of all, for a way to save the Jews. After an extended
visit to Palestine, he concluded that the objective could not realis-
tically be achieved there.

Hibbat Zion regarded Palestine as the solution to both the
problem of the Jews and the problem of Judaism. Herzl was troubled by the problem of the Jews and wanted to win them their right
to live as human beings; Palestine was not a necessary condition
for him. Ahad Ha'am argued that whoever wished to solve the
problem of the Jews could not lead them at the end of the nineteenth century to Palestine. In an essay titled *The Jewish State and
the Jewish Problem,* written several months after the First Zionist
Congress, he explained that

> Every state must acquire its [economic] share through unceasing
> toil. Therefore, only a near-crazy delusion could allow us to
> believe that immediately upon establishing the state, millions
> of Jews could come and find themselves a sufficient means of
> livelihood.

Unlike Herzl, Ahad Ha'am did not present a detailed program
for leaving Europe or a guide for establishing a spiritual center in
the Land of Israel. But the words he wrote after returning from his
first trip to Palestine in 1901 were very clear:

> The real answer is therefore: both America and Palestine. The
> economic aspect of the Jewish question should seek its solution

in America, while the idealistic side, the need to create for ourselves a spiritual center . . . if it has a chance of being fulfilled . . .
can only be in the land of Israel.

One year before the First Zionist Congress, Ahad Ha'am attributed to Pinsker a sentence that is the quintessential expression of
his own view. "The land of Israel cannot be a safe refuge for the
Jews, but it can and should become such for Judaism." More than
one hundred years later, these words are equally true, even if the
circumstance and reasons are quite different.

Ahad Ha'am appeared to be criticizing Herzl's enthusiasm for
establishing a Jewish state in a land (Palestine) that was incapable
of successfully absorbing millions of immigrants. In fact, he was
criticizing Herzl's opponents, who were not prepared to consider
any alternative to the Land of Israel, even if only as a temporary
solution. They rejected the notion of a "night refuge" even though
they also understood that it was unrealistic to expect to establish a
Jewish state that could immediately absorb all of European Jewry.
Not sharing the same sense of urgency as Herzl, Nordau, and Ahad
Ha'am, they preferred to wait.

After the League of Nations approved the Balfour Declaration,
at least half a million Jews could have immigrated to Palestine, but
the Zionist Organization was apprehensive about absorbing such
a large number of immigrants and asked the British Mandatory
authorities to deny visas to Jews who requested them. At the London Conference in 1920, Max Nordau called for the immediate
transfer of half a million Jews from Eastern Europe before new
developments occurred that might prevent this. But the conference rejected his proposal, in effect abandoning its Zionist activities. Like many other decisions taken then, one can understand the
logic behind it, but in retrospect it was simply one of the most
dreadful mistakes of Zionism in the post-Herzl era.

If it were possible to push back the hands of time, Herzl may have joined Ahad Ha'am and tried to transfer the Jews to those countries still willing to accept them, especially the United States. He would have viewed this as a "night refuge" and would not have objected to the establishment of a Jewish community in Palestine that would express a nationalist ideology and prepare the groundwork for additional Jewish immigrants.

Herzl did not form a national liberation movement; his objective was a movement for national salvation. He was driven by an individualistic Jewish conception, not by a historic mission. He wanted a state right away, since European Jewry could only be transferred to a state. Herzl's special character, his considerable charisma, and his absolute devotion to the idea that captured his heart—all of these combined to turn him into the leader of a national liberation movement, and a messiah—King of the Jews. Herzl was a brief flash in Jewish history, appearing on the stage for eight years and five months, from the publication of *The Jewish State* in February 1896 until his death in July 1904. After his sudden death, which transformed him at once from controversial to mythical, Herzl became the torch of the Jewish national movement. He became the accepted symbol of Wolffsohn and Ussishkin, Weizmann and Ben-Gurion, Jabotinsky and people like my grandfather. Herzl, who near the end of his life, on the way to Uganda, swore that he hadn't forgotten Jerusalem, was returned to the land of his forefathers after his death.

If Herzl's Zionism was intended to save European Jewry from the mounting storm, then it was an awful failure. Zionism after Herzl did not continue his policy of "first of all leave Europe and then favor the Land of Israel." The group that continued to lead the Zionist movement became passionately Palestine-centric and identified the late Herzl with their leadership, thus creating an ideological fellowship of Ben-Gurion and Jabotinsky.

The establishment of the State of Israel, which became possible mainly due to the shock of the Holocaust, was a victory for Zionism. It turned an idea that initially seemed so fanciful into reality. But Israel can also be seen as a victory for anti-Semitism, as an admission by the Jews that there is really no place for them in non-Jewish society—just as anti-Semites claim.

The anti-Semitic German composer, Richard Wagner, believed, for example, that the Jews were faced with only two options: complete assimilation in Europe until no trace of Jewishness remained, or the creation of an independent national entity where they could live as real Jews, just like the French or the Germans.

Contrary to the hopes of the Zionist visionaries, the state did not bring an end to anti-Semitism. Rather, it bred new anti-Semitism in the form of anti-Zionism—anti-Semitism aimed at the State of Israel. The establishment of the state provided world Jewry with a source of identity, pride, and occasional worry. It also intensified their anxiety over charges of dual loyalty and exposed them to Arab terror aimed at inflicting revenge on Israel. Paradoxically, this combination of factors helped to strengthen and maintain the unique character of Diaspora Jewish communities.

It is very difficult to make a separate and objective assessment of the world's two most important Jewish communities. In retrospect, it becomes clear that it is quite hard to analyze the Israeli Jewish community without considering the enormous influence of America and its Jewish community on Israel's development. Similarly, it is impossible to know if American Jewry would have achieved the same measure of success were it not for Israel as a unifying factor and object of identification.

The Jews of the United States represent the greatest victory of the Emancipation. As individuals, the several million American Jews who escaped the Holocaust have successfully integrated in their adopted society. Unlike the traditional nation-state, America was more open to diverse national groups. It was former President Ronald Reagan who said, "You can't be English or French when you move there to live. But everyone can be an American!" The Jews have certainly proved him right.

Still, this claim should always be made with some reservation. Full American openness toward Jews, pride in being Jewish, integration in various fields—these are all characteristics of recent decades, especially since the 1960s. The years of intensive immigration were accompanied by hatred of the Jews and even anti-Semitism, which peaked in the 1920s with severe immigration restrictions. The closing of the gates to America meant that most European Jews became Holocaust victims. One is always tempted to put the idyllic portrayal of American Jewry in perspective by noting that the Emancipation in Europe lasted for more than a century and it was precisely when the last restrictions against the Jews were being lifted that the most virulent hatred began to accumulate against them.

The collective past also haunts the Jews of the United States today. They sense anti-Semitic trends—particularly among other minority groups—and are very concerned about charges of divided loyalty. This is why the Jonathan Pollard episode was so traumatic for many of them. Likewise, they fear that economic downturns might be attributed to the fact that many of the leading players in the American economy are Jews.

For American Jews, the United States was "Zion" from the moment they landed on its shores. People like Louis Brandeis, Stephen Wise, and Abba Hillel Silver, who together led the American Zionist movement during the first half of the twentieth century, were not prepared to identify with European Zionism, which linked the movement with immigration to Palestine. They viewed Zionism as a way to identify with an important Jewish trend and thus prevent assimilation. It was important for them to emphasize their complete loyalty to the United States and their perception of America as their home.

For its part, the State of Israel is a surprise in its very existence, as well as in the obstacles it has overcome and in the prominence it has attained in the world. The failure of other such attempts in the modern era, like the efforts to revive the Gaelic language in Ireland, prove how great Israel's success has been. The rapid economic progress, democratic structure, military successes, scientific achievements, and its continued survival—all are a great credit to a state that few believed would even be established.

There is some similarity between the Israeli and American Jewish communities. In both countries, there was an attempt to forge a "melting pot" that, in both cases, turned out to be more myth than reality. During the peak of the "melting pot" era, people tended to change their names and deny their past in order to secure a better future for their children. As this concept started to show cracks, the old names returned, with nostalgia for the past.

Zionism, for its part, created a tremendous challenge for the Jewish people, especially for its younger generations. It brought forth collective energies for the unique experience of fashioning a new society in the face of many obstacles, physical and otherwise. This was something of enormous moment. The question "What is best for the individual?" cannot be quantified. I can imagine that the emotions my parents felt at the time of the UN Partition Plan vote in 1947 were much more meaningful to them than the fact that they were still using an icebox long after their American counterparts had electric refrigerators and television sets.

The question "What is best for the people?" is, likewise, one that cannot be answered quantitatively. Nowhere in the world is there a place more open to Jews than Israel, while the United States is probably the most secure place for the Jews of today. Yet conversely, Israel may be the most secure haven for secular Jewish culture.

If our main aim is to prevent another Holocaust, it is no longer certain that Israel is the best solution. In fact, the concentration of so many Jews in one area, confronted by hostile threats and weapons of mass destruction, makes Israel a problematic danger zone. If, on the other hand, the aim is to guarantee Jewish continuity far into the future, the United States does not seem capable of assuming this challenge.

Israel is an attempt to enjoy the advantages of the Jewish ghetto without paying the price. This experiment is being tested every day. Life in this framework is especially good for someone who does not want to worry when he leaves the room that someone may comment, "He's awfully nice—for a Jew." The rare Jewish feeling of belonging to a national majority is significant in an era in which nationalism still plays an important role. Many of the immigrants who arrived in Israel from the West were influenced by unflattering references to their Jewishness. Others, apparently, do not encounter this problem, or do not take it too seriously, or do not consider it serious enough to warrant the heavy price of emigration and life in Israel.

Most Diaspora Jews prefer assimilation to *aliyah*. Most of the Jews in the world do not seek to live in Israel, and most of those who do live in Israel are the first or second generation of immigrants who had no place else to go. Only a relatively few came to Israel for reasons of Zionist ideology. After fifty years, Israel has not succeeded in changing this immigration pattern of many poor Jews and a few idealists.

Zealous advocates of Zionism insist that there is only one solution: every Jew should immigrate to Israel. This solution holds considerable power for Israelis themselves. It is important to support those who make the decision to immigrate and understand that their decision entails hardships. It was the recognition of these hardships that prepared us to go so far as to call the early immigrants "the generation of the desert."

This problematic epithet expressed our understanding that many of them would not find their place in the new country and that only their children would be able to take full advantage of the decision to move to Israel. Young people in their thirties suddenly became very old upon disembarking in Israel, focusing all their hopes on their young children entering Israeli elementary schools.

The Jewish history curriculum in Israeli schools culminates with the Holocaust and then turns to the story of the State of Israel. The story of other Jewish communities in the world today is simply not there. It took a good deal of self-confidence, and even impudence *(hutzpah)*, for the small community of 630,000 Jews in the early days of Israel to omit to mention in its textbooks the community of 6 million American Jews. For decades, Israeli students were taught that American Jews were living in exile, having made the mistake of immigrating to the United States instead of Israel. In this light, what difference does it make whether the Jews initially arrived in America in waves from Portugal, then Germany, and then Russia? Why is it of interest to know the difference between the American Jewish Committee and the American Jewish Congress? Why is it important to understand what types of activities are being conducted in American Jewish communities, and why so many American Jews are affiliated with the Reform and Conservative movements?

Herzl did not consider his campaign to save the Jews of Europe a secular commandment or moral duty; for him it was simply a salvage operation. He himself made only one brief visit to Palestine, in order to meet Germany's Kaiser Wilhelm II. Dov Ber Borochov, the theoretician of Marxist Zionism, believed that Jewish immigration to Palestine was inevitable ("stychic") and needed no encouragement. He himself never visited the Land of Israel.

Zealous advocates of Zionism hurt their own cause by insisting that American Jewry was just another exile community, like those of Babylon, Spain, and Poland. When Israeli leaders "solve" the problems of American Jews by concluding "The only solution is *aliyah!*" they are missing a chance for real dialogue on issues shared by Israel and the Diaspora. This outlook makes it only harder to build a Jewish world that commits itself to work for Jewish continuity.

If there was ever a chance to attract large numbers of idealistic immigrants, it was during the period immediately following the Six-Day War. Identification with Israel was at an all-time high and pride in Israel's achievement was enormous. In virtually all of the nearly two hundred Jewish communities in America there are people in their early fifties who came to Israel at that time, spent several years on a kibbutz, lived in one of Israel's cities, and then returned to the United States. They speak a little Hebrew, have friends in Israel and look back fondly on the time they spent there. A few, of course, remained in Israel, but most did not succeed in creating for themselves a strong enough focus of attraction.

It is difficult to argue with the success of American Jewry. It is not merely a matter of their successful integration in all walks of life after many years of (mainly informal) restrictions. They have not only fully integrated, but have risen to dominant positions in the most important areas of American society. The Jews comprise 2 percent of the population of the United States, but account for 10 percent of the Senate and nearly the same proportion of the House of Representatives. They also hold senior positions in the president's administration.

According to figures published in 1996, sixteen of the forty richest people in the United States are Jews, as are 26 percent of the most prominent journalists, 40 percent of America's top attorneys, and 59 percent of the most prominent figures in the movie industry. From the Hollywood of Steven Spielberg to the Broadway of Neil Simon to the television series of Jerry Seinfeld, America is influenced by the Jews, absorbs Jewish concepts, and easily identifies with this group of people who have long ceased to be newcomers to the American scene.

Just like the rabbis who have been willing to give up on many Jews, Israeli leaders have given up on many Israelis. For years, official Israel has ostracized the Israeli expatriate press in America, refusing to grant them interviews or access. In public meetings with former Israelis, only one question is voiced: "When are you finally coming home?" The Israeli leadership may have succeeded in creating guilt feelings among the first generation of emigrants, but these feelings usually dissipate in the second generation.

This attitude toward *yordim* is similar to the attitude of the labor movement's leadership toward those who leave the kibbutz. A complete generation spent some time on a kibbutz, most generally leaving after a few years, opting for a different lifestyle. The stigma attached—even by city-dwellers—to those who left the kibbutz did not dissuade those who chose to leave; it merely burdened them, unnecessarily, with a guilty conscience. For the rest of their lives, they felt obliged to explain why they left the kibbutz. (Curiously enough, it turned out that most of these ex-kibbutzniks attributed their decision to leave the kibbutz to their spouses!)

Many of the former Israelis now living abroad are well-educated and highly mobile. The "parents' committee" should be exerting efforts to integrate them in the Jewish federations, maintain contact with them, cooperate with their media, and create opportunities for them and their children to visit Israel more frequently. If Israel continues to reject them, they will only grow more alienated. Through efforts to reach out to them, it may be possible to bring some of them back to Israel for at least part of their lives. Israel is a democratic and open society—it is possible to join and permissible to leave, even if it makes us sad when people emigrate. But we are hurting ourselves as much as we hurt those who choose to leave Israel when we impose this sort of psychological punishment on them.

Two large Jewish communities sit on opposite sides of the planet, suspicious of each other. Israel is worried about the emigration of its children, while American Jews worry about the charge of divided loyalties. The latter are not thrilled about efforts to convince their children to immigrate to Israel. The former, even at the beginning of the twenty-first century, continue to view American Jewry as an "exile" community, while American Jews ride camels in the streets of Atlanta on Israel's Independence Day to symbolize warm ties with Israel. America is not the exile and Israel is not the desert. We need to get over this Jewish fear and replace it with strong, ongoing, relevant, and institutionalized relations. One of the things that this would enable is a new, nonreligious definition of who is a Jew in the twenty-first century.

The ultra-Orthodox told us in the eighteenth century: "Don't leave the ghetto and don't take part in the Emancipation!" In the nineteenth century, they warned us: "Don't try to force the hand of Jewish fate. Don't emigrate to Israel!" At the beginning of the twenty-first century, they are telling us: "Don't change the definition of who is a Jew. Decrease the number of Jews in the world!" In addition, time and again, the ultra-Orthodox lend support to the Israeli right in forging governments that block the continuation of the peace process.

The ultra-Orthodox are not carrying the torch of Jewish continuity in the Diaspora. They are continuing something foreign and strange based upon a perpetuation of distress. It is no coincidence that Rabbi Shlomo (Shneur) Zalman of Lyady prayed for the czar's victory over Napoleon. He believed that only suffering would preserve the Jewish people and feared that Napoleon's victory could put an end to this suffering! If Orthodox zealots succeed in their aspirations to keep their version of Judaism as the only one in the Diaspora, this would mean, in effect, the end of the Jewish world outside of Israel. This is precisely the trend we must work to prevent in the twenty-first century.

In the same way, we must work against the trend that would turn Israel into a new version of the old ghetto—with religious laws governing central areas of life, with hatred for the State of Israel replacing the old anti-Semitism, with unresolved conflict with its neighbors, and dangerous security threats, and a capital that is not recognized by other nations. Such a state cannot be a focus of attraction and provide a second home for world Jewry. In fact, those currently living in Israel might even abandon it as their first home. If Israel becomes a religious-rightist ghetto, it would not only betray Herzl and his vision, but, more important, it would betray Israeli citizens and the Jewish world.

Israel must offer more Jewish content to the young generation, devote more classroom hours to the study of Jewish thought, Bible, and Oral Law, while at the same time working to prevent religious coercion and the perception of such coercion. In an atmosphere free of religious legislation, young people will be more open to explore and choose from the treasure of the Jewish heritage.

A normal state, living at peace with its neighbors, whose existence is no longer threatened, where military service is not so long—and perhaps not compulsory—and whose law books are liberated from the invasion of religious legislation, would be much more attractive to the hundreds of thousands of Jews remaining in Russia, Ukraine, and other parts of the Commonwealth of Independent States. This is currently the most available reservoir of potential immigrants and Israel should make a supreme effort to attract these Jews. Israel today offers a great advantage for those immigrating from the former Soviet Union: over the last decade, there has emerged a community of about one million Russian-speakers who help assimilate newcomers in a cultural setting more comfortable than that which awaited the earlier waves of immigrants.

I am not worried about Russian "autonomy"—the Russian newspapers, the use of Russian in stores and as the language of conversation among these immigrants, and so on. This is a welcome phenomenon that makes the adjustment easier for the first generation of immigrants but rarely outlasts the second generation. My parents' generation also read newspapers in Hungarian, German, and Polish, while their children are satisfied with reading the Hebrew press. In the same way, the children of recent Russian-speaking immigrants will readily enough become part of the Hebrew culture. Indeed, I hope that these immigrants will pass on some Russian-language skills to their children, unlike our parents, who kept this knowledge from us out of concern that we might not be "Hebrew" enough.

If we succeed in making Israel a focus of Jewish and universal attraction, if it becomes both a normal state and a Jewish state that assumes special missions in the world, perhaps even Herzl would choose to immigrate to Israel. This will require action. The change in the definition of who is a Jew is the most revolutionary change, and will require careful consideration and communication between central elements of American and Israeli Jewry. This sort of discussion can take place only if a common table is established for the two communities, and only if this becomes the backbone of a new and institutionalized world Jewish organization. It would be a historic decision not to push away those who consider themselves Jews. It would unify and expand the Jewish people, despite the contentions of some opponents that it might cause a rift.

The new American-Israeli Jewish Forum would handle, among other things, the annual administration of the "birthright" program, including its funding, the updating of programs offered to the young Jews visiting Israel, and the management of follow-up activities. In short, this organization would be responsible for the central national project of the Jewish world in the twenty-first century.

It would also have many other tasks. It would refer young people from Israel and the Diaspora to projects in Jewish communities throughout the world that require assistance. It could also direct the Jewish activities in the Third World and make aid to those countries one of the great challenges shared by young people in Israel and the rest of the Jewish world. In addition, the Forum would respond to incidents of anti-Semitism in the world and speak out against racism, neo-Nazism, and neo-fascism.

Jewish education would be a central mission for the Forum. Israel could serve as a laboratory for education experiments, just as it has for meaningful social experiments. For example, Israel could test one of the ideas I personally favor: starting school at age four and graduating from college by age eighteen. This would realize the relative advantage that the "people of the Book"—that is, a people of students—still retain, before this advantage gradually disappears.

Israel, for its part, must complete the peace process with its neighbors. An agreement with the Palestinians is at the heart of the Arab-Israeli conflict, and its solution is possible and practical. Peace with the Palestinians will make it easier to achieve peace with Syria and Lebanon. A comprehensive peace will significantly decrease the danger that Israel will be attacked by extreme outer-rim states wishing to win the support of Arab states.

Peace will lead to normalization and will bring Israel to a stage when a professional army can replace compulsory military service. This development will have positive implications on relations with the ultra-Orthodox, while also encouraging immigration to Israel. As long as there is this compulsory service, the young ultra-Orthodox will remain cloistered in *yeshivot*—unlike any other time in Jewish history—since only the *yeshivah* is authorized to confirm that a student qualifies for a "deferment" that, in effect, becomes an exemption from army service. The moment army service becomes voluntary, we will stop forcing all of the ultra-Orthodox youth to study in *yeshivot*. There is no doubt that many would prefer to enter and become part of the Israeli economy rather than live in poverty on government handouts.

In the realm of religion-state relations, the most crucial decision is to enable civil marriage and divorce. Another important matter is to deny preferred status to any one of the religious streams of Judaism. It is not absolutely necessary to separate religion and state. Israel could decide to completely separate itself from the Jewish, Muslim and Christian frameworks, and announce that, from now on, they would need to finance themselves. But Israel could also continue to fund them, in proportion to the number of people requiring religious services in each group.

If this progressive approach triumphs, the twenty-first century will witness a growing number of Jews, and the creation of a Jewish world that finally, for the first time in history, works together to handle common problems and chart a shared future.

I wonder about my grandfather Yossel. The world turned over twice—two world wars, including the Holocaust—between his meeting with Herzl in 1903 and his death in 1946. I don't know if he left the world feeling contented. He was not a content man, so in all likelihood he went to his grave still protesting. In his sixties, did he look back on himself at age twenty-three with understanding, or did he feel regret? After the Holocaust, was he sorry that he was among those who blocked the implementation of the majority decision to at least explore the Uganda option? Or was he happy that he acted as he did and took pride in the impressive achievements of the *yishuv?* I'll never know.

The advantage that the perspective of time affords us is unfair toward the passionate and intelligent people who wrote and acted without the benefit of knowing what would transpire in the next century. No one, not even the most pessimistic, anticipated the Holocaust. They expected more of what they already knew: hatred of the Jew, job restrictions, and pogroms. Herzl perhaps expressed the most urgent sense of an impending catastrophe, though he had no way of knowing exactly what it would be. The search by Herzl and Nordau for a "night refuge" was, in retrospect, the most correct approach. But it is impossible to know whether it would have been feasible. Ahad Ha'am was right in noting that America could more easily accommodate millions of immigrants than Palestine. My grandfather and his friends were correct in their concern that the "night refuge" would soon become a new "Zion." That is, the Jews who fled Europe and arrived in Canada, Australia, Brazil, Argentina, and certainly the United States, would not be quick to abandon these countries in order to move to the real Zion. Herzl's successors were also correct when they sought to prepare Palestine for new immigrants from Eastern Europe, and were concerned that a sudden flood of hundreds of thousands of Jews would overwhelm Palestine before these preparations were completed. But in retrospect, the Holocaust makes just about everyone look mistaken.

If three or four million Jews had immigrated to America instead of only two million, the scope of the Holocaust could have been diminished. If the gates to Palestine had been open after the Balfour Declaration and British conquest, another half a million European Jews could have been saved. But these are only "what if" scenarios, though very tempting to consider. Facts were created on the ground, including unexpected ones. My grandfather and his colleagues, their children and grandchildren, developed auto-emancipation in Israel—a reality of heroism, creativity, constant interest, impressive achievements, a special way of life, and a unique mosaic of cultures. Israel is not a Viennese coffeehouse: contrary to Herzl's vision, the rabbis do not confine themselves to synagogue affairs, and the army is not composed solely of career soldiers. But an Israeli history has been forged, together with Israeli nostalgia. A complete world has been created, constituting a new reality that stands on its own. It is this reality alone, and not the "what if" scenarios, that we can and should address.

A very interesting and completely different Jewish reality has been created in America, which represents the ultimate success of the Emancipation. This is a different "Zion"—without the heroism, without the myths, much more individualistic—one that has an amazing impact on the society around it.

On both sides of the Atlantic Ocean, we speak in terms of eternity—"forever" and "never"—and tend to forget how prone we are to make mistakes and how transitory reality is, even when it appears permanent to us. It is enough to look to the past to realize how easy it is to be mistaken about the future.

# Epilogue:
# Two Options

JEWS NOW COMPRISE a smaller percentage of the world's population than in the past, although Jewish influence and prominence is quite disproportionate to these smaller numbers. At the end of the second millennium, only one out of every 445 people in the world was a Jew. When we look at the two largest Jewish communities, we find the Jews in America worried that their grandchildren might not live as Jews, while the Jews in Israel are worried about whether or not their Jewish grandchildren will live in peace.

There has been a proliferation of books and articles warning about the disappearance of the Jewish people. In 1963, *Look* magazine ran a lead article titled "The Vanishing American Jew." A year later, the French sociologist Georges Friedman published *The End of the Jewish People?* In the wake of the new statistics on growing rates of intermarriage, the rabbi of Great Britain, Jonathan Sachs, published *Will We Have Jewish Grandchildren?* in 1994. Bernard Wasserstein predicted that the Jews of Europe would completely assimilate during the twenty-first century in his book *Vanishing*

*Diaspora,* published in 1996. After his son's marriage to a Catholic woman, Alan Dershowitz wrote *The Vanishing American Jew,* which proposes universal values—justice, altruism, study, and so on—as the basis for Jewish continuity in a world where Jews are neither religious nor anxious to immigrate to Israel.

But are we really disappearing? It is very hard to predict. It also is a question of definition. If being Jewish is solely a matter of religion, defined exclusively by our rabbis, the Jewish world will continue to shrink. However, if Jewishness implies being part of a people, and if the definition of a Jew is inclusive, the Jewish people may even grow. The lines along which this definition is made is up to us.

While the Jews as a people have, unlike many other nations, survived conquest and exile, many individual Jews have disappeared over the centuries, becoming part of other civilizations. Those who remained Jews have done so because they remained part of a community—whether of their own accord or because they were forced to live in a ghetto. Jews who sought to live outside of Jewish communities did not succeed in preserving their Jewish identity over generations.

In looking back over the last several centuries of Jewish history, I am impressed by the explosion of creative energies unleashed by the Emancipation in the late eighteenth century, and impressed as well by the wide range of solutions—including Zionism—proposed toward the end of the nineteenth century to counter the rise of anti-Semitism. While Israel may be seen as a victory for Zionism, this solution did not prevent the Holocaust. In fact, when I look at Herzl's portrait in the Knesset, he always seems to be crying.

We are faced with two basic options: either wring our hands and heave sighs of concern over the state of the Jewish world at the beginning of the twenty-first century, or take action. The first approach says that a reliable peace cannot be achieved with Israel's hostile Arab and Muslim neighbors. In addition, pessimists who say there is nothing to be done would discount efforts to stem the tide of assimilation and intermarriage in the Diaspora, contending that attempts to establish a new type of dialogue between Israel and world Jewry are doomed to failure.

On the other hand, the second option (taking action) means pushing forward with the peace process and working for religious pluralism in Israel, including a broad definition of "Who is a Jew?" This path of action would explore creative new ways to bring the Jewish world closer together, seeking to draw upon the respective strengths of each community.

One thing is clear from a study of the past century of Jewish history: the Jews who paid the heaviest price were the ones who did nothing. Many who took action survived, whether by seeking refuge in America or Israel, or even in the unsuccessful Siberian settlement in Birobidzhan. Those who remained in the Vienna cafés and Jewish ghettos were the ones who perished.

For this I am grateful to my grandfather Yosef Bregman, who, after roaming across Russia with his family, finally arrived in Palestine. The lesson I draw from all of this is that I cannot allow myself to look out from my balcony on Israel and the Jewish world, admiring the successes and sighing over the problematic trends. I am convinced that our actions can make a difference. We do not need to undertake such grandiose schemes as Herzl's plan to transfer an entire people from one continent to another. Far more modest steps are likely to ensure that the twenty-first century will be remembered as a wonderful time for the Jewish people. But this means that we must stop sighing and start acting—now.

# Appendix A:
# The Ben-Gurion–
# Blaustein Statements (1950)

PRIME MINISTER DAVID BEN-GURION:

WE ARE VERY HAPPY to welcome you here in our midst as a representative of the great Jewry of the United States to whom Israel owes so much. No other community abroad has so great a stake in what has been achieved in this country during the present generation as have the Jews of America. Their material and political support, their warm-hearted and practical idealism, has been one of the principal sources of our strength and our success. In supporting our effort, American Jewry has developed, on a new plane, the noble conception, maintained for more than half a century, of extending its help for the protection of Jewish rights throughout the world and of rendering economic aid wherever it was needed. We are deeply conscious of the help which America has given to us here in our great effort of reconstruction and during our struggle for independence. This great tradition has been continued since the establishment of the State of Israel.

You, Mr. Blaustein, are one of the finest examples of that tradition, and as an American and as a Jew you have made many and significant contributions to the Jewish cause and to the cause of democracy. We are therefore happy on this occasion of your visit here as our guest, to discuss with you matters of mutual interest and to clarify some of the problems which have arisen in regard to the relationship between the people of Israel and the Jewish communities abroad, in particular the Jewish community of the United States.

It is our great pride that our newly gained independence has enabled us in this small country to undertake the major share of the great and urgent task of providing permanent homes under conditions of full equality to hundreds of thousands of our brethren who cannot remain where they are and whose heart is set on rebuilding their lives in Israel. In this great task you and we are engaged in a close partnership. Without the readiness for sacrifice of the people of Israel and without the help of America this urgent task can hardly be achieved.

It is most unfortunate that since our State came into being some confusion and misunderstanding should have arisen as regards the relationship between Israel and the Jewish communities abroad, in particular that of the United States. These misunderstandings are likely to alienate sympathies and create disharmony where friendship and close understanding are of vital necessity. To my mind, the position is perfectly clear. The Jews of the United States, as a community and as individuals, have only one political attachment and that is to the United States of America. They owe no political allegiance to Israel. In the first statement which the representative of Israel made before the United Nations after her admission to that international organization, he clearly stated, without any reservation, that the State of Israel represents and speaks only on behalf of its own citizens and in no way presumes to represent or speak in the name of the Jews who are citizens of any other country. We, the people of Israel, have no desire and no intention to interfere in any way with the internal affairs of Jewish communities abroad. The Government and the people of Israel fully respect the right and integrity of the Jewish communities in other countries to develop their own mode of life and their indigenous social, economic and cultural institutions in accordance with their own needs and aspirations. Any weakening of American Jewry, any disruption of its communal life, any lowering of its sense of security, any diminution of its status, is a definite loss to Jews everywhere and to Israel in particular. We are happy to know of the deep and growing interest which American Jews of all shades and convictions take in what it has fallen to us to achieve in this country. Were we, God forbid, to fail in what we have undertaken on our own behalf and on behalf of our suffering brethren, that failure would cause grievous pain to Jews everywhere and nowhere more than in your country. Our success or failure depends in a large measure on our cooperation with, and on the strength of, the great Jewish community of the United States, and, we, therefore, are anxious that nothing should be said or done which could in the slightest degree undermine the sense of security and stability of American Jewry.

In this connection let me say a word about immigration. We should like to see American Jews come and take part in our effort. We need their technical knowledge, their unrivalled experience, their spirit of enterprise, their bold vision, their "know-how." We need engineers, chemists, builders, work managers and technicians. The tasks which face us in this country are eminently such as would appeal to the American genius for technical development and social progress. But the decision as to whether they wish to come—permanently or temporarily—rests with the free discretion of each American Jew himself. It is entirely a matter of his own volition. We need *halutzim*, pioneers, too. *Halutzim* have come to us— and we believe more will come, not only from those countries where the Jews are oppressed and in "exile" but also from countries where the Jews live a life of freedom and are equal in status to all other citizens in their country. But the essence of *halutziut* is free choice. They will come from among those who believe that their aspirations as human beings and as Jews can best be fulfilled by life and work in Israel.

I believe I know something of the spirit of American Jewry among whom I lived for some years. I am convinced that it will continue to make a major contribution towards our great effort of reconstruction, and I hope that the talks we have had with you will make for even closer cooperation between our two communities.

JACOB BLAUSTEIN, PRESIDENT OF THE
AMERICAN JEWISH COMMITTEE:

I am very happy, Mr. Prime Minister, to have come here at your invitation and to have discussed with you and other leaders of Israel the various important problems of mutual interest.

This is the second time I have been here since the State of Israel was created. A year and a half ago my colleagues and I, of the American Jewish Committee, saw evidence of the valor that had been displayed, and felt the hopes and aspirations that had inspired the people to win a war against terrific odds. This time, I have witnessed the great achievements that have taken place in the interval and have discussed the plans which point the road upon which the present-day Israel intends to travel.

I find that tremendous progress has been made under your great leadership; but also, as you well know, tremendous problems loom ahead. The nation is confronted with gigantic tasks of reconstruction and re-habilitation, and with large economic and other problems, as is to be expected in so young a state.

I am sure that with your rare combination of idealism and realism, you will continue to tackle these matters vigorously; and that with your usual energy, resourcefulness and common sense, you will be able to overcome them.

Traveling over the country and visiting both old and newly established settlements, it has been a thrill to observe how you are conquering the Negev and the rocks of the Galilee and are thus displaying the same pioneering spirit that opened up the great West of my own country. It has been satisfying to see right on the scene, how well and to what good advantage you are utilizing the support from the American Jewish community. I am sure, too, that the American tractors and other machinery and equipment acquired through the loan granted by the Export-Import Bank will further contribute to the technological development of your country.

## A Stronghold of Democracy

But more than that, what you are doing and creating in this corner of the Middle East is of vital importance not only to you and the Jews, but to humanity in general. For I believe that the free and peace-loving peoples in the world can look upon Israel as a stronghold of democracy in an area where liberal democracy is practically unknown and where the prevailing social and political conditions may be potential dangers to the security and stability of the world. What President Truman is intending to do under his Four Point Program, in assisting underdeveloped peoples to improve their conditions and raise their standards of living, you here to a large extent have been doing right along under most difficult conditions and at great sacrifice.

Important to your future, as you recognize, is the United States of America and American Jewry. Israel, of course, is also important to them.

In this connection, I am pleased that Mr. Elath has been here during our stay. As your Ambassador to the United States, he has rendered invaluable service in bringing our two countries and communities closer together.

I thought I knew it even before I came to this country on this trip, but my visit has made it still more clear to me—and as an American citizen and a Jew I am gratified—that the Israeli people want democracy and, in my opinion, will not accept any dictatorship or totalitarianism from within or from without.

Democracy, like all other human institutions, has its faults; and abuses are possible. But the strength of a democratic regime is that these faults and these abuses can be corrected without the destruction of human rights and freedoms which alone make life worth living.

There is no question in my mind that a Jew who wants to remain loyal to the fundamental basis of Judaism and his cultural heritage, will be in the forefront of the struggle for democracy against totalitarianism.

The American Jewish community sees its fortunes tied to the fate of liberal democracy in the United States, sustained by its heritage, as Americans and as Jews. We seek to strengthen both of these vital links to the past and to all humanity by enhancing the American democratic and political system, American cultural diversity and American well-being.

As to Israel, the vast majority of American Jewry recognizes the necessity and desirability of helping to make it a strong, viable, self-supporting state. This, for the sake of Israel itself, and the good of the world.

The American Jewish Committee has been active, as have other Jewish organizations in the United States, in rendering, within the framework of their American citizenship, every possible support to Israel; and I am sure that this support will continue and that we shall do all we can to increase further our share in the great historic task of helping Israel to solve its problems and develop as a free, independent and flourishing democracy.

## Israel Means Much to Jews

While Israel has naturally placed some burdens on Jews elsewhere, particularly in America, it has, in turn, meant much to Jews throughout the world. For hundreds of thousands in Europe, Africa and the Middle East, it has provided a home in which they can attain their full stature of human dignity for the first time. In all Jews, it has inspired pride and admiration, even though in some instances, it has created passing headaches.

Israel's rebirth and progress, coming after the tragedy of European Jewry in the 1930s and in World War II, has done much to raise Jewish morale. Jews in America and everywhere can be more proud than ever of their Jewishness.

But we must, in a true spirit of friendliness, sound a note of caution to Israel and its leaders. Now that the birth pains are over, and even though Israel is undergoing growing pains, it must recognize that the matter of good-will between its citizens and those of other countries is a two-way street: that Israel also has a responsibility in this situation—a responsibility in terms of not affecting adversely the sensibilities of Jews who are citizens of other states by what it says or does.

In this connection, you are a realist and want facts and I would be less than frank if I did not point out to you that American Jews vigorously repudiate any suggestion or implication that they are in exile. American

Jews—young and old alike, Zionists and non-Zionists alike—are profoundly attached to America. America welcomed their immigrant parents in their need. Under America's free institutions, they and their children have achieved that sense of security unknown for long centuries of travail. American Jews have truly become Americans; just as have all other oppressed groups that have ever come to America's shores.

## Democracy's Future Rests in U.S.

To American Jews, America is home. There, exist their thriving roots; there, is the country which they have helped to build; and there, they share its fruits and its destiny. They believe in the future of a democratic society in the United States under which all citizens, irrespective of creed or race, can live on terms of equality. They further believe that if democracy should fail in America, there would be no future for democracy anywhere in the world, and [then] the very existence of an independent State of Israel would be problematic. Further, they feel that a world in which it would be possible for Jews to be driven by persecution from America would not be a world safe for Israel either; indeed it is hard to conceive how it would be a world safe for any human being.

The American Jewish Committee, as you, Mr. Prime Minister, have so eloquently pointed out, has assumed a major part of the responsibility of securing equality of rights and providing generous material help to Jews in other countries. American Jews feel themselves bound to Jews the world over by ties of religion, common historical traditions and in certain respects, by a sense of common destiny. We fully realize that persecution and discrimination against Jews in any country will sooner or later have its impact on the situation of the Jews in other countries, but these problems must be dealt with by each Jewish community itself in accordance with its own wishes, traditions, needs and aspirations.

Jewish communities, particularly American Jewry in view of its influence and its strength, can offer advice, cooperation and help, but should not attempt to speak in the name of other communities or in any way interfere in their internal affairs.

I am happy to note from your statement, Mr. Prime Minister, that the State of Israel takes a similar position. Any other position on the part of the State of Israel would only weaken the American and other Jewish communities of the free, democratic countries and be contrary to the basic interests of Israel itself. The future development of Israel, spiritual, social as well as economic, will largely depend upon a strong and healthy Jewish community in the United States and other free democracies.

We have been greatly distressed that at the very hour when so much has been achieved, harmful and futile discussions and misunderstandings have arisen as to the relations between the people and the State of Israel and the Jews in other countries, particularly in the United States. Harm has been done to the morale and to some extent to the sense of security of the American Jewish community through unwise and unwarranted statements and appeals which ignore the feelings and aspirations of American Jewry.

## Had Been Harmful to Israel

Even greater harm has been done to the State of Israel itself by weakening the readiness of American Jews to do their full share in the rebuilding of Israel, which faces such enormous political, social and economic problems.

Your statement today, Mr. Prime Minister, will, I trust, be followed by unmistakable evidence that the responsible leaders of Israel, and the organizations connected with it, fully understand that future relations between the American Jewish community and the State of Israel must be based on mutual respect for one another's feelings and needs, and on the preservation of the integrity of the two communities and their institutions.

I believe that in your statement today, you have taken a fundamental and historic position which will redound to the best interest not only of Israel, but of the Jews of America and of the world. I am confident that this statement and the spirit in which it has been made, by eliminating the misunderstandings and futile discussions between our two communities, will strengthen them both and will lay the foundation for even closer cooperation.

In closing, permit me to express my deep gratitude for the magnificent reception you and your colleagues have afforded my colleague and me during our stay in this country.

# Appendix B:
# The Distribution of the Jewish People in the World

THE YEAR 1881 was a turning point in the dispersion of world Jewry. The largest Jewish community in the world was concentrated in the "Pale of Settlement," a region of the Russian Empire that had once been Poland. In March of 1881, Czar Alexander II, whose sweeping reforms had brought a brief period of hope to the impoverished Jewish masses, was assassinated by an anarchist. A mass assault on the Jews of Yelisabatgrad followed during Easter of that year. News of the murder, rape, and plunder spread rapidly throughout the Pale. This, together with the feeling that the government authorities were encouraging similar attacks (pogroms) throughout southern Russian in 1882, finally convinced the Jews that it was an illusion to think that they could ever integrate into Russian society. The waves of pogroms fueled by anti-Semitism were even harder to bear than the oppressive edicts and laws that had become normal before the enlightened reign of Alexander II. Jews fled Russia in increasing numbers.

Czar Alexander III reinstated restrictions on the Jews, including quotas that made it difficult for them to achieve higher education. He evicted many Jews from their places of residence and encouraged the Jewish exodus by announcing to Russia's five million Jews that the country's western border was open to them.

Between 1881 and 1914, some 2,370,000 Jews left Eastern Europe in the biggest wave of emigration in Jewish history. Of this number, about 1,300,000 emigrated from Russia, with the rest from Austria, Poland and Romania. Pogroms continued to occur from time to time throughout this period. In the wake of the harsh pogrom in Kishinev in 1903, some 400,000 Jews fled to the United States.

Most of the Jews who left Eastern Europe arrived in the United States, with smaller groups immigrating to South America, Canada, and Great Britain. A very small number of them reached the shores of Palestine.

## At the Time of the First Zionist Congress in 1897

At the time of the First Zionist Congress in 1897, the Jewish world was in the midst of an emigration frenzy. There were approximately 10.5 million Jews in about 2 million households. At that moment, 5 million Jews lived in Russia, 1 million were already in the United States, and most of the rest were in other European countries or in settlements all around the Mediterranean basin. Most of the Jewish world was characterized by poverty and suffered restrictions regarding where they could live, what professions they could pursue, what public offices they could hold, and where they could study.

In Max Nordau's brilliant speech, titled "The General Condition of the Jews," he contended that in the flush of Emancipation fever, in pursuing rationalistic logic to its inevitable conclusions, the nations of Western Europe had thrown open the gates of the ghettos and suddenly granted the Jews civil rights. Taken entirely by surprise, the Jews had no time to emotionally adjust to this Emancipation. France led the way, and other Western countries followed its lead. Apart from England, where, according to Nordau, Jewish rights were a natural matter, emancipation was a matter of imitation. The Jew, who had previously accepted his limited rights and found his complete world in the ghetto, anticipated becoming an equal among equals at the end of the nineteenth century, but instead encountered harsh discrimination.

Nordau sung the praises of the ghetto as a sanctuary, rather than a prison for the Jews:

> In the ghetto, the Jew had his own world; it was his sure refuge and it provided the spiritual and moral equivalent of a motherland. His fellow inhabitants of the ghetto were the people whose respect he both wanted and could attain. His goal and ambition was to gain its good opinion, and its criticism or ill will was the punishment that he feared. . . . What did it matter that those values that were prized within the ghetto were despised outside it? The opinion of the outside world did not matter, because it was the opinion of ignorant enemies. One tried to please one's brothers, and their respect gave honorable meaning to one's life. In the moral sense, therefore, the Jews of the ghetto lived a full life.

For several decades in the nineteenth century, Nordau claimed, Jews enjoyed a new sense of equality, hurriedly abandoning their ghettos:

> Well nigh intoxicated, the Jews rushed to burn all their bridges immediately. They now had another home, so they no longer needed a ghetto; they now had other connections and were no longer forced to live only among their coreligionists. Their instinct of self-preservation adapted itself immediately and completely to the new circumstances.

But by the end of the century, Jews were both disillusioned about equal rights in Europe and unable to return to the ghetto. They realized that anti-Semitism in Europe prevented them from integrating into the life of the continent. Some opted to convert to Christianity—not for religious reasons, but out of sheer desperation. This group, according to Nordau's account, simply concluded that being Christian was the only way to avoid encountering hatred and to truly integrate into European society.

While sympathizing with their "spiritual misery," Nordau "contemplates with horror the future" of these "new Marranos." His review of the state of contemporary Jewry continued with the Zionist option:

> Some Jews hope for salvation from Zionism, which is for them not the fulfillment of a mystic promise of the Scripture but the way to an existence wherein the Jew will at last find the simplest and most elementary conditions of life, which are a matter of course for every non-Jew of both hemispheres: that is, an assured place in society, a community that accepts him, the possibility of employing all his powers for the development of his real self instead of abusing them for the suppression and falsification of his personality.

Nordau continued his address to the First Zionist Congress with a review of the various Jewish communities in the world at that time. The vast majority of the Jews were in Russia and subject to a series of limiting edicts. Permits were required for living in many areas of the country, with exceptions being made only if one was involved in trade or well educated. "All those able to leave the country do so in order to find in foreign lands the light and air denied them in their homeland. Anyone who is not bold enough to do so, remains in place and withers away spiritually, morally, and physically."

In Galicia, there were some 772,000 Jews and, according to Nordau, "70 percent of them are beggars." Dr. Abraham Salz told how the Jews there were kept out of the professions and worked as craftsmen, traders, small shopkeepers, middlemen, agents, waiters in taverns, and that 38,000 were supported by charity.

There were about 400,000 Jews living in western Austria at that time. While the law accorded them equality, they were not able to enjoy their rights, as they were socially ostracized. It was very difficult to make a living, and many Jews did not even reach the income threshold for paying taxes. Catholic anti-Semitism grew stronger, as part of a mass movement supported by the Church and the government. A certificate of baptism was required for all candidates for the military academy. It was very difficult for Jews to find work as doctors or lawyers. Dr. Alexander Mintz of

Vienna told the congress that Jews did not have the right to become citizens of Vienna, and that the slogan "Don't buy from Jews!" was heard far and wide.

In Hungary, there were some 300,000 Jews who enjoyed full civic rights and an excellent economic situation. They were permitted to work in any professions and acquire any property. However, Nordau explained, "Those familiar with the situation are sure that even in Hungary, hatred for Jews is simmering under the surface and will violently erupt upon the first opportunity."

There were 250,000 Jews living in Romania amidst considerable difficulties. Shmuel Pineles explained:

> It's forbidden for a Jew to be a peddler, to sell tobacco and matches, to be an attorney or pharmacist. A Jew cannot be an officer or hold any public position, meaning that he is prohibited from being a judge or public official, policeman, customs clerk, mail, telegraph or telephone clerk, train or bank employee, government or city engineer, professor, teacher at local or government public schools, doctor in a public hospital, produce merchant or shipping agent, and so on. A Jew is not even allowed to be a street sweeper!

In light of this, Pineles concluded that fervor for Zionism was especially great in Romania.

Dr. Sauer, who spoke about the condition of the 300,000 Jews of Germany, also referred to the gap between their formal rights and their actual situation. Here again they were unable to take advantage of these rights due to widespread anti-Semitism.

Jacob de Haus's report on the Jews of Britain turned out to be the only positive report on Jewish communities presented at the congress. Most of the Jews in England were first-generation immigrants; only 20 percent were born there. Yet they enjoyed true and complete equality and were able to choose any profession. The British government supported Jewish education. Only one position was off-limits to the Jews: Lord Chancellor, since he is, technically, the confessional priest to the queen and therefore must be Anglican.

No Jew in England needed to turn to local authorities for the stipend distributed to the poor. Affluent Jews financed the Jewish community's institutionalized welfare system, which was headed by a board of representatives from all of the communities and had a regular operating budget. "The Jews are avid fans of opera, music and concerts . . . and the Jews of England especially love horse racing, while the foreign Jews become hooked on cards and dice."

In Bukovina, reported Dr. Meir Avner, the 60,000 Jews comprised more than 10 percent of the country's population. For many years, the Jews there considered themselves Germans and rejected Romanian influence; but when the German-Christian Party appeared and barred them from joining it, the Jews transferred their allegiance to Romania. About 1,000 affluent Jews lived in Bukovina. The rest were wretchedly poor; many of them worked as bartenders. Most of the law graduates were Jewish, as were half of the secondary school students. Many of the Jews were university graduates, but were unable to attain positions. The only road to advancement was through conversion to Christianity.

Professor Zvi Balkovsky told the congress that the 27,000 Jews in Bulgaria lived in terrible poverty and crowded conditions. Equal rights existed only on paper, while in reality there was harsh discrimination. Whenever a Jew was elected to the Parliament, ostensibly legal means were always found to nullify the voting. Parents sold their daughters as servants when they were only six or seven, and young Jewish women were raped without anyone raising a fuss. Jewish women converted to Christianity in order to marry Bulgarian men.

Yaakov Bahar, from France, reported on the Jews of Algeria, where he spent five years. Algerian Jews, most of whom were descendants of slaves sold by the Spanish to the Arabs, were granted emancipation in 1870 and became French citizens. Of the 45,000 Jews in Algeria at that time, some 30,000 lived in poverty, the objects of the hatred of both Christians and Muslims.

The Jews of Morocco and Persia received only passing mention at the First Zionist Congress. Nordau said the following about these two Jewish communities:

> I must be brief about the 15,000 Jews of Morocco and the Jews of Persia, whose number I don't know. They are the poorest of the

poor, and even lack the spirit to rebel against their poverty. They
bear it with dull resignation, they don't complain and only draw
our attention when the mobs attack their ghetto, looting, raping
and killing.

There were no reports on the Jews of Iraq, Egypt, Yemen, and South
America at the First Zionist Congress.

Adam Rosenberg spoke about the one million Jews of the United
States. "Twenty years ago," he said,

one came to America to seek one's own happiness and there are
many who succeeded in finding happiness there. Later there were
those who, unfortunately, came in search of a homeland, who
hoped to improve their economic condition there and having
been hitherto unsuccessful, hoped that they would now succeed.

The Jewish proletariat in the United States was growing, Rosenberg
told the delegates, and many were critical of the large waves of immigration, noting the burden they placed on the American economy,
and demanding that immigration be limited. Anti-Semitism existed, he
reported, but was latent. The Jewish community was highly institutionalized, and there were many Jewish organizations. Zionism was popular
mainly among Jewish immigrants from Eastern Europe, whose dreams of
finding happiness in America had not been realized.

Rosenberg's description was naturally very limited. The delegates to
the congress could hardly have imagined that, within a few decades, the
United States would displace Russia as home to the largest Jewish community in the world. More than anywhere else in the world, America was
perceived by those immigrating to it as a home and not merely a "night
refuge."

## The U.S. Jewish Community

The Jews of Germany were the first large wave of nineteenth-century
Jewish immigration to America. The first national organization of U.S.
Jews, B'nai B'rith, was founded in 1843. The failed revolutions of 1848 in

Europe made conditions worse for the Jews and many non-Jewish intellectuals who were, sometimes justifiably, suspected of taking part in the rebellion against the old regime. Tens of thousands of German Jews arrived in America in a brief span of time and soon found a place in American society. Unique among Jewish communities of the world, they established Reform Judaism as their largest and most organized Jewish movement.

When the mass immigration of Russian Jews began, America's basic Jewish institutions were already well-established. For a long time, the Russian Jews found themselves considered "greenhorns" (as compared to the German Jewish "old-timers"). The German Jews felt confident enough in 1906 to form the American Jewish Committee, in an effort to improve the situation of Jews not only in America but throughout the world.

With the outbreak of violent anti-Semitism in Eastern Europe, increasing numbers of Russian Jews journeyed to the New World. During the forty-three years between the assassination of Czar Alexander II in 1881 and the restrictive U.S. immigration laws of 1924, some two million Jews immigrated to the United States. Immigration peaked in 1906, when 200,000 Jews arrived from Eastern Europe in a single year.

The millions of Jews who found themselves refugees in the wake of World War I and the Bolshevik revolution tried vainly to reach America, only to discover that they were suspected of being Communists and the harsh immigration quotas kept them from entering the country. If the flow of immigration had not been halted in 1924, millions would have been saved from the Holocaust, but xenophobia and anti-Semitism were not confined to Europe.

Anti-Semitism was also on the rise in America. In 1919, the most prominent American industrialist, Henry Ford, republished the "Protocols of the Elders of Zion," a spurious document concocted twenty years earlier by Russian anti-Semites, in his anti-Semitic daily, *The Dearborn Independent*. From this bully pulpit, he also voiced his own prejudiced opinions, which found a responsive audience.

During the 1920s and thirties, viciously anti-Semitic remarks were openly expressed in the United States; it was a time when many new Jewish immigrants were quick to blur their identity, change their names, and even convert to Christianity. It was not easy to be a Jew in the New World during those years. The number of Ku Klux Klan members reached four million, and universities set restrictive quotas for the admission of Jewish students. Congressional debate on limiting immigration took place between 1909 and 1924. The main argument raised in these discussions was that certain immigrants lower the average national intelligence. The immigrants specifically referenced were Jews, Italians, Greeks, and Slavs. During the 1920s, the Jews reached their relative demographic peak, comprising 3.85 percent of the U.S. population. The American leadership sought to prevent this proportion from growing.

In the end, Congress passed the Reed-Johnson Immigration Reform Act of 1924, which set immigration quotas for the groups mentioned above. The quota was 2 percent annually of the 1890 immigration statistic for groups already present in the United States. This allowed for the immigration of 6,000 Jews per year from Poland, 2,000 from Russia, and 600 from Romania. In essence, this meant a virtual closing of the gates. Some Jews prevented from immigrating to the United States left for Palestine, but most remained in Europe in straitened circumstances.

President Calvin Coolidge chose not to veto the Reed-Johnson legislation. Apparently, it corresponded to his own preferences. In fact, these U.S. immigration restrictions remained in effect for forty-one years. In 1942, President Roosevelt asked the Congress to temporarily suspend these laws, but the Congress refused to accede. Anti-Semitism persisted even at the highest levels of government until after the Holocaust. Laws discriminating against Jews were then slowly abolished, as Jewish organizations began cooperating more closely and waged successful legal campaigns, pursuing the overturn of these laws even to the Supreme Court. In a 1963 Supreme Court ruling, enforced school prayer was abolished, and during President Johnson's administration in 1965, the Reed-Johnson immigration restrictions were finally removed.

As officially sanctioned discrimination ended, anti-Semitism moved to the fringes of American society, to be practiced mainly by pariahs like the Reverend Louis Farrakhan. One reason for the decline of anti-Semitism in the United States was that, through intermarriage, Jews were becoming an integral part of many Christian homes.

The last few decades have been the golden years of American Jewry.

The Six-Day War gave them pride, strengthened their identity with Israel, intensified their fund-raising activities, and created a new cadre of leadership among philanthropists. The struggle for the liberation of Soviet Jews in the 1970s served as a rallying cause for the Jews of America and enhanced the self-confidence of their organizations in approaching the administration and the Congress. The commemoration of the Holocaust also became a central issue on the agenda of American Jewry. Since the 1980s, more and more attention has been devoted to this subject, resulting in the establishment of Holocaust museums and the comprehensive academic study of the Nazi period in secondary schools and colleges.

Jews have filled central positions in several U.S. administrations, and have reached a new peak during President Bill Clinton's tenure. Today's American Jews are proud of their Judaism, feel no need to change their names, and certainly do not feel compelled to convert to Christianity. At 5.6 million souls, they constitute the largest Jewish community in the world. Most are liberal Democrats. They generally support liberal causes like abortion rights, equal opportunities for minorities, and humanitarian aid to countries in distress. Despite occasional pockets of poverty, American Jews are an affluent group, earning far above the national average.

In 1990, the most comprehensive survey ever conducted on American Jews was published, revealing shocking statistics on intermarriage. The survey discovered that some 52 percent of Jews in the United States marry non-Jews. This intermarriage rate has undoubtedly increased during the past decade. Successful integration in all walks of life has facilitated closer contacts with potential marriage partners who are not Jewish, while the dispersion of Jews throughout America has made it harder to find Jewish partners. The second and third generation of Eastern European immigrants have largely accepted the fact that their children will not be Jewish and hope that their grandchildren will retain some connection with their Jewish roots.

American Jewish organizations are considered a success story. They are influential and enjoy a myth of power, although, in fact, most American Jews are not represented by them; and their titles often seem bombastic. The American Israel Public Affairs Committee (AIPAC) is a Jewish pro-Israel lobby whose effectiveness stems partly from its ability to influence congressional campaigns, providing or withholding support from candidates according to their stance on Israel.

AIPAC was formed in 1944 as the Washington branch of the Zionist movement. After the establishment of Israel, it became a lobby with offices in various Jewish communities. Even if it does not always succeed, AIPAC has maintained a successful image and still has a significant influence on Congress. Jews living in many other countries have sought to learn the secret of AIPAC's success, but have been unable to duplicate its record.

Another group that myth and reality combine to serve is the Conference of Presidents of Major American Jewish Organizations. Established in 1953 as an informal framework for coordinating the contacts of Jewish organizations with the U.S. government, it was intended to remedy the conflicts caused when each Jewish organization made separate approaches to the various government offices. The Conference's first leader was Nahum Goldmann, president of the World Zionist Organization. The Conference of Presidents later became the umbrella organization of American Jewish institutions and the principal official voice of U.S. Jews. Its organizational structure has grown to encompass some sixty institutions, five times the number of its member groups in 1953.

The most significant Jewish organizations represent the three main streams of American religious Judaism: the Reform, comprising the majority of American Jews; the Conservative, the second-largest group; and the Orthodox, who account for about 10 percent of U.S. Jews. These organizations have a more palpable connection with average American Jews. They are represented by synagogues, have varying degrees of financial assets and power, and have proven their ability to influence Israel on issues of religious legislation.

An important and influential American Jewish organization is the Anti-Defamation League (ADL), which is devoted to uncovering anti-Semitism and other expressions of racism in the United States and the world. It publishes reports on these subjects, and its opinions have a significant impact. Established in 1913 as part of the B'nai B'rith organization, the ADL became extremely active in the 1920s and thirties. It even infiltrated the cells of fascist organizations in the United States and reported on their activities to the Federal Bureau of Investigation. Despite the waning of anti-Semitism, the ADL still has an essential role in the struggle against racism, neo-fascism, and Holocaust deniers.

Two important organizations that have lost much of their luster are the American Jewish Congress and the American Jewish Committee. As mentioned earlier, German Jews established the Committee in 1906 mainly in order to pressure the Russian government to fight anti-Semitism. Despite its elitist nature and the fact that internal elections were never held, the Committee emerged as the main spokesman for American Jewry. Its moment of greatest achievement came when it convinced the U.S. Congress in 1911 to cancel a trade agreement with Russia in light of the severe, officially tolerated anti-Semitism there.

The American Jewish Congress was formed in 1917 in response to the demand by Russian immigrants for an elected, nonelitist organization. Elections were indeed held in 1917, but these were the first and last elections in this organization. Under the leadership of Rabbi Stephen Wise and his successors, the American Jewish Congress soon became a second elitist organization. A number of attempts to unite the Congress and the Committee—which have only about 30,000 members each—have consistently failed and they have settled into a position of polite cooperation.

B'nai B'rith, established in 1843, is the oldest American Jewish organization and the one most widely spread throughout the United States and the world. It was started by a dozen youngsters who, spurned by non-Jewish organizations, decided to form an association to promote their own goals and those of humanity. Beginning as a secret order to promote philanthropy and patriotism, it later evolved into an open organization with offices adjacent to the United Nations, in Israel, and in many Jewish communities throughout the world. Despite enjoying a large membership and a democratic framework, B'nai B'rith has lost much of its influence over the years.

The Jewish communities themselves have become more influential than the national organizations, with some 180 Jewish federations supporting educational, religious, and welfare institutions. The federations, which have recently taken over control of the United Jewish Appeal, determine how UJA funds will be allocated. These federations, and not the national organizations, run Jewish community life in America. Even the umbrella Council of Jewish Federations does more coordinating than directing. The recent merger between the CJF and UJA came as a result of the declining strength of both. It is apparent that local communities wish to determine their own futures and today's major contributors believe it is their right, and not the prerogative of national organizations, to decide how their donations should be allocated.

The federations will continue to exist, since they offer Jews in their local community a range of services from which to choose. Assimilation means that there are Jews leaving the community, and in some places less than half of the Jews are registered with the local federation, but it remains an orderly system, and one that is often very active and creative.

Most of the national organizations in the United States were created to respond to an immediate need, most often to express defiance. In this way, B'nai B'rith was born when Jews were not accepted in any other clubs; the American Jewish Committee was created to assist Jews throughout the world; the American Jewish Congress came into being as a result of a dispute with the American Jewish Committee; and AIPAC was established to protect Israel from harm. Some of the organizations lost sight of their original goals a long time ago. The American Zionist Movement had a reason to exist, for example, when there were anti-Zionist streams in American Jewry. Today, most of American Jews consider themselves Zionists, though only a few ever consider immigrating to Israel. Clearly, there is no longer any justification for a group such as the American Zionism Movement, but it continues to exist.

In the Conference of Presidents there are active organizations like Hadassah and other organizations mentioned above; but there are also dozens of obscure organizations that are decrepit vestiges of the past and continue to exist in name only. It is no wonder, then, that American Jews look skeptically upon their national organizations and prefer the local community. The exceptions to this rule are the powerful organizations representing the main religious streams of American Judaism, which have a national rather than a local character.

The American Jewish community may be characterized as a sort of plutocracy, dominated by its most affluent members. Since it is a voluntary system supported mainly through donations, large contributors play a decisive role in American Jewish organizations. Fund-raisers concentrate on courting the few major donors rather than bothering to pursue smaller contributions from a larger number of Jews.

A group of a few hundred individuals dominate the American Jewish institutions. This group is composed of two main parts: the professionals who work for several years managing a particular organization or community before moving on to another similar position, and the millionaires (and billionaires) who fund the organizations and communities. The latter are awarded titles of leadership and honorific chairmanships, but generally they yield nearly unlimited freedom of action to the Jewish professionals.

The end result is that the professionals actually lead the Jewish organizations in America. But this does not mean that the philanthropists feel left out. On the contrary, heading an important institution means widening their circle of social, political, and business connections. Titles carry considerable significance, and this reality informs the unwritten "deal" between the benefactors and the professionals. In many cases, the professionals play an important role in choosing "their leaders," generally preferring those who are not particularly assertive, so as to preserve their own autonomy.

A consequence of this development is a weakening of the Jewish leadership in the United States. For years, there has not been an outstanding Jewish leader who could speak on behalf of American Jews and influence them. The forced rotation of voluntary leaders does not allow them to have a meaningful voice in the organizations they head, and by default the professionals become the address to which Israeli and American officials turn. But these professionals do not seem to aim to become leaders in any real sense, or else they are incapable of leading.

Whoever does not fit into one of these two categories—major contributor or Jewish professional—is, in effect, excluded from the inner circle. Jewish intellectuals do not find their way onto the playing field of Jewish leadership in America, and the absence of this large group of potential leaders is acutely felt. Senior Jewish politicians, including members of the Senate and the House of Representatives, play no leadership role in the Jewish world. They are the first address for the pro-Israel or pro-Jewish lobbies, but are not the leaders.

The Jews of the United States have replaced the Russian Jews of a century ago, the time of the First Zionist Congress, as the largest Jewish community in the world, with 5.6 million Jews. But here the similarity ends. While the Judaism of the Jews of Russia was taken for granted, there is a real question of Jewish continuity in America. The more the United States is ready to integrate the Jews in all walks of life, the faster assimilation accelerates.

The process of secularization took away the religious common denominator that existed for Jews in Russia. The process of Americanization took away the common language (Yiddish) that Jews shared. The further the Jews are from their original generation of immigrants, the less likely they are to maintain Jewish connections, live in Jewish neighborhoods, join Jewish clubs, and send their children to Jewish summer camps. Interactions between Jews become more infrequent and opportunities to meet Jewish marriage partners likewise decrease. The American bear hug has led to unprecedented rates of assimilation and intermarriage, which are steadily diminishing the numbers of Jews in America.

According to one estimate, the population of Jews in America will plummet to 10,000 by the year 2067. In any case, during the twenty-first century, which promises to be the first century in history when Jews will not face an external threat, American Jewry will lose its numerical preeminence and Israel will become the largest Jewish community in the world—for the first time in thousands of years.

## Canadian Jewry

The Jewish community of Canada, unlike the U.S. Jewish community, is steadily growing. It is a younger community and currently numbers some 360,000, concentrated mainly in Toronto and Montreal. Immigrants and the second-generation comprise a significant part of the community. The new Jewish immigrants to Canada come from Russia, South Africa, and even from Ethiopia. An earlier wave of immigration arrived from Morocco.

About 40 percent of the children in the community attend Jewish elementary day schools and some 20 percent continue in Jewish high schools. While only 10 percent of the U.S. Jews identify themselves as

Orthodox, the proportion in Canada is 40 percent. Another 40 percent are Conservative and 20 percent align themselves with the Reform movement. A Jewish press has developed in Canada and there are Jewish clubs. The intermarriage rate is rising, but it is still much lower than the prevailing rate in the United States.

Canada is the fifth-largest Jewish community in the world. Most of its Jews are organized under the Canadian Jewish Congress, the community's umbrella group. The first Jews arrived in Canada after the British defeated the French in the second half of the eighteenth century, but during the next one hundred years, the community grew very slowly. Some 2,500 Jews arrived from Lithuania and settled in Montreal.

The Jews of Russia are the ones who made Canada the home of hundreds of thousands of Jews. Large-scale immigration began in the 1880s, and by 1921 there were about 126,000 Jews in Canada. As in the United States, the gates of immigration to Canada closed during the most critical years for the Jews—the 1930s and forties. After the end of World War II, the Jews of Canada lobbied for the renewal of immigration and the number of Jews in Canada by 1961 reached about 260,000.

The next wave of Jewish immigration to Canada came from North Africa—Jews who settled comfortably in the French-speaking milieu of Montreal. Over the past thirty years, the Jewish community in Canada swelled by 50 percent, making it the fastest-growing Diaspora community in the world. Approximately 30,000 Jews have emigrated from Israel to Canada, while only some 8,000 Canadian Jews have immigrated to Israel since 1948.

Recent years have seen a steady flow of Jews—mainly English-speakers—from Montreal to Toronto. These Jews are concerned that Montreal, the capital of Quebec, will become part of an independent entity that will secede from Canada. At the end of the 1970s, there were about 100,000 Jews in each of these cities, but two decades later, there are some 175,000 Jews in Toronto, while the Jewish population in Montreal remains at 100,000.

Canada will continue to absorb Jewish immigrants in the coming years, especially from the former Soviet Union and South Africa. The number of immigrants will likely offset the number of Jews lost to assimilation. In the twenty-first century, the situation in Canada will probably come to resemble that in the United States: fewer fourth-and fifth-generation Jews will attend Jewish schools, and the rate of intermarriage will significantly increase.

## European Jewry

The Jewish community in Europe, decimated earlier in the century by emigration and by the Holocaust, is diminishing at an accelerated pace due both to assimilation and low birthrates. On the eve of World War II, there were about ten million Jews in Europe, including the European parts of the Soviet Union. In 1944, less than five million remained, and in 1994 there were less than two million.

The gates of the world were closed to the Jews at just the time they sought to flee the Nazi regime in Germany. For example, only 50,000 Jews managed to escape Germany and Austria during the years 1933 to 1939, most finding refuge in Britain. Even after the war, the gates remained shut, the victorious Allies intending to settle the Jewish survivors in their countries of origin, mainly in Poland.

This was a terrible mistake. Many Jews who tried to return to their homes were expelled or murdered. Hundreds of Jews were killed in pogroms in Poland after the war and before the end of 1945. A serious pogrom occurred in 1946 following the dissemination of a blood libel against the Jews in Poland. From the end of the war in 1945 to 1947, some 1,500 Jews were murdered in Poland. The property of Jews was transferred to non-Jews or nationalized by the new Communist regimes in Eastern Europe. With no place to return and no possibility of immigrating to the West or Israel, they found themselves languishing in displaced-persons camps. The number of displaced persons reached 150,000 in 1947, and the camps did not finally close until 1957, after most of the Jews had immigrated to Israel or America.

## Jews of the Former Soviet Union

The largest concentration of European Jews was, and still remains, in the area of the former Soviet Union. Of the five million Jews living in the Soviet Union on the eve of World War II, the Nazis murdered nearly two million.

Life was also very difficult in the postwar period, Stalin's last years, for the more than three million Soviet Jews who survived the war and the Holocaust. They were forbidden to leave the country or maintain contact with their relatives in Israel. Restrictions were imposed on the Jews as a "middle-class" group, limiting their business and academic options. Hebrew instruction and Jewish schools were completely shut down. In 1948, the Soviet Union outlawed all Jewish publications. After briefly supporting the establishment of the State of Israel, the Soviets transferred their support to the cause of Arab nationalism in order to weaken the influence of the West in the Middle East.

The hostility toward Jews in the Stalinist period peaked during the Writers' Trial, in 1952, and the Doctors' Trial, in 1953, when an important segment of the Soviet Jewish elite was put to death. To a certain extent, the Jews were able to breathe a sigh of relief during the Khrushchev period.

The first census in the U.S.S.R. in 1959 indicated a Jewish population of 2,267,000. The Jews were mostly urban, highly educated professionals. Yiddish was the language of only a few, and assimilation was rampant. In 1970, the Jews numbered only about 2,150,000, most of them living in Moscow, Leningrad, and Kiev. They were prominent in the fields of physics and mathematics, comprising 14 percent of Soviet scientists in the 1970s.

Immediately following the Six-Day War, all of the Communist Bloc countries—except Romania—cut off relations with Israel. Soviet Jews were urged to publicly criticize Israel, and many were accused of divided loyalty. In 1968, Jews began to disseminate underground publications, mostly Russian translations of Israeli and Jewish literature. Some signed petitions demanding the right to emigrate to Israel, and in 1970, a group of young people tried to hijack a plane in an attempt to reach Israel.

In 1971, when emigration to Israel was first permitted, many Jews grabbed this opportunity, with great excitement. At one point, the Soviet authorities tried to impose a ransom on Jews with higher education, amounting to thousands of dollars for each Soviet émigré, depending on his or her academic degree. However, the large movement formed in the West on behalf of Soviet Jews pressured the U.S.S.R. to drop their ransom demand.

During the eight years in the 1970s when emigration was permitted, some 250,000 Jews left the Soviet Union, most of them arriving in Israel. This window of opportunity closed in 1979 as the Soviet invasion of Afghanistan led to a deterioration of the relations between the U.S.S.R. and the West.

In the 1980s, several thousand Jews were allowed to leave the Soviet Union, most of them migrating to the United States. Israel and international Jewish organizations lobbied to open the gates of the U.S.S.R. for Jewish emigrants. The Jewish organizations, however, did not stipulate a destination, while Israel demanded that the Jewish emigrants must come to Israel. Israel understood that, given a choice of destinations, most Soviet Jews would choose America. For this reason, Israel called on the U.S. to deny them "refugee" status, since, under Israel's Law of Return, Soviet Jews could claim immediate citizenship in Israel.

In 1989, the United States ended refugee status for the Russian Jews and limited the immigration of Soviet Jews to less than 50,000 per year. In the same year, the gates of the U.S.S.R. were opened to all Soviet citizens wishing to emigrate, with no limitation. Concerned for their future—and their safety—as the Soviet Union began to break apart, they did not gamble on the chance of getting a rare visa to America and arrived in Israel in large numbers, even if this was not really their destination of choice.

Since 1989 some 1,000,000 Jews from the former Soviet Union have immigrated to Israel, about 200,000 to America, and tens of thousands to Germany. The scope of anti-Semitism in Russia has proven to be less than anticipated by some of the emigrants, though hostility toward Jews is spread by the magazine *Pamyat* and is manifest in the anti-Semitic platform of Vladimir Zhirinovsky, who won significant support in the Russian elections in 1996.

Emigration from the former Soviet Union has slowed in recent years, but a steady flow of immigrants to Israel continues. Less than 100,000 Jews leave the Commonwealth of Independent States (C.I.S.) each year, with approximately 50,000 arriving in Israel. The number of Jews in Russia today is about 360,000; the Jewish population of Ukraine is approximately 180,000.

The Jews who chose to remain in Russia and Ukraine now live in a system in which they are free to shape their institutions as they choose. They are forming Jewish federations and trying to resurrect a community life that was nonexistent during the seventy-five years of Communist rule. But at the current rate of emigration, the combined Jewish population of Ukraine and Russia will soon dip to less than 500,000. Moreover—and paradoxically—now that the restrictions on synagogues and Jewish cultural activities have finally been lifted, the Jews in Russia and Ukraine will likely assimilate more quickly than they did during the Communist period.

The instability of their situation makes it difficult for Jews to forge a complete institutional system in Russia and other states of the C.I.S. The two largest Jewish communities in the world—the United States and Israel—prefer to view the Jews in the C.I.S. as a community in transition that will virtually disappear after a few years through emigration. Nevertheless, there are groups of Jews trying to build an institutionalized local system, on the assumption that hundreds of thousands of Jews will choose to remain in their countries of origin.

During the Communist period, the Jews of the U.S.S.R. were able to regard themselves as Jews living in a multinational society. The breakdown into smaller national units has made the question of identity more acute for them. (This also applies to Czechoslovakia, which was divided into two national entities, and to Yugoslavia.) The possibility of creating a structure for Jewish communities to deal with issues of education, culture, and other matters of Jewish concern is largely dependent on the structure of the states in the C.I.S.—on their level of democracy and the scope of civic activities permitted outside the governmental realm.

The natural leaders of Soviet Jewry were the first to leave the country and immigrate to Israel. In the process of realizing their own dreams, they left behind a weak and hesitant community, which soon learned of the difficulties new immigrants faced in Israel. Some have clearly decided to remain where they are, but others are still wavering. Anti-Semitism or an economic crisis could change the minds of the undecided.

In December 1989, the Assembly of Jews of the Soviet Union gathered for the first time, and Jewish federations began to form in the various states of the U.S.S.R. In Russia, a Zionist "council" was established, which first emphasized the issue of Jewish culture but quickly turned to promoting *aliyah*. Later, the focus shifted back to building the community and assisting Jewish refugees within Russia, including those who fled the fighting in Chechnya. Jewish education has increasingly become the central issue, and the main questions facing Russian Jewry are: Who are the Jews of Russia? How many of them will remain in Russia, and how many of these will want to retain a Jewish connection?

In June 1996, the Russian Duma passed the Cultural Autonomy Law, which enables Jews to organize and promote their culture on a recognized legal basis. It remains to be seen whether the remaining Jews in Russia will be interested in this kind of autonomy.

Ukraine was the most important Jewish center of what was called "Russian Jewry." It was also the scene of the Chmielnicki pogroms in the mid-seventeenth century and brutal attacks against the Jews during the nineteenth century. Most of the major cities of Ukraine were captured by the Nazis during World War II, and most of the Jews who did not manage to flee were murdered by the Nazis or their Ukrainian accomplices. The terrible slaughter at Babi Yar remains for many in the former Soviet Union the most potent symbol of the Holocaust. Under the Communist regime, all official Jewish activity was banned; any religious or cultural activities took place underground. Following the large wave of emigration earlier in the decade, and amidst an ongoing, albeit smaller, emigration trend today, the Jewish population of Ukraine is aging. The median age is fifty-six, with ten deaths registered for every birth.

Following the breakup of the Soviet Union, no less than four Jewish organizations vie to represent the community. There are Jewish day schools and Sunday schools, Jewish newspapers, theaters, and other cultural institutions. Hebrew and Yiddish are taught, and there are synagogues and other religious services. There is tension between those wishing to establish regular community life and those who see the Jews of Ukraine mainly as potential emigrants. Local activists complain that world Jewry invests ten times more promoting Jews to emigrate than in support of those seeking to establish their own institutions in Ukraine.

It is hard to predict how the Ukrainian Jewish community will develop in the twenty-first century. Demographically, emigration is decreasing its numbers. Jewish parents are not quick to send their children to Jewish schools, fearing that this would alienate them from their Ukrainian neighbors. The unstable economic and political situation in Ukraine could easily speed up emigration, and this aging and declining community would further shrink in stature.

A shrinking Jewish population and assimilation characterize all of the European communities of the former Soviet Union. The demise of the Communist regime and the subsequent cultural freedom extended to the Jews may have come just in time to allow some chance for Jewish life to be rehabilitated. That is, Soviet Jewry might well have become an abstract concept if another generation or two had passed with no possibility of maintaining any Jewish life. The fact that the Soviet regime collapsed while some Holocaust survivors and other Jews connected to their "roots" were still alive, and while there were young people willing to take risks to assert their Jewish nationality, enabled the large-scale emigration of Soviet Jews, most of whom arrived in Israel.

There are, of course, Jews who feel that their fates are tied to that of Russia, Ukraine, Belarus, Moldavia, or Latvia, and believe that they can preserve their identity as Jews and even develop this identity in an open and democratic society. But it is safe to say that most of those who decide to stay are prepared to give up their Jewish identity. If there indeed remain significant Jewish communities in the Commonwealth of Independent States, it would not be surprising if they assimilate in the twenty-first century at a faster pace than they did in the twentieth.

## Hungary

Outside of the Commonwealth of Independent States, only one large Jewish community remains in the former Communist region of Europe: Hungary, with its 54,000 Jews. The Jews of Hungary stayed because of the positive attitude evinced by Hungarian leaders toward the country's Jews ever since the state became independent in 1867. Equal rights were extended to Hungarian Jews shortly before the First Zionist Congress. Despite this, many assimilating Jews chose to convert to Christianity. During the short-lived Hungarian republic established after World War I, Jews filled 161 of the top 203 government positions. The right-wing regime that replaced the republic after only 133 days sought revenge against the Jews. The subsequent "White Terror" led to the murder of about 3,000 Jews, and a series of anti-Semitic legislations was passed in Hungary in the 1930s.

During the Holocaust, approximately 600,000 Hungarian Jews were killed, some as a result of cooperation between the Nazis and Hungarian fascists. Anti-Jewish feelings persisted after the end of World War II, and pogroms occurred in a number of places throughout Hungary. The return of the Communist regime in Hungary also brought renewed involvement of many Jews in government, a prime example being Mátyás Rákosi, who led the Stalinist regime in Hungary until the uprising of October 1956.

The Soviet tanks that crushed this uprising ushered in a new nationalistic, anti-Jewish wave. Tens of thousands of Hungarians fled on foot toward the Austrian border, including many Jews who feared for their lives. Of the 20,000 Jews who left Hungary during this period, some 9,000 arrived in Israel, with the rest landing in the United States, Canada, and Great Britain.

However, a relatively comfortable period for the Jews ensued. The regime installed by the U.S.S.R. and led by János Kádár allowed unrestricted religious ritual and other nationalistic cultural expressions. Dozens of synagogues were established in Budapest, as well as a kosher restaurant, a Jewish day school, a hospital, an orphan's home, and a radio station that broadcast Jewish prayers. In 1970, Jews comprised 25 percent of the Central Committee of the Hungarian Communist Party, but emigration and Zionist activities were prohibited, except for the annual memorial for Theodor Herzl.

In 1967, Hungary was the last Eastern European country to cut off diplomatic relations with Israel. From 1967 until 1989, when relations were renewed, Jews lived in Hungary under a relatively tolerant regime that allowed them either to maintain a Jewish lifestyle or freely assimilate. This toleration explains the fact that Jews did not hurry to leave Hungary when the gates were finally opened after the collapse of the Communist regime. There are, similarly, no signs that Hungarian Jews will choose to emigrate in the twenty-first century. There is thus a larger degree of stability in the Jewish presence in Hungary, as opposed to that of many communities in the former Soviet Union, where emigration is ongoing.

## Other Eastern European Communities

There are only some 14,000 Jews remaining in Romania today and this number will continue to decrease. Fewer than 8,000 Jews live in Poland, about 6,000 are in Lithuania, 3,000 in Estonia, the same number in Bulgaria, 2,500 in Yugoslavia, and 2,000 in Croatia. The reality underlying these numbers is that very few Jews will be living in Eastern Europe in the twenty-first century, the possible exceptions being the communities in Russia, Ukraine, and Hungary.

Romania was the only Communist state not to break off diplomatic relations with Israel and to allow Jews to emigrate (albeit in return for a ransom payment of about $3,000 per Jewish émigré). Prior to World War II, some 850,000 Jews lived in Romania and about half—420,000—remained after the war. During the postwar period, Jews enjoyed religious freedom, but were subject to anti-Semitic outbreaks, and were eager to leave Romania if given the chance. Some 273,000 Romanian Jews emigrated to Israel since 1948.

Poland, which became the cemetery of European Jewry during the Holocaust, continued to be anti-Semitic after World War II and its remaining Jews fled whenever possible. By 1951, some 106,000 Polish Jews immigrated to the State of Israel. Up until 1956, there were still some Jews in positions of power in Poland, but they were at that time removed from positions in government, academia, and the media for not being "proletarian."

After the Six-Day War in 1967, the situation of Polish Jewry became even worse. Wladyslaw Gomulka, the Polish leader, charged Polish Jews with divided loyalty and portrayed them as a fifth column. Following a wave of anti-Semitism, some 14,000 Jews left Poland in the years 1968 through 1972, some 10,000 of them reaching North America and the rest arriving in Israel. During the 1970s, there appeared to be almost no Jews remaining in Poland. Only later did it emerge that the number of Jews was greater than earlier reported, as several thousand Jews revealed their Jewish background once the Communist regime was replaced by a democratic one.

Anti-Semitism in Poland did not end with the disappearance of the

Jews. At election rallies, it is still common to ascribe Jewish roots to political rivals, who are quick to deny any such background. This was the case, for example, when the leaders of the Solidarity movement came to power and felt compelled to explain that they had no Jewish roots.

The Jewish population in Czechoslovakia stood at 375,000 before World War II, but only 55,000 of them survived the war. During the 1950s, there was an atmosphere of anti-Semitism in the country that peaked in a series of showcase trials in which Jews were accused of subversive activities in the name of Zionism. The hopes that attended the reforms of Dubcek in the spring of 1968 were quickly dashed, and in the wake of systematic anti-Semitic incitements unleashed by the pro-Soviet media, about one-half of the Jews of Czechoslovakia left the country. The division of the country into two national states on January 1, 1993, awakened nationalistic emotions and revived anti-Jewish feelings, especially in Slovakia. Prior to this partition of the state, it was often joked that the only real Czechoslovakians were the Jews.

In Yugoslavia, Jews enjoyed full equality of rights under the Tito regime, but this came too late for most of the Jews in Serbia, who were annihilated in the wake of the German invasion during World War II. Unlike the Jews of Eastern Europe, the Jews of Yugoslavia maintained contact with the Jewish world and Israel. However, just as in Czechoslovakia, anti-Jewish emotions were awakened when the state was divided into separate national entities in 1991–92. The civil war found the Jews in a very difficult situation. The Jews of Sarajevo emigrated to Israel, and the remaining Jews live in Serbia. The aging Jewish community in Serbia, with its high rate of intermarriage in the younger generation, will likely cease to exist during the twenty-first century.

## Western European Communities

The largest Jewish community in Western Europe is found in France, home to 525,000 Jews. Of the 300,000 Jews who lived in France prior to World War II, some 70,000 were killed by the Nazis, aided by the French police. During the first three years after the war, about 80,000 Jews from Eastern Europe arrived in France. Another group of about 10,000 Jews came to France from Egypt in the 1950s. However, the biggest influx of

Jews came as a result of Algeria's war against France, and the Jewish population of France doubled after Algeria gained its independence.

The Jews of France are an integral part of the political-cultural-social fabric of the country. Jews are prominent in the field of literature and are represented in the National Assembly. There are Jewish ministers in every government and Jews have also served as prime ministers of France. Approximately 40 percent of French Jews are registered in synagogues or Jewish organizations, and about 25 percent of Jewish children receive Jewish education. Two national organizations represent the community: the Conseil Représentatif des Institutions Juives de France (CRIF) is a secular organization that handles the political and social affairs of French Jewry, while the Consistoire de Juifs de France is a religious framework that supervises the chief rabbinate and the rabbinical court.

Recent anti-Semitic incidents in France have included acts of terror against Jewish targets and the desecration of the Jewish cemetery in Carpentre, near Avignon, in 1990. Anti-Semitism is also reflected in the rise of the extreme right led by Le Pen. Still, French Jewry is undaunted, deeply rooted, and organized.

The significant impact of French Jews has accorded the community special consideration in election campaigns since 1973. While comprising only 1 percent of French citizenry, they number 7 to 10 percent of voters in some areas. Most French Jews tend to vote for the left, and candidates vying for their votes try to portray themselves as more fervent supporters of Israel than their opponents.

The Jewish community in France, nevertheless, is shrinking. The rate of intermarriage stands at about 60 percent, while the natural increase of French Jews is low. Only some 34,000 French Jews have arrived in Israel since 1948. It has been a community that has absorbed more immigrants than it has produced. If the current trends continue, we can expect that French Jewry will continue to constitute one of the most prominent Jewish communities in the world in the twenty-first century, while its numbers gradually decrease.

The Jewish community in Great Britain is shrinking at an even faster rate than that of France. Home to some 292,000 Jews, it is the second-largest Jewish community in Western Europe, built upon several waves of immigration. German Jews arrived toward the end of the nineteenth century, but between 1881 and 1914 a wave of Russian Jewish immigration made this group the largest component of the community. British Jews numbered about 300,000 on the eve of World War I. Another wave of Jewish immigrants from Germany arrived during the 1930s.

The Jews of Great Britain were the only large Jewish community in Europe (besides the Jewish communities of Sweden and Switzerland) to survive the Holocaust intact. The Jewish population peaked in the 1950s, when the number of Jews climbed to 410,000; yet their very low rate of natural increase and their high rate of intermarriage have steadily eroded the community. It is not an emigrant community: only about 26,500 of its members have immigrated to Israel since 1948, and many of them eventually returned to live in Great Britain.

It is, instead, an established community whose members belong to the British middle class. There are well-developed community organizations, and Jewish education reaches about one-third of the children. The long-lived *Jewish Chronicle* (London) is still the most important Jewish newspaper in the world that is not written in Hebrew. The Board of Deputies was established to represent British Jewry in the nineteenth century and still exists, although the most influential segment of the population are the affluent British Jews who finance the community's activities.

Most Jews tend to support the Labour Party, though the number of Jewish ministers and members of Parliament peaked during the days of Prime Minister Margaret Thatcher, when a number of Jews served as Conservative Party representatives. Despite their relatively small numbers, British Jews play a significant role in the country's political life. Similar to the situation in the United States, but to a lesser extent, their political fund-raising is an important source of their influence.

While the Jewish communities in London and Manchester are maintaining their substantial size, the smaller Jewish communities in Great Britain are gradually disappearing and the overall trend is clearly one of contraction. It will remain an important Jewish community in the twenty-first century but will likely drop to half its current size or less if current trends continue.

Germany is one of the few European Jewish communities whose population is on the rise. (Spain and Sweden also have growing Jewish communities.) There were 503,000 Jews in Germany in 1933 and some of them managed to flee to England, the United States, and Palestine. From 1938, there was no place of refuge open to German Jews, and 180,000 of them were murdered in the Holocaust. At the end of World War II, only a few Jews remained in Germany. They were joined by displaced Jews from Eastern Europe and 2,500 German Jews who returned from their wartime refuge in Shanghai.

In 1956, there were already 16,000 Jews in Germany. When the gates of the Soviet Union and other Eastern European states were opened, the members of the German Jewish community tried to absorb the emigrants. This happened in the case of Soviet Jewish emigrants in 1970 and in other situations. Israelis also contributed to the growth of the community: some 9,000 of them settled in Germany during the 1980s. German Jews now number about 62,000, including those living in the former East Germany.

The communities are confederated under the officially recognized Central Council of the Jews of Germany. The Central Council deals with the everyday concerns of the Jewish community, handles the reparation payments to victims of the Nazis, and tracks the persistent manifestations of neo-Nazism in Germany. There are some eighty extreme-right-wing groups in Germany, with a total membership of about 65,000; these groups are responsible for the desecration of Jewish cemeteries and vandalism of synagogues.

The Jewish community in Germany is well established and offers its members Jewish services including schools, synagogues, cemeteries, and kosher food. There are Jewish museums in Germany, as well as regular Jewish publications in German and Yiddish. It is a Jewish community whose growth is not due to natural increase, but to newcomers who join. It is reasonable to assume that Germany will continue to attract Jews from Eastern Europe as long as the community is interested in growing and as long as the German government continues to lend its hand to this immigration.

In reviewing the distribution of Jews in Europe today, it becomes apparent that, for the first time since the eighteenth century, the number of Jews is less than two million: there are about 1,741,000 Jews in Europe today, including both the West and the East; and for the first time since the Middle Ages, there are more Jews in Western Europe than in Eastern Europe.

Throughout Europe, the rate of natural increase among Jews is lower than that of the surrounding population, and the Jewish birthrate is not keeping pace with the death rate. The population, therefore, is aging and shrinking.

The wave of immigration from the former Soviet Union, which began in 1989, is the largest since World War I and is directed mainly at the West and Israel. If the situation in the Commonwealth of Independent States does not significantly improve, this immigration trend will continue and perhaps grow, bringing hundreds of thousands more to the West and Israel during the next century.

Anti-Semitism exists in both Western and Eastern Europe, yet it is less severe than ever before and is not now a catalyst for Jewish emigration. In most of the places where Jews live today in Europe, their Jewishness is not considered a disadvantage. Jews do not feel compelled to convert to Christianity, or even to change their names, in order to feel part of European society. They are integrated and accepted in society, and they find it natural to pair off with non-Jewish spouses and distance themselves from the Jewish collective.

Is a rejuvenation of European Jewry possible? On the face of it, there are reasons to believe so. Never have European Jews lived as they do today. Throughout Europe, there are no restrictions on Jewish emigration. All of the Jews live in democratic countries and enjoy equal rights. They no longer feel obliged to be greater "patriots" than their Christian neighbors in order to experience this equality.

The downfall of the Communist regimes in Europe and the diplomatic relations between the Vatican and Israel enable Jews to be influential in a Europe that is undergoing a process of unification. Jewish history—with a special emphasis on the Holocaust of European Jewry— is now being studied everywhere and is of great interest even to non-Jews.

With the weakening of nationalist sentiments as the European Community develops, Jews are in a position to build connections across a continent where they have given so much of themselves. The Jews are, in fact, the old-timers of the continent, who created the Judeo-Christian culture and have always flourished in multinational communities.

A pan-European Jewish community has not yet emerged. If this does happen, the European community will comprise one of the three points in a triangular relationship between the Jews of North America, Israel, and Europe. A triangle like this could strengthen European Jewry and prevent the scenario that some predict—in which no Jews would remain in Europe by the end of the century.

## Jews in Latin America

The two largest Jewish communities in Latin America are found in Argentina and Brazil. There are about 206,000 Jews in Argentina today, most of them living in Buenos Aires, the capital city. A large wave of immigrants arrived in Argentina from Russia after 1881, while others chose to land in the United States. Argentina's advantage in those years was in its openness to immigrants. Baron Maurice de Hirsch formed the Jewish Colonization Association in 1891 to provide for the creation of Jewish colonies in Argentina and Brazil. A small portion of the Russian Jewish immigrants settled in these colonies, but most made their homes in the big city.

Prior to this large wave from Russia, there was Jewish immigration from France and Central Europe in the mid-nineteenth century. Marranos from Portugal and Spain arrived in Argentina in the sixteenth and seventeenth centuries but quickly assimilated into the Christian population. Some 15 percent of the Jews of Argentina came from Muslim countries, in particular Turkey, North Africa, and Syria.

Jewish life in Argentina is highly organized, with 20 percent of the children receiving Jewish education and some belonging to Zionist youth movements. Since 1948, about 45,000 Jews from Argentina have immigrated to Israel. The Delegation of Jewish Associations in Argentina (DAIA) is the central political organization of Jews in Argentina, dealing with education, culture, and social welfare. It is also forced to confront the incidents of anti-Semitism that occur from time to time. In 1992, there was a terrorist attack on the Israeli Embassy in Buenos Aires, and in July 1994 a bomb exploded in the Jewish community center in the city, killing one hundred people and destroying the building. Both of these incidents followed Israeli attacks against Hezbollah leaders in Lebanon.

The story of Brazilian Jewry is similar to that of the Jews of Argentina. Russian Jews arrived at the beginning of the twentieth century, settling in the southern part of the country in Baron de Hirsch's colonies, as well as in the cities. Earlier, Moroccan Jews had arrived shortly after Brazil's declaration of independence in 1822. (As in Argentina, Marrano Jews had arrived also in Brazil in the sixteenth century.) In the 1930s, Brazil closed its gates to immigration, but after World War II, Jewish immigrants came to Brazil from Hungary and several Muslim countries, including Turkey, Syria, Lebanon, and Morocco.

Today there are about 100,000 Jews living in São Paulo and Rio de Janeiro. Most of them are economically prosperous. Brazilian Jews are organized under the Jewish Federation of Brazil (CONIB) umbrella group, which maintains Jewish educational institutions, clubs, and a social-welfare system. Only 8,400 Jews have immigrated to Israel from Brazil during the last fifty years.

## Australian Jewry

Approximately 92,000 Jews currently live in Australia, mostly in Melbourne and Sydney. The Jewish community of Melbourne is largely composed of Jews of Polish extraction, while most of the Jews of Sydney came from Germany or England. This is a relatively new community. The first Jews to arrive in this former penal colony were prisoners expelled from Britain in the eighteenth century. In the nineteenth century, Jews followed from Britain and Eastern Europe during Australia's gold rush. The first large wave of immigration came in the 1930s, when some 7,000 refugees arrived from Germany and Austria.

After World War II, tens of thousands of Holocaust survivors arrived in Australia, making it the Jewish community with the largest proportion of Holocaust survivors in the world. During the 1970s, Jewish immigrants from the Soviet Union landed in Australia and, in recent years, many Jews from South Africa are moving there.

Since many of the Jews of Australia are the first- or second-generation, there is a strong Jewish consciousness in this community. The Zionist movement is also significant in Australia. Jewish education is well developed, and the Mount Scopus school in Melbourne is considered the largest Jewish day school in the world. The Shalom Aleichem school in Melbourne is still affiliated with the Bund and children still learn Yiddish there. The percentage of pupils registered in Jewish schools is high. There is a Jewish press, as well as Jewish radio broadcasts in English, Hebrew, and Yiddish. Jewish student activities abound and the rate of assimilation, at 10 percent, is one of the lowest in the world.

The Executive Committee of Australian Jewry is the umbrella organization of this community. Zionist youth movements and organizations belong to the Zionist Federation of Australia. More than 3,500 Jews have immigrated to Israel from Australia since 1948.

This community is likely to grow during the century due to Australia's relative openness to immigration and the continuing flow of Jews from South Africa and the former Soviet Union. And even if the pace of assimilation in Australia increases, it will still be far less than that being experienced in either the United States or Europe.

## Jews in South Africa

There are approximately 95,000 Jews in South Africa today. It is a relatively new community in a country where Jews were not allowed to live until the beginning of the nineteenth century. A large wave of immigration began in the 1880s from Lithuania and the number of Jews in South Africa reached 40,000 by 1910. Immigration restrictions were imposed in the 1930s, and Jewish immigration from Germany was prohibited in 1937. Still, some 8,000 Jews managed to escape Europe and arrive in South Africa. Jews came to South Africa in the 1940s from Germany and Britain. They first settled in Johannesburg, which continues to be the major center of South African Jewry, and later in Cape Town.

South African Jews tend to hold liberal views and were consistently among the opponents of apartheid. However, the end of apartheid created a new situation of insecurity for the Jews who have achieved financial success in South Africa. This community has a Zionist tradition and 16,300 Jews have immigrated to Israel since 1948. Some 10,000 Israelis have also settled in South Africa.

The Council of Community Representatives of South Africa represents the Jews of the country and is recognized as the liaison to the government. The Jewish educational system is well developed, and the Zionist youth movements are represented. On the other hand, it is an aging community with a growing rate of intermarriage, which, at least to date, remains lower than that in most Jewish communities in the world.

South African Jewry is in transition and its numbers are shrinking. If Jews there feel their security and influence eroding at the beginning of the twenty-first century, they may decide to leave the continent, as the Jewish community in Rhodesia/Zimbabwe did in the 1970s. Israel has failed to attract significant numbers of Jewish emigrants from South Africa, and they apparently will continue to immigrate instead to North America (especially Canada) and Australia.

# Glossary

*Aliyah*  Jewish immigration to the Land of Israel (literally, "ascent"). Until the late nineteenth century, *aliyah* had a specifically religious character. From 1882 on, Jewish immigration from the Diaspora acquired a more secular character. Several major waves of immigration are clearly identifiable: the First Aliyah (25,000 immigrants in the 1880s); the Second Aliyah (35,000 from 1904 to 1914); the Third Aliyah (37,000 from 1919 to 1923); the Fourth Aliyah (83,000 from 1924 to 1928); and the Fifth Aliyah (235,000 from 1930 to 1939).

*Canaanite*  A movement in the late 1920s that called for the creation of a new "Hebrew" nation that would disassociate itself with the Jewish people and include all residents of Palestine—Jews and Arabs alike.

*Haganah*  An underground military organization affiliated with the labor movement in prestate Israel. The Haganah, active in defending Jews in the years 1920–48, was the largest of several underground military groups and became the core of what is today the Israel Defense Forces.

*Halachah*  The religious laws and rules that define the lifestyle of Orthodox Jews. Religious political parties in Israel have invoked the *halachah* in their efforts to withhold recognition from Reform and

Conservative rabbis, and from those who have been converted to Judaism by them.

*Haredim*   Ultra-Orthodox Jews who, for the most part, view the establishment of the State of Israel before the coming of the Messiah as a rash and mistaken endeavor.

*Hovevei Zion (Lovers of Zion)*   Members of the Hibbat Zion movement formed in Russia in the early 1880s under the leadership of Dr. Leo Pinsker. This movement called on the Jews of Europe to move to Palestine in order to renew their lives there. Many Hovevei Zion joined the Zionist movement when it was formed by Herzl.

*Keren HaKayemet (Jewish National Fund)*   A fund initiated in 1901 for acquiring land in Palestine for Jewish settlement.

*Keren HaYesod (Foundation Fund)*   A Jewish fund-raising organization established in 1920 by the Zionist Organization primarily to finance immigration and absorption in Palestine. During the prestate years, Keren HaYesod also funded economic projects, agricultural settlements, and defense costs.

*Kvutzah*   A cooperative framework for communal living, based on mutual assistance and guarantees, and including both private and collective ownership. (Similar to the *kibbutz,* later development of the *kvutzah.*)

*Sanhedrin*   A body of seventy-one sages who served as the supreme religious court for the Jews living in the Land of Israel from the sixth century B.C. through the first century of the Common Era.

*The Land of Israel*   The area between the Mediterranean Sea and the Syrian Desert, referred to as Palestine since the second century. The borders of the land of Israel changed frequently under various rulers. At the time of the British Mandate, the Land of Israel, or Palestine, included what is now the Kingdom of Jordan, the West Bank, and Israel.

*Yishuv*   The community and social-political framework of Jewish immigrants who arrived in Palestine beginning in the late 1800s. This term refers to the period preceding statehood in 1948, but does not include the "old yishuv," the community of religious Jews who have lived in the Holy Land continuously throughout the centuries, particularly in the cities of Jerusalem, Hebron, Safed, and Tiberias.

*Zeirei Zion*   An organization of young people advocating a life of labor in the Land of Israel, first organized as a political party in 1903 in Russia, Romania, and Galicia. Some of the members of this organization immigrated to Palestine during the Second Aliyah (1904–14).

*Zionei Zion*   A group of delegates to the Seventh Zionist Congress who opposed the Uganda proposal. Organized under Menahem Ussishkin's leadership, they asserted that only the Land of Israel could be the goal of Zionist activity.

# Bibliography

## BOOKS IN ENGLISH

Yossi Beilin. *Touching Peace: From the Oslo Accord to a Final Agreement.* London: Weidenfeld & Nicolson, 1999.

Avraham Ben Zvi. *Partnership Under Stress: The American Jewish Community and Israel.* Tel Aviv: Jaffe Center for Strategic Studies, Memorandum 52, August 1998.

Barry Chazan. *What We Know About the Israel Experience.* New York: Israel Experience Inc., 1998.

Alan M. Dershowitz. *The Vanishing American Jew.* Boston: Little, Brown & Company, 1997.

Carol Diament, ed. *Zionism: The Sequel.* New York: Hadassah, 1998.

Daniel J. Elazar and Shmuel Trigano. *How European Jewish Communities Can Choose and Plan Their Own Future.* Jerusalem: World Jewish Congress, 1998.

J. J. Goldberg. *Jewish Power.* Reading: Addison-Wesley, 1996.

Anthony Gordon and Richard Horowitz. *Will Your Grandchildren Be Jewish?* Manuscript, 1997.

Arthur Hertzberg. *The Zionist Idea.* New York: Atheneum, 1979.

Baruch Kimmerling. *Zionism and Territory.* Berkeley: Institute of International Studies, 1983.

David Mittleberg. *The Israel Visit and Jewish Identification.* New York: American Jewish Committee, 1994.

Samuel Norich. *What Will Bind Us Now?* New York: Center for Middle East Peace and Economic Cooperation, 1994.

Jonathan Sachs. *Will We Have Jewish Grandchildren?* Ilford: Vallentine Mitchele, 1994.

Henry H. Weinberg. *The Myth of the Jew in France 1967–1982.* Oakville: Mosaic Press, 1987.

Geoffrey Wheatcroft. *The Controversy of Zion.* Reading: Addison-Wesley, 1996.


Articles and Lectures in English

Shlomo Avineri. "Dreyfus Was Not the Reason." *Midstream,* May/June 1998, pp. 16–17.

———. "Jews of the Former Soviet Union, Yesterday and Tomorrow," in *Jews of the Former Soviet Union.* The American Jewish Committee, 1996, pp. 5–9.

Elihu Bergman. "The American Jewish Population." *Midstream,* October 1977, pp. 9–19.

Michael Chlenov. "Jewish Community and Identity in the Former Soviet Union," in *Jews of the Former Soviet Union.* The American Jewish Committee, 1996, pp. 11–16.

Steven M. Cohen. "The Impact of Varieties of Jewish Education Upon Jewish Identity, An Inter-Generational Perspective." *Contemporary Jewry 16,* 1995, pp. 68–95.

Sergio Della Pergula. "World Jewish Population 1995," in *American Jewish Year Book 1997.* New York: American Jewish Committee, 1997, pp. 513–44.

Eli N. Evans. "Telecommunications and World Jewish Renewal." Keynote Address at the Conference on Media and Technology in Jewish Education, Brandeis University, June 1997.

Craig Horowitz. "Are American Jews Disappearing?" *New York,* July 14, 1997, pp. 101–8.

Charles S. Liebman. "Diaspora Influence on Israel: The Ben-Gurion–Blaustein 'Exchange' and Its Aftermath." *Jewish Social Studies,* vol. 36, nos. 3–4, July–October 1974, pp. 271–80.

P. London and A. Hirshfeld. "Youth Programs in Israel: What the Findings Mean." *The Journal of Communal Service*, vol. 66, no. 1, 1989, pp. 71–87.

## BOOKS IN HEBREW

Ahad Ha'am. *Kol kitvei Ahad Ha'am* (The Collected Writings of Ahad Ha'am). Tel Aviv: Dvir, 1959.

Avi Backer, ed. *Hakihilot hayehudiot biolam* (Jewish Communities in the World). Tel Aviv: Yedioth Ahronoth, 1997.

Avraham Burg. *Brit 'Am* (A Covenant of the People). Jewish Agency for Israel, 1995.

Yigal Elam. *1000 yehudim bi'ate hachadasha* (One Thousand Jews in the Modern Era). Tel Aviv: Zemora Bitan Modan, 1974.

Amos Elon. *Herzl.* Tel Aviv: Ofakim-Am Oved, 1975.

Yosef Gorny. *Hasheala ha'aravit vehaba'aya hayehudit* (The Arab Question and the Jewish Problem). Tel Aviv: Ofakim-Am Oved, 1985.

Arthur Hertzberg. *Hayehudim biamerica* (Jews in America). Tel Aviv: Schocken, 1994.

Theodor Herzl. *Altneuland* (Old-New Land). Tel Aviv and Haifa: Steimatzky, 1961.

———. *Medinat hayehudim* (The Jewish State). Jerusalem: Keshetarbut, 1996.

Ze'ev (Walter) Laqueur. *Toldot hatziyonut* (A History of Zionism). Tel Aviv: Schocken, 1974.

Yehiam Padan. *Hahalom vehagshamato* (The Dream and Its Realization). Tel Aviv: Ministry of Defense, 1979.

Anita Shapira. *Yehudim chadashim, yehudim yeshanim* (New Jews, Old Jews). Tel Aviv: Ofakim-Am Oved, 1995.

Eliezer Shveid. *Hayehudi haboded vehayahadut* (The Individual Jew and Judaism). Tel Aviv: Ofakim-Am Oved, 1974.

Yossi Shtrom, ed. *Tziyonut—maazan baynayim vmegamot le'atid* (Zionism—An Assessment and Future Trends). Jerusalem: Israel Zionist Council, 1997.

Ze'ev Sternhal. *Binyan umah oh tikun chevrah?* (Building a Nation or Improving Society?). Tel Aviv: Ofakim-Am Oved, 1995.

Ephraim and Menachem Talmi. *Lexicon tziyoni* (A Zionist Lexicon). Tel Aviv: Ma'ariv, 1977.

## Articles and Lectures in Hebrew

Michael Livne. "Protocol diyunai si'at artzeynu" (Protocols of "Artzenu" Faction Debates), pp. 43–47.

Nathan Rotenstreich. "Hamachshava haleumit hachadasha" (The New National Thinking). Tel Aviv: Machbarot lisafrut, n.d., pp. 107–16.

Yehuda Slotzki. "Hahagira kegoram betoldot hayehudim bemizrah eropa ad 1881" (The Role of Emigration in the History of the Jews in Eastern Europe Through 1881). Jerusalem: Israeli Historical Association, 1973, pp. 67–79.

# Index

# ABOUT THE AUTHOR

Yossi Beilin, who currently serves as Israel's Minister of Justice, has set the agenda for Israeli politics over the last decade. In his various public roles—as a member of the Knesset since 1988, a leader of Israel's Labor Party, and a minister in the governments of Yitzhak Rabin, Shimon Peres, and Ehud Barak—Beilin has proven himself a unique type of politician. He began the process that resulted in the 1993 Oslo Accords and has led the public movement for a unilateral withdrawal from Lebanon. Beilin also serves as Israel's foremost thinker on issues of Jewish continuity and the changing relationship between Israel and Diaspora Jewry. He was an initiator of the Birthright program, which aims to bring thousands of Jewish youth on a free trip to Israel and which is just one of the many ideas discussed in this book. Born in Israel in 1948, Beilin lives in Tel Aviv with his wife and two sons.